More Praise for *The*

"Here is an absolutely original work ... erning your days and nights. Reader,
  —Christopher Merrill, author of *Self-Portrait with Dogwood*

"*The Thinking Woman*, the first work of non-fiction by acclaimed novelist Julienne van Loon (whose career began with a Vogel win for her first novel, *Road Story*, in 2004) is a knotty, charismatic exploration of the intersection between ideas and lived experience, through six central themes . . . a surprising and resonant work that cements Julienne van Loon's status as a thinking woman well worth reading and following."
  —Jo Case, *The Sydney Morning Herald*

"There is so much life in these conversations. Words and ideas feel hot, propulsive, uncontained in their implications. Above all else, this feeling of thinking, of thinking out loud, of thinking together, of thinking *with* and *alongside*, it's a very special kind of high."
  —Maria Tumarkin, author of *Axiomatic* and
  winner of the Melbourne Prize for Literature 2018

"It's heartening to read a book that encourages us to challenge our assumptions. To think expansively, and to look at those who do, and how that may be relevant to our everyday. An invitation to a thoughtful life. Julienne van Loon's *The Thinking Woman* is that kind of book."
  —Melissa Cranenburgh, Feminist Writers Festival

"A compelling portrait of the relationship between thinking and feeling."
  —Amanda Lohrey, winner of the Patrick White Award

"A fascinating book that will have us all thinking, whether or not we are women."
  —Anne Summers, author of *Damned Whores and God's Police*

"*The Thinking Woman* is also much more than a thematically organised collection of essays that bring the dense theories of living feminist and female philosophers to a general readership. In many ways the book is also a revelation, as it marks van Loon as an extraordinary memoirist, able to draw convincing parallels between her own life and the academic arguments of her philosopher subjects without descending into cant or mawkishness. Van Loon manages to move confidently and convincingly between discussing her early love of trees and her first job working at a Dagwood Dog truck, to Julia Kristeva's theory of subjective horror and Rosi Braidotti's concept of bios/zoe."

—Johanna Leggatt, *The Australian Book Review*

"Towards the end of van Loon's journey through her interviews with these impressive women, she asks: where are you at? It is a question she says we should all be asking each other, not so much for our physical whereabouts—though that can be crucial when a friend is in trouble—but to enquire about our own journey of becoming in the precarious world we inhabit . . . *The Thinking Woman* does a lot to help us think about how we can, how we could, even how we should, deal with our own feelings, and find the fluidity of imagination to live thoughtfully and fully. I await volume two."

—Drusilla Modjeska, *Inside Story*

"Show[s] us why and how philosophy matters in achingly personal, human terms . . . The quiet delight of this book is not just in watching its women think but understanding how and why they slice the world the way they do; locating their ideas in a biographical context, as the unique product of a life. A woman's life."

—Beejay Silcox, *The Australian*

The
Thinking
Woman

JULIENNE VAN LOON is the author of three critically acclaimed novels: *Road Story, Beneath the Bloodwood Tree* and *Harmless*. She lives in Melbourne, where she holds a Vice Chancellor's Senior Research Fellowship with the writing and publishing program at RMIT University. Julienne's honours include the *Australian/Vogel's* Award and an appointment as Honorary Fellow in Writing with the University of Iowa. *The Thinking Woman* is her first work of non-fiction.

For Francis

The Thinking Woman

Julienne van Loon

Foreword
by Anne Summers

RUTGERS UNIVERSITY PRESS

NEW BRUNSWICK, CAMDEN, AND NEWARK, NEW JERSEY, AND LONDON

Library of Congress Cataloging-in-Publication Data

Names: Van Loon, Julienne, 1970– author.
Title: The thinking woman / Julienne van Loon.
Description: New Brunswick, New Jersey : Rutgers University Press, [2020] | "First published in Australia by NewSouth, an imprint of UNSW Press"—Verso. | Includes bibliographical references and index.
Identifiers: LCCN 2020025412 | ISBN 9781978819900 (paperback ; alk. paper) | ISBN 9781978820081 (hardcover ; alk. paper) | ISBN 9781978819917 (epub) | ISBN 9781978819924 (mobi) | ISBN 9781978819931 (pdf)
Subjects: LCSH: Holmstrom, Nancy (Nancy Christina Louise) | Braidotti, Rosi. | Hustvedt, Siri. | Kipnis, Laura. | Kristeva, Julia, 1941– | Warner, Marina, 1946– | Women—Social conditions. | Women—Conduct of life. | Female friendship. | Women employees—Social aspects.
Classification: LCC HQ1397 .V35 2020 | DDC 305.4—dc23
LC record available at https://lccn.loc.gov/2020025412

A British Cataloging-in-Publication record for this book is available from the British Library.

First published in Australia by NewSouth, an imprint of UNSW Press

∞ The paper used in this publication meets the requirements of the American National Standard for Information Sciences—Permanence of Paper for Printed Library Materials, ANSI Z39.48–1992.

www.rutgersuniversitypress.org

Manufactured in the United States of America

Contents

It falls to us now to go on thinking ... Think we must. Let us
think in offices; in omnibuses; while we are standing in the
crowd watching Coronations and Lord Mayors'; Shows; let
us think as we pass the Cenotaph; and in Whitehall; in the
gallery of the House of Commons; in the Law Courts; let us
think at baptisms and marriages and funerals. Let us never
cease from thinking – what is this 'civilization' in which we
find ourselves? What are these ceremonies and why should we
take part in them? What are these professions and why should
we make money out of them? Where in short is it leading us
...?

– Virginia Woolf

Foreword
by Anne Summers

We women are so accustomed to having unfriendly or even abusive adjectives and epithets hurled at us that it is a rare, and very welcome, experience to be described as 'thinking'. It is, when you think about, so unusual, contradictory even, that it is startling. Instead of the usual descriptions – 'bitch', 'aggressive', 'shrill', 'ball-breaking' – that portrays us as upsetting the natural order of things, we are characterised as thoughtful, as people who want answers to the big questions of life.

This book aims to 'connect philosophical thinking and everyday life' and Julienne van Loon has done this in an intriguing way. The book is partly a memoir, telling often disturbing stories of her childhood, becoming a mother, joining the academy, leaving a long-term relationship, losing a best friend to a violent end, travelling, learning, thinking. It is also an exploration of the themes that have preoccupied her in life and at work and which are the organising themes of this book. The six chapters explore love, play, work, fear, wonder and friendship, through interviews with 'thinking women' and stories of her own experiences. It is an absorbing and, at times, challenging brew. I found myself stopping to think on almost every page as ideas swirled up in new ways, or new contexts, and forced me to ask the same questions of myself that van Loon was asking as part of her meditation.

It is an energising and provoking experience and that it is so unfamiliar is a testament to the originality of this book. We are not used to such philosophical explorations being linked to the stuff of everyday existence, yet we should be. How else do we arrive at understanding, or enlightenment? At the insights that brace us to continue to propel ourselves forward? There are many in this book but perhaps the one that resonated most with me was the description of friendship as 'a project that has no end'. What a perfect way to think about the wonderful, rewarding yet often infuriating relationships we have with our close friends. I am still turning this thought around in my mind and using it to examine the friendships I value.

Of the six thinking women she interviews, only one, Nancy Holmstrom, she says, can be labelled 'a capital P philosopher' in that she is employed as such at a university. The others are the novelist Siri Hustvedt, the feminist philosopher Rosi Braidotti, the media studies professor Laura Kipnis, the writer and historian Marina Warner and Julia Kristeva, a psychoanalyst, novelist and feminist philosopher. But they are each women who continue to think deeply about the fundamental questions of life and who were willing to share their thoughts, as well as their precious private time, with their Antipodean interrogator. The result is a fascinating book that will have us all thinking, whether or not we are women.

Introduction

The thinking woman exists: she is alive and well. Browsing through the philosophy sections of some of the world's best bookshops, and indeed through the staff listings in philosophy departments at any of our most prestigious universities, one has to be sharp-eyed and persistent to find her. Sometimes, she has been cast out from capital-p Philosophy as a discipline and a category. Often, she was never admitted to those schools in the first place. In fact, the thinking woman can frequently be found having a better and more playful time elsewhere: she is with and amongst the novelists, artists and activists; she has flourished in the social sciences and humanities more broadly; or she has made it on her own as an independent scholar. Life, for the thinking woman, can be messy and complicated. She is and is not a philosopher. She is rarely a household name. When she gets too powerful, there is a remarkably consistent method for bringing her down: a combination of ridicule, smear campaign and forced exile. These are some of the reasons why her work has so much to offer.

Six years ago, I set out to write a book profiling living female philosophers, a book I hoped would work to connect philosophical thinking and everyday life in a manner that values and validates the work of some of our leading female philosophers, and that speaks to those of us trying to make sense of how to live now. I had particular themes in mind: love, friendship, work, play, fear and wonder. I had questions, too. Is love a good investment? In what form should women participate in work under capitalism? How necessary, how vital, is friendship? I began reading widely, in earnest. I began to wonder who we might define as a female philosopher.

And then, what is philosophy?

AS I WRITE THIS INTRODUCTION, SITTING AT A FAMILIAR CAFÉ benchtop on an ordinary weekday morning, I look to the other end of the long room, and see a woman looking back at me. She is dark-haired and spectacled, her profile eerily similar to my own, and as she leans forward, elbow on the table, she tilts her face slightly to rest against her hand. She is looking back the length of the room at me, not with recognition but with an open, contemplative gaze. She is thinking. For a second, I mistake her for another version of myself.

Philosophy need not be a closed and cloistered corridor. It need not be a space exclusively for the Y chromosome and the elite. In a secular, contemporary world, many of us who are untethered from organised religion – or at least less firmly bound by it than our parents or grandparents might have been – can find both solace and instruction in the rich and rigorous examination of meaning that goes on and through the work of philosophy. It is, in its broadest definition, the art of making sense of things. By *things*, in this instance, we can mean those pertaining to the bigger picture: existence, reality. And yet the work I profile here frequently knits together the big picture and the small: I find the role of lived experience in the work of the women I profile in this book vivid and impactful.

In my view, the purpose of philosophy is to help us to analyse and therefore to understand our experiences of the world in which we live. Those physical, social and institutional structures we find ourselves negotiating every day – work, family, the neighbourhood, domestic coupledom – are themselves the products of particular ways of thinking. Reading the work of the female thinkers I profile in this book has helped me to think more deeply about the circumstances into which I have been cast, and into which I have cast myself. Their work has led me to examine – often with considerable discomfort – not just the choices I have made, but the extent to which those choices have been complicit in furthering forms of thinking that I don't actually subscribe to myself, including some that I actually would prefer to outright reject.

Are my key subjects in this book philosophers, then? No and yes. Yes and no. Given the problems of philosophy as a category that so frequently excludes women, and as a discipline so enamoured by logic as method, I came to categorise the women whose work I write about here as, first and foremost, thinkers. Their work prompts insightful questions about the big things and the small, and this too became a key objective for my own book. I wanted to braid their questions with my own. I wanted to try their observations on. Further, I wanted to prompt and provoke my own readers to look at what happens when we apply philosophy to our own everyday circumstances. It's not an easy thing to do. It can lead to a radical change of attitude to things we have come to accept. It can prompt us to investigate more fully our own motivations, or, as has sometimes happened to me, give us a deeply uncomfortable feeling of anger or shame.

To develop this book, I travelled widely, spending considerable hours with my interviewees. I sat with Siri Hustvedt in her artfully decorated home in Brooklyn as we shared with one another playful anecdotes about childhood and parenting. I climbed the stairs to Laura Kipnis's apartment in Manhattan, and shared a Thai meal with her while talking fidelity and control in domestic partnerships. In London, the following year, I fell a little bit in love with Marina Warner's summertime urban garden. I carried the memory of its lively colour with me across continents as I sat down at my kitchen table in Australia to read more deeply her work on botanical artist Maria Merian. Gradually, *The Thinking Woman* began to take shape. I travelled again, this time to trace a path along the old canals of the Netherlands to the magnificent front room of the Centre for the Humanities at the University of Utrecht, where Rosi Braidotti and I commenced a friendship through intense discussions about the meaning and potential of friendship. Later, I met with Helen Caldicott in her newly planted back garden in the southern highlands of New South Wales, where we talked about what it takes to care so deeply for the planet that you turn to full-time activism for a period of forty years. Finally, I returned to the United States and to Manhattan, where I met with one of the few women in the book to forge a career in a conventional philosophy department: Nancy Holmstrom. In addition to philosophies of work, Nancy and I compared my experiences of road cycling to hers with running marathons. I still remember fondly the beautiful poise of her cat. With Julia Kristeva, I exchanged several emails, but, regrettably, we did not meet in person. I still hope one day to change that.

While I was writing this book, there was plenty happening to prompt one's thinking about feminism in the public sphere. Hillary Clinton's presidential campaign was dogged by gendered discourse, including ridicule, and ultimately failed. Rebecca Solnit published *Men Explain Things to Me*. Then the #MeToo movement took flight with the outing of Harvey Weinstein, and many other men in positions of privilege who have been revealed to be sexual predators since. As this book goes to press, Julia Kristeva has come under the spotlight due to allegations about her relationship with the Bulgarian government when she was a young student in France. Was she a spy? The facts are still disputed, but my inclination is to see the allegations against her as part of a fairly common trend: she is possibly the most well-known living female philosopher. She has considerable influence. Tracking the work of the women in this book over decades, including the reception of their work in the public sphere, I am inclined to approach attempts at reputational damage with considerable caution. One sees patterns, over time, and the cumulative effect is dispiriting.

As I wrote, the world kept turning. Rosie Batty won some hard-fought battles for domestic violence policy reform in Australia, even while one woman per week in this country continues to be killed by her partner or ex-partner. Rosi Braidotti's work on posthumanism has found an increasingly widespread audience in recent years, particularly in the light of the serious effects of climate change. My own life circumstances changed too. I left the father of my son. I moved cities. My child grew from preschooler to confident tween.

I stuck to the themes I had begun with – work and play, fear and wonder, love and friendship – and to my original intentions for the book. I wanted to write a companionable book that validates the work of living female thinkers and at the same time provides its readers with a sense that the questions those thinkers are asking are not so different from those we all ponder from time to time. I wanted to celebrate the contribution made by women in the intellectual sphere at the same time as considering their ideas thoroughly, by applying them to my set of circumstances. Women like Laura Kipnis and Nancy Holmstrom (to name just two) have thought deeply about such questions as: why do relationships seem like work; what alternatives are there for the way we organise our labour? Their endeavours deserve our serious attention.

The book you hold in your hand has far more of my own story in it than I intended at the start, and, for this reason, it has not been easy to write. The writing has required some deeply reflective thinking of my own, much of which I share with you. I have tried to recreate events, locales and occasional conversations from my memories of them. Sometimes I have changed names and identifying details to protect privacy. The eight women I have chosen to profile in the book – both intellectuals and activists – all play themselves, of course, and I generally quote from transcriptions of our conversations, recorded over a three-year period (2014–2016). These women are indeed alive and well, and their thinking speaks to the particular cultural moment we find ourselves in right now. I thank them for their extraordinary work, and also for their support for this project. I urge you to consider their ideas with some depth, to apply their thinking to your (our) own circumstances and to move towards your own mode of answering back, in whatever form that may take.

The woman I observed earlier at the other end of the long room has moved on, and I watch as another takes her place. Younger, the new visitor sports short spiky hair, a dark floral print on her dress, boots. She puts down her heavy backpack and takes off her headphones. She looks at the menu a moment, then glances towards the window. I wonder what she is thinking, and further, where her thinking might take her next.

CHAPTER
ONE
Love

One day during the summer of 2013 I stumbled into a moment of recognition that would turn my whole world on its head. I hadn't seen it coming. Looking back, I suppose it was the kind of epiphany that I'd often coached my undergraduate students to weave into their short stories in the manner of James Joyce and Flannery O'Connor. Fiction intensifies such experiences for dramatic effect. I had written such events into fiction myself, but I'd always reserved judgment on whether they happened quite so neatly in real life. The religiously inspired Flannery O'Connor seemed to believe that the mind could regularly flood with the kind of grace that leads to profound new understandings, and that one might frequently alter one's life according to them. Perhaps this is the way she genuinely lived, but it seems to me that most of us stumble through our daily lives without much grace, occasionally half-glimpsing the possibility of change, rarely investing the time and attention to gain the full benefit of insight.

My year had begun ordinarily. I was busy, in that interminable way familiar to so many of us in modern life. A working parent, and a senior professional, I rarely felt on top of things. I was always running from one appointment to another, always behind in replying to my emails. I was also the willing victim of a long commute, which I had been doing for more than a decade, and at home the daily labour of co-parenting a preschool-aged child was insistent and demanding. I was tired. My relationship with my partner of two decades was also tired. In the little bit of down time he and I shared at home together of an evening, he watched television. I read books. So it went on.

One morning, I was about to give a seminar to new PhD students on how to navigate their way through their first year of university bureaucracy, when I got talking to a colleague. The Dean of Research was there to welcome the students and to introduce my session. He was new to the job, perhaps six months in. I had been working in the place for fifteen years. There were a few minor administrative issues we needed to speak about. We discussed a plan for sorting those issues through, speaking in hushed tones in the corner of the half-populated lecture theatre while we waited for the session's scheduled commencement time to draw closer. And then we made small talk.

The dean and I did not know each other all that well, at that time. He was the chair of a monthly meeting I'd recently begun to attend. We were in frequent email contact about work-related matters. I respected his opinion. I suppose you could say we were friendly, but that's about all. That morning, we talked, however briefly, about a novel we both knew. His reading of it was smart, articulate and thoughtful. When he smiled at me I recognised in him something that disarmed me. It was the possibility of profound intimacy: strange, improbable and completely unexpected.

AFTER MY SEMINAR, I LEFT THE DEAN, WHO WAS TO INTRODUCE the next speaker, and walked out into the late summer morning.

The academic year was only just beginning and the campus was bustling with newly enrolled undergraduate students finding their way to their next tutorial or lecture, or gathering on the grass beneath tall trees. A couple of staff members from my own building passed me by and nodded in my direction. I nodded back. The whole setting was very familiar to me, and yet something was distinctly *not right*. I felt fearful. I felt exhilarated. I felt inhabited by the acute sense of vertigo that only dangerous knowledge can invoke.

In the days and weeks that followed I started to think a lot about the dean. I thought about him while I was cycling to work. I thought about him while putting my little boy to bed at night. I thought about him when I was supposed to be reading. I tried to talk myself out of thinking about him, but inevitably failed (then, in failing, rejoiced). On that morning in February, my perspective on what mattered had buckled. It was a shock. The attraction was more than just physical: it was intellectual, it was emotional, it was deeply human. As Roland Barthes so beautifully suggests in his seminal essay, *A Lover's Discourse*, language is both too excessive and too impoverished a medium for expressing what happens to us in such circumstances. I had drifted into a parallel realm: 'the realm of sleep, without sleeping'.

One day, in March, I was driving to an appointment and happened to tune into a drama on Radio National. In the course of the narrative, the narrator described the character of a secretary who was in love with her boss. The setting was the 1950s and the boss was married with children. The long-suffering woman remained single. She went on living with her mother. As it turned out, she would work for the man in question for thirty years and never tell him how she really felt. She was a woman of her era, perhaps. In any case, her heart-breaking reticence, coupled with her respect for (or oppression on account of) social convention made me squirm. I made a determination: I would not be like her.

At the same time, I said nothing about my affliction to anyone, least of all to the dean.

At home, I began to look at my long-term partner with a mournful sort of gaze. Every choice I had made for the past two decades of adulthood had led me to this: a predictable, slightly exhausting routine involving work, mortgage repayments, driving, domestic labour. There was nothing uplifting about it. I began to suspect I was trapped in the wrong narrative. I stopped sleeping so easily at night.

After all, love is everything, right?

IT WAS DURING THE YEAR PRIOR TO MY LATE-SUMMER EPIPHANY that I first came across the writing of Laura Kipnis on adultery. An essay she published in *Critical Inquiry* – which later became the chapter 'The Art of Love' in her book *Against Love* – presents a delightfully scandalous argument for the adulterer as artful saboteur. To the question of whether adultery is a political act, Kipnis's considered response is a resounding 'Yes!'. Her essay made me laugh out loud, and on the strength of it, I ordered her book. Kipnis's dark humour, coupled with her capacity for robust cultural critique, is both confronting and refreshing. While I was not about to subscribe to her (tongue-in-cheek) political call to arms, and it's notable that I feel the need to reassure both myself and others about that fact, *Against Love* had a powerful effect on me. Through reading it I was able to draw more fully into focus many aspects of the constraint I had been feeling for so many years. I didn't know then how generative the author's articulation of the complexities and contradictions inherent in domestic coupledom was to be for me.

Laura Kipnis is a professor of media studies at Northwestern University in Chicago, to which she commutes from her home in New York. Her first book was the well-known *Bound and Gagged*, which focused on pornography. A later publication, *How to Become a Scandal*, looks at our cultural fascination with scandal and her most recent, *Unwanted Advances*, takes a frank look at the politics of sexual assault on university campuses. Kipnis's writing is the product of an acute and playful intelligence and a fascination for complication and paradox. She is an art school graduate, and during her early career exhibited work as a video artist. At Northwestern she teaches a combination of screen production and critical cultural theory, including a long-running course on Roland Barthes.

The title of Kipnis's *Against Love* makes clear the provocative nature of the book itself. To be against something might mean to stand opposed to it, but the word can also mean to bolster or to fortify, as in to lean against or hold against oneself. 'Against' is one of only a handful of words in the English language that can mean both itself and its opposite, Kipnis tells me when we meet at her home base in Manhattan in the winter of 2014. 'Cleave' is another such word; and so is 'fast'. These, I discover, are known as contronyms. 'Who would dream of being against love?' asks Kipnis in her book's introduction. 'No one', her playful teaser continues, 'but is there something worrisome about all this uniformity of opinion? Is this the one subject about which no disagreement will be entertained, about which one truth alone is permissible? Consider that the most powerful organised religions produce the occasional heretic; every ideology has its apostates; even sacred cows find their butcher. Except for love. Hence the need for a polemic against it.'

I have always considered myself on the sceptical side when

it comes to the form of romance dished up to us in simplistic narratives via contemporary media. As a feminist, I am also suspicious of the marriage contract, having chosen to steer clear of ever signing one myself. In practice, I am a loyal monogamist, mainly because I find sex a more meaningful and fulfilling practice when it involves somebody I care deeply about, but also because honesty and trust are important to me. And yet I have never invested any of my relationships with promises of lifelong devotion. Change is the only certainty, in so many aspects of life. And, having made an incredibly naïve but ultimately successful attempt at saving my own mother's life at age ten, as her husband (my father) tried to strangle her to death, I have tended towards being fairly philosophical about the capacity for love (and our loved ones) to change. I am generally up-front with the important gentlemen in my life: 'If this gets bad for my health', I've been inclined to say, at the beginning, 'then I'm out.' I will not stay the way my mother stayed.

HERE IS A SCENARIO PERHAPS FAMILIAR TO MANY: TWO PEOPLE fall in love. They have mutual interests, some friends in common. They enjoy each other's company. The sex is good. After a time, they move in together and share the domestic labour along with the relevant household expenses. Their togetherness provides a source of comfort and belonging. Both work, mainly full time. Somewhere along the line, they buy a house. It's further away from the city than they would both prefer, but they can afford the mortgage repayments this way. They go out into the world together less often, and some years down the track they become parents. The schedule becomes a little more demanding. The daily routine includes less and less time alone together. Their sex life wanes. Their topics of conversation become less and less engaging.

Nothing is particularly, drastically wrong. There are not a lot of arguments. Small things irritate: one party doesn't tidy up in the kitchen sufficiently. The other pisses regularly on the lemon tree, leaving the scent of urine too close to the house. The share of dog-walking leans too heavily in one direction. Strategies for managing the toddler's behaviour differ. Gradually the relationship becomes little but a fragile pattern of habitual repetitions and minor annoyances. The main players are barely present.

They fall out of love.

HERBERT MARCUSE, A GERMAN-AMERICAN SOCIOLOGIST, philosopher and political theorist, was the author of two influential books – *Eros and Civilization* (1955) and *One-Dimensional Man* (1964) – and is perhaps best known for his critique of modern industrial society, which remains unhappily relevant to life under 21st-century capitalism. Marcuse's critique of social domination included the observation that every aspect of life is reduced to work. Heavily influenced by both Sigmund Freud and Karl Marx, he argued that under modern industrialism and consumer culture, workers and consumers alike become extensions of the objects they produce or consume. We recognise ourselves in these commodities and as such, our consciousness is not only manipulated, it is false. Workers, therefore, cannot be relied upon to be the agents of political and social change. We are dulled and repressed by the system to which we inevitably capitulate. If change is to come at all, it must come from a combination of radical intellectuals and social outcasts: those sufficiently outside the system to be able to see it for what it is.

In *Against Love*, Laura Kipnis equates those of us engaged in marriage or long-term coupledom with Marcuse's workers. It's a disturbing equation. 'We all know that Good Marriages Take Work', she writes:

> Work, work work ... are you ever not on the clock? ...
> When monogamy becomes labor, when desire is organized
> contractually, with accounts kept and fidelity extracted like
> labor from employees, with marriage a domestic factory
> policed by means of rigid shopfloor discipline designed to
> keep the wives and husbands and domestic partners of the
> world choke-chained to the status-quo machinery – is this
> really what we mean by 'a good relationship'?

For me, in the months following my encounter with the dean, Kipnis's argument for applying Marcuse's work to the concepts of marriage and domestic coupledom was deeply convincing. While I don't mind conceding that all relationships take some degree of effort – whether to understand another, to resolve conflict, to deepen our empathy and compassion, or not to simply walk away when things become difficult – Kipnis's thinking urged me to consider that my own form of domestic-coupledom work was part of a much bigger picture. She refers to the Frankfurt School's Wilhelm Reich, for example, who subscribed to the opinion (as did Freud) that the suppression of sexual curiosity leads to intellectual atrophy, including the tendency to lose any real capacity for dissent. Hence Kipnis's polemic on adultery, which was prompted to a large degree by America's extraordinary response to the Monica Lewinsky scandal. While adultery is certainly not the only form of breaking free from monogamy, or, indeed, of expressing one's sexual curiosity – as I shall discuss later – Kipnis's use of it in Against Love acts as a kind of case study: perhaps it is a form of behaviour or release that really does have the capacity to wake us up from our dull state of repression. Read in this light, adultery becomes a political act. Kipnis brings a great deal of humour to her thesis. Equally, however, her thinking is very alert to how power operates in the domestic scene. I couldn't stop myself from thinking about her various provocations.

KIPNIS'S RESPONSE TO MY REQUEST TO MEET WITH HER TO talk about *Against Love* was enthusiastic, even though the book had been published a decade earlier. Before we met, she made it clear to me that she did not want to be interrogated about her personal life. This was not surprising given the way the book had been received when it was published.

Several reviewers of *Against Love* took the book to be a quasi-confessional argument for adultery. One journalist who visited the author at home went so far as to surreptitiously check how many toothbrushes she kept beside her bathroom sink, reporting (inconclusively) on her detective work in her article. Others interpreted the work as falling into the self-help genre, a kind of advice manual for those hankering to depart a sagging domestic arrangement. Actually, the genre is most helpfully understood as Cultural Studies. It interrogates adultery, marriage and domestic coupledom through the lens of contemporary culture: consumption patterns, *New Yorker* cartoons, film, television and popular literature. It contains no confessions or advice. It does include the thoughtful contemplations of a wonderfully articulate thinker and social commentator.

My discussion with Kipnis began with the question of work: is it inevitable in long-term monogamy?

'I think so,' she said. 'I was kind of struck and also gratified when I did start reading these relationship advice books and they

ALL use that same phrase: "Good relationships take work" or "Marriage takes work". And there was this moment when a lot of it crystallised for me.' That moment was the linking together of the self-help 'relationships take work' mantra with Marxist thinking on the politics of labour. 'I thought of Marcuse's phrase "surplus labour", and it just hit me, you know: surplus monogamy … It opened up this whole set of analogies.'

In Marcuse's terms surplus labour is the difference between 'necessary labour' and the length of your work day. This difference equates with profit or, as Marx would see it, exploitation. Carry this idea across to a marriage or monogamous relationship that takes 'work' and it may be that you never actually knock off. Things not working out? 'Work harder!' the self-help books and an army of relationship counsellors barrack.

We 'shuttle between two incompletely theorised spheres – love and work', writes Kipnis, 'punching in, punching out, trying to wrest love from the bosses when not busily toiling in the mine shafts of domesticity. Or is it the reverse?' Given how long monogamy's 'marriage' of domestic and emotional labour can last, the sheer volume of the surplus, especially for women, can be chilling to contemplate.

As we talked about the process of writing *Against Love*, Kipnis described the way her thinking about adultery took flight the more she pursued metaphors and jokes. *New Yorker* cartoons about marriage, for example – 'Man watches TV as wife makes dinner. Caption: "Life without parole"' – spurred on her thinking about the domestic space as a kind of gulag.

I asked her about a line that resonated with my own observations from a section of the book in which she considers the centrality of romantic love to the way we think about ourselves. That is, we seem to treat its pursuit as fundamental, and those deemed to have succeeded at it are endlessly revered. Kipnis acknowledges the influence of the novel in all this, and the way that entering into romance provides us a story to tell about ourselves, one that counsellors and therapists can 'work with' when things go wrong. The particular line that struck me in this section of the book was that 'secular society needed another metaphysical entity to subjugate itself to after the death of God, and love was available for the job'.

'I want to ask you about this need to subjugate.'

'Yes. It's huge, huge, huge!' said Kipnis. 'I mean to the point that it's also invisible. I think that was also the fun of the book: it was pointing out the obvious. You know, I taught a junior seminar, it was a seminar on love, and I had this student who I always thought was a girl who was not brilliant at all, but she had this thing, she said: "Love has power over us." And you know, it was just the most obvious thing to say but for some reason for the first time I understood it.'

MEANWHILE, BACK AT THE OFFICE, I SPENT SIX MONTHS NOT doing anything about the dean. Circumstances required us to tackle some challenging problems, such that we were in regular phone and email contact. We got along well. We had lunch together. But could I manage to voice how I felt? It was not just about trepidation over a confession, or a simple fear of rejection. I was deeply aware that my fascination for him placed me on ethically shaky ground, both personally and professionally.

I spent much of this period reflecting on my existing relationship, mapping its demise over two decades. I spoke to a couple of close friends about it. One friend suggested relationship counselling, but I sensed it was already too late for that. Besides, it sounded a little too much like work, in the sense implied by Marx and Marcuse, and I felt as if I had put plenty of that in already. And it occured to me, bluntly, that maybe I had no interest in saving the relationship. Another friend – then single – spoke more philosophically about the inevitability of change, and the way it can completely surprise you. But she talked also, from personal experience, about the deep-felt nature of rejection. The way it can take years to recover.

In the very middle of the year, when my decision to leave my existing relationship was just about sealed, an email arrived in my inbox at the university. The divisional office announced the dean's sudden resignation; he had accepted an offer for a job interstate. The new position had a sense of urgency about it; it involved work at the national policy level. The dean cut short an overseas trip to return to campus to clear out his office and hand over to the hastily appointed new incumbent. He would be leaving at the end of the week.

I was quietly bereft.

We arranged to meet at a local café on a Sunday morning, the day before he was due to fly east. We talked about work, and we talked about politics, but my mood was kind of low and I could not properly say what I was thinking. I could not properly talk. The already-former dean was gracious enough to fill the silences with content that steered clear of the heart of the matter.

'I'm going to miss you', I managed.

'I'll keep in touch,' he countered. 'There are a few colleagues here I'd like to keep in touch with. You are definitely one of them.'

The formality of his comment was excruciating.

Early the next morning, my partner made me a cup of tea. The sun was not yet up; our child was not yet awake.

'You know what?' I said. 'I think this is over. I think this thing between the two of us is finally over. Really.'

'Yeah, I think so too', he said. 'I've been thinking the same thing for some time.'

And so it was. The former dean was gone. And within the very same week, so was my partnership of twenty years.

'I WILL SAY ON THE PERSONAL SIDE THAT AT THE TIME THAT I wrote the book, I was not a part of any kind of official couple', Laura Kipnis told me during the course of our discussion about *Against Love*, 'and I think, now, looking back, I do not think I would have been able to write that book if I was part of an established couple. So, it's something I've thought about, like the constraints that coupledom puts on, you know, probably not on writing across the board, but certainly on writing on certain subjects.'

I remain acutely aware of her point. The challenge of writing honestly about love and its contradictions seems particularly difficult in the context of the personal essay, whether or not one is presently under the influence of love's sometimes dramatic peaks and troughs. We write to investigate, to reflect, to trace a path of understanding through complexity. But the writing can never properly encompass the intricacy, the convolutedness, *of what's really going on.*

One of the frustrations in writing about complex ideas is that one's project is inherently reductionist: language has its limitations and narratives must, inevitably, cohere. At the same time, however, reflection through writing can change our perspective on things that matter, or it can reveal a perspective we might not have been capable of expressing before. It can articulate meaning that already exists, but it can also generate new meaning. The end product can be truthful, in its way. It can also be hurtful, controversial, misunderstood.

'I know that you have talked in a previous interview,' I said to Kipnis, 'about avoiding writing in the first person because of what you've recognised as the saturation of contemporary culture with the confessional mode. So, have you changed your mind on this?'

'I kind of think I have capitulated,' she admitted, reflecting on a more recent collection of essays in which she employs the first-person mode of address. 'I think editors rely on it and I think readers rely on it.' Kipnis's hesitation with writing in the first person has in some ways been about more than fear of exposure. 'My own life seems to me more confusing than other people's,' she told me. 'My life doesn't feel like it has narrative coherence.'

'Does anybody's, really?' I wondered out loud.

If the books in Laura Kipnis's body of work have something in common, it is this: the writing is unashamedly provocative. Her interest in errant behaviour is central to everything she has written, and this, coupled with her easy, direct tone, combines to lead readers quickly into complex territory. 'The best of Kipnis's writing has the force of a shot slap,' wrote the reviewer of a recent book. 'It goes down easy but it hits you hard.' Her tendency to provoke has resulted in a complex relationship with feminism. She admits she has spent a lot of time over the last two decades reading feminist and cultural theory, but her primary concern is in paying attention to what is going on in the culture and using what she has read to inform her observations. She is certainly not afraid to shake up women's assumptions about ourselves.

'Let's hear it for paychecks!' Kipnis writes in an essay on the topic of women and envy. 'In fact, women can now be entirely free from men, should they so choose. Interestingly, it turns out that despite the new possibilities for economic liberty, the majority of women do not so choose.'

Here is the heart of the dilemma: contradiction. How it tails us. Who amongst us hasn't desired another, even if just fleetingly, while in the very arms of the one we're with? Twice, during my relationship with my son's father, I tested the limits of my own desire to stray. Ten years before we separated, a chance meeting with a young man in a bar, while I was interstate at a conference, led to a lunch date and a short series of phone calls and email exchanges, shot through with lascivious suggestions. When my work took me to his city once more, I dialled his number, but it turned out he had sobered up. 'I can't do it, I can't go through with it,' he said, which left me wondering why, conversely, I felt I could have done so, and probably fairly easily.

A few years previously, I spent some months working in the far north-west, thousands of kilometres away from my partner, and out of frontier-town boredom took to occasional drinking and dancing at a local hotel with a girlfriend. There, on a Friday night, I picked up a virginal apprentice mechanic. He was eighteen. I was twenty-six. The sex felt like a kind of extended flashback to early teenage-hood: he was awkwardly self-conscious. Afterwards, I wanted to see him again, but for various reasons, that first evening in my temporary government-employee housing turned out to be both the beginning and the end. And so it was a classic one-night stand. I regretted that – not the infidelity, as such, at least not then – but the casual, almost tangential nature of the meeting. I was interested in this stranger. I don't know why. I have never been good at separating sex and friendship and affection. Indeed, I've now come to understand that casual sex is something I'd never really enjoyed, not at any point in my life. I no longer feel the need to pursue it.

For reasons I find hard now to explain, I confessed the incident with the eighteen-year-old to my partner. Out of what, I wonder now? A plea for honesty? A misguided sense of faithfulness?

Perhaps, I'm shocked to find myself asking, out of cruelty? The confession changed things between us, as you can imagine, and although we stayed together for many, many years beyond it, I can see now how it shadowed us both. I had transgressed, and though it was a minor offence in the scheme of things, it was an offence nonetheless. Paradoxically, in the longer term, I suspect its confession had the effect of doubling my sense of loyalty.

AS A CHILD, I DECIDED I WOULD NEVER MARRY. I OBSERVED THE complications inherent in my parents' marriage and came to the conclusion, rightly or wrongly, that marriage was not the place to find happiness. By way of explanation, I offer three memories from somewhere between the age of eight and twelve.

One. My mother and I were taking a holiday interstate. She had let a small cottage near The Coorong. There were two bedrooms, one of which I had to myself. The other, the main room, my mother was to share with a man named Martin. Martin drove a very swish car. He did not drink. He and my mother seemed happy in one another's company. I liked that about this holiday. I enjoyed their happiness too. I also sensed that they were very keen for me to go to bed on time, and I obliged them. One morning, my mother asked me how I would feel about us leaving my father and coming to live in Adelaide with Martin. 'I don't want to,' I replied. I surprised myself with this answer. In fact, I had been dreaming for a long time about some way for my mother, my siblings and me to get away from my father's violent alcoholism. 'I don't want to,' I repeated. 'I want us to stay with Dad.'

Two. Back in our country town in New South Wales, I listened regularly to a school friend talking about one of her favourite uncles. She didn't realise that I'd met him. She didn't know he'd once sat at the head of our kitchen table on a school night. 'What do you think about your mother and me?' he'd asked me. I was ten. There was no further explanation necessary, as far as I was concerned, and I was painfully aware of how careful I needed to be in responding to his question. My mother was standing in the kitchen, directly behind Uncle P, and she seemed flattered to have him in the house. At the same time, she was extremely anxious. She was doing that nervous sort of laugh she sometimes did. My father was already sleeping in the front room, a post drinking–session torpor. As my mother caught my eye, I responded to Uncle P. 'It's all right', I said softly. This man, too, had been drinking. I cleared my throat. 'It's all right', I repeated, giving it a little more volume. The man's face dropped a little, a brief wave of sobriety. My answer was insufficient. I knew that. At the same time, it was an attempt at a kind of salve for each of us.

Three. It was early evening on a school night. My father was sobbing in the front bedroom of our old house. Presumably my mother was in the room with him, though I could not see either of them directly. I was in the living room at the other end of the house, reading a book. All the doors were open. I listened as my father related a botched attempt at suicide. Apparently he had tried to drown himself in the river. He was bereft, not because he had felt the desire to kill himself, but because he seemed to feel he lacked the courage to see it through. As usual, he had been drinking. I don't remember my mother saying anything at all in response, although she must have said something. She must have said something.

AS KIPNIS'S STUDENT AT NORTHWESTERN SO ASTUTELY OBSERVED: love does have power over us. But how? And can it ever be completely benign? 'What offers greater regulation of movement and time, or more precise surveillance of body and thought to a greater number of individuals?' Kipnis asks in *Against Love*. Indeed, one of the main tenets of the book is the notion that marriage (or long-term monogamy) is a modern form of enclosure. In this, the author draws heavily on the ideas of French cultural historian Michel Foucault.

A considered treatise on the complex relation between knowledge and power, Foucault's *Discipline and Punish: The Birth of the Prison* was first published in 1975 and has long been considered a central work in the field of critical cultural theory. It focuses on the way the modern prison system developed simultaneously with the discourse of Enlightenment. Foucault notes the way in which, over time, punishment became less focused on physical torture and more closely linked to social function. Disciplinary power can thus be seen to operate increasingly via various social institutions, and marriage is no doubt one of the longest serving of these.

In *Against Love*, Kipnis documents some of the ways in which individuals who form a couple discipline one another, both overtly and covertly, through setting up specific prohibitions. She interviewed a number of subjects and posed the question, 'What can't you do because you're in a couple?' Their responses run to almost ten pages:

> You can't leave the house without saying where you're going
> ... You can't watch soap operas without being made fun of
> ... You can't eat what you want ... You can't take risks, unless
> they're agreed-upon risks, which somewhat limits the concept
> of 'risk' ... You can't say 'cunt' ... You can't issue diagnoses,
> even when they're glaringly obvious.

'I did interview a lot of people,' Kipnis told me. 'But you know, I was thinking about it just recently. My father, who is married to a woman who is not my mother, gets really mad if her best friend calls after ten. And, you know, he says, "She should not call after ten, that's my time." These prohibitions become kind of fascinating.'

'It's that thing about subjugation, again,' I observed. 'How willingly we enter into it, don't we?'

'Yes! I get really angry when my boyfriend uses the word "puke",' confessed Kipnis. 'I just don't like the word. So, I mean, I can write a whole list of my own prohibitions. It's the specificity that's funny. Someone told me that they read that section of the book at a wedding rehearsal, you know, as a joke.'

We laughed.

MANY SOCIAL THEORISTS, ALONG WITH CONSERVATIVE politicians, read marriage as our fundamental social structure. Tony Tanner, in *Adultery in the Novel* (1979) calls it 'the all-subsuming, all-organising, all-containing contract'. Indeed, the history of marriage reveals an institution far more caught up with the contractual and the authoritative than with matters of the heart. In *Marriage, A History* (2005), Stephanie Coontz illuminates the ways in which love and marriage were often considered antithetical. In pre-20th-century Europe, as in many other places, property ownership and the accumulation of wealth and power were the primary reasons for families to seek marriage for eligible sons and daughters. In ancient India, love before marriage was considered a disruptive, antisocial act. The ancient Chinese read excessive love between husband and wife as a threat to the solidarity of the extended family. Today, at least in Western democracies, marriage without love is generally frowned upon: it is considered an empty vessel. And yet the conservative anxiety in many of those same democracies in regards to same-sex marriage reveals just how deeply embedded the marriage contract remains in notions of state, church and nationhood. Back in 1998, the Monica Lewinsky scandal that resulted in an attempt to impeach former United States president Bill Clinton, and that, coincidentally, spurred Kipnis to begin her book, was treated not just as a personal marital issue, but as tantamount to an act of treason against the nation state. The perception seems to be that any *risk* of mucking with the status quo of marriage can put all sorts of other things at risk.

There are two key factors that prevent most of us in the midst of coupledom from engaging in, or perhaps even considering engaging in, adultery. These are its disregard for honesty, and its predication on betrayal. But what if you take those two factors away? The philosopher Simone de Beauvoir did just that. De Beauvoir never married, and maintained a mutually open relationship with her long-term partner Jean-Paul Sartre. Their agreement was that they would openly discuss their affairs with other lovers whenever they arose. The two saw each other almost every day, but never lived together. Of course, under the circumstances these two agreed to, loving another is not, by definition, adultery. It's interesting, however, that commentators on the relationship between de Beauvoir and Sartre often employ the phrase 'an open marriage' to describe the agreement the two put in place. They were together for fifty-one years and they were largely emotionally and intellectually loyal to one another, but part of the philosophy of their approach was precisely to eschew *marriage*. 'We were two of a kind,' de Beauvoir wrote of her relationship with Sartre, 'and our relationship would endure as long as we did: but it could not make up entirely for the fleeting riches to be had from encounters with different people.' De Beauvoir documented her relationships with women and men in her journals, and justified her approach in her book *The Second Sex* (1949), now widely agreed to be the most influential of the philosophical works to come out of the French existentialist movement. Her arrangement with Sartre was an adventurous pact for its time. You could call it ahead of its time, except, curiously, it seems just as unusual now.

WHEN I WAS STILL IN PRIMARY SCHOOL, MY OLDER COUSINS, many of whom were then in their early twenties, lived in de facto relationships, and this was accepted and generally discussed among the women in my extended family as a form of progress. When children began to arrive, it neither prompted nor required a marriage contract, and this too, was generally met with approval by my parents and their siblings. When I was a student at university in the 1990s, couples I knew would declare their relationship serious by moving into the same dwelling. 'They're living together,' was the expression we employed. The subtext was that this implied they would be monogamous: to flout this would be to meet with widespread disapproval. Virtually nobody talked about marriage at that time. One young woman among my circle of friends openly declared that she aspired to get married, and that this was her main reason for attending university. She was looking to meet her future husband. My friends and I laughed heartily at this idea. We all thought it a mad sort of conceit.

A decade later, as we entered the new millennium, something about my generation's social milieu changed significantly. Friends who had been living together for a decade or more began to announce their intention to marry. Ceremonies were designed

according to particular philosophies and with respect to, or sometimes in reaction to, particular traditions. 'We're writing our own
vows', became a common line among women I knew, usually, I
assumed, to enable them to remove that awful phrasing common
to the Christian marriage service: 'to love and obey'. *What's happening?* I wondered. *All my friends are getting married. Why?*

Curious to me now is my own compliance with the *spirit* of
the married life I engaged in with the father of my son, even in
the face of my long-held rejection of the formal marriage contract.
We met when I was twenty-one, in a share house, and so there
was no need to announce intentions to move in together. We were
already cohabiting. This went on, virtually uninterrupted, for the
next twenty-two years.

Unlike de Beauvoir and Sartre, my ex-partner and I came to
no formal agreement about the exclusivity of our sexual relationship. It was assumed but never really properly discussed. We shared
our money when one or the other was un- or under-employed. We
travelled together and relocated interstate together. Eventually, we
signed up to a shared mortgage and became co-owners of a property. And then we had a son. Written this way, the whole episode
seems impossibly passive, the players happily shunted along, the
arrangement entirely continuous with standard conventions, as if
we were mere carriages on a track laid down by others.

One of the things that interests me about the way Simone de
Beauvoir and Jean-Paul Sartre have been so revered as the celebrity
poster-couple of the French existentialist movement is the way the
discourse around them tends to emphasise the *enduring* nature
of their relationship. Like a successful marriage, it is regularly
described, approvingly, as 'a lifelong relationship', often evidenced
by the fact that their ashes now rest side by side in Montparnasse.
Much, too, has been made of de Beauvoir's declaration that her

relationship with Sartre was her primary achievement in life. Surely, I find myself thinking, that could not really be the case. Is that really what she thought? What about her contribution to philosophy?

'WE ... FEEL LIKE FAILURES WHEN LOVE DIES', WRITES LAURA Kipnis in an article in the *New York Times*. 'We believe it could be otherwise. Since the cultural expectation is that a state of coupled permanence is achievable, uncoupling is experienced as crisis and inadequacy – even though such failures are more the norm than the exception.'

In *Against Love*, Kipnis points to the anti-love story – the films *Fatal Attraction* (1987) or *Sid and Nancy* (1986), for example, or Edward Albee's play, *Who's Afraid of Virginia Woolf?* (1962) – where love is fundamentally a kind of misrecognition. The gist is that the wrong kind of love is delusional: intoxicating and therefore toxic.

I'm not sure that I ever felt radically anti-love upon the end of the relationship with my son's father. There was a mixture of emotions. In darker moments, I grieved for the loss of the future I had sometimes imagined for the three of us. And yet, the overarching feeling was of positive change. Why do we stay? I wondered. Why do we stay so long in a relationship in which there is nothing left to keep us together?

A friend of mine – the very one who suggested counselling as a means of hanging on to my long-term relationship – was married to her husband for more than fifty years. She was twenty when she married him, and seventy-two when he collapsed and died of a heart condition on the footpath right beside her. Maureen and I have had wonderfully frank conversations over the years about

men and about love. She is someone who came to higher education and to feminist scholarship quite late in life, and who has
embraced it with enthusiasm, but the gravity of some of its claims
have forced her to deeply reassess so much of what she had hitherto
thought of as 'normal' or 'straightforward' in her life. Why did she
marry at twenty? 'I epitomised the good girl,' she once told me.
Why did she launch straight into pregnancy and childbirth and
not think, terribly much, about doing anything else? Maureen
explains those decisions as partly being of the times – there was
no oral contraception then, for example – but also as being closely
connected to feelings of self-worth, which in the late 1950s, for
women at least, were dependent on your 'ability to nurture, to
be the compliant, non-thinking wife' – as Maureen put it. But as
her children grew, and Maureen and her husband withdrew from
physical intimacy, due in large part to her husband's suppressed
childhood experiences of sexual abuse, she felt increasingly ill at
ease. She felt inadequate in the role of wife and mother, and unat-
tractive. Her husband drank to cope with his inadequacies. After
the sudden death of a close sibling, everything seemed to lack
purpose. She sought medical help and was hospitalised, where she
received shock therapy without counselling.

My friend eventually struggled back to mental health, and
she credits tertiary education as having been enormously helpful
in helping her to achieve that. When I asked Maureen recently
to read Kipnis's work, and to tell me her thoughts, her response
was first and foremost to the author's tone, particularly her sense
of playfulness. Maureen reminded me of a quote from the French
writer Hélène Cixous: 'This place with no laws is similar to the
one occupied in a dream: there are no borders to cross; the reader/
writer/dreamer is instantly in the world of the text ... moorings
are severed with the already written – the already known'. Cixous

describes such a place as a liminal zone, where instead of seeing the connection with self and 'other' as alienating, there is a feeling of openness, a feeling that is aligned with creative productivity. Perhaps, posited my friend, Kipnis's conception of adultery is also the conception of a place of possibilities, of potential, of surprise.

Maureen, having completed a PhD informed by critical cultural theory, is these days far more acutely attuned to the politics of power and gender, and to the personal effects of the kinds of Foucauldian enclosures we've been discussing here, than she was as a woman of twenty. I can say the same for myself. Of course, our attunement to Foucauldian notions of enclosure, as to many of the other key concepts explored by Kipnis in *Against Love*, is not a get-out-of-jail-free card, but such knowledge does become a tool for making sense, and can work as a prompt that enables us to pause and reassess with caution those 'normal' and 'straightforward' routines and relationships we women stumble into regularly. 'It's not that we … don't register the contradictions of our collective existence,' writes Kipnis in her essay for *Critical Inquiry*, in fact we often 'register them painfully and seek relief, salve, treatment'. But even then, counsellors and therapists tend to treat our excess desires as a personal issue, rather than a psycho-social one. Excess desires are frequently understood in developmental terms, argues Kipnis, and as 'something maturity will eventually cure'.

A DECADE OR MORE INTO 'LIVING TOGETHER' AND MANY OF us no doubt feel that we have invested so much of our efforts into a particular institution (marriage, coupledom, domesticity, even the mortgage) that to pull down the structures we have built is to lay decades' worth of our own labour to waste. So post-relationship there is a feeling of residual guilt: what have I destroyed? But there is also, of course, the fear of being alone. And the dominant cultural narratives around the centrality of sex and romance do nothing to allay such a fear, especially if you have no interest in joining in the roving hook-up culture of Tinder.

In fact, the thing that most frightened me immediately after the break-up was the same fear that had prevented me from not taking action sooner: it was the challenge of coping with the economic and domestic labour pressures of being a sole parent. For all the drudgery and perceived work involved in conjugal domesticity, it can be a pretty efficient and cost-effective way to live. Immediately upon the end of our relationship, my ex-partner moved to the other side of the country. The onus was suddenly completely on me to attend to all of the needs of our young child. Each week became a carefully mapped itinerary of drop-offs and pick-ups, carving out hours for being physically at work, for working late at home. Childcare bills increased. For the first time in a decade, I applied for a credit card. I was reminded of one early reader's response to Simone de Beauvoir's *The Second Sex*. When British reader Joyce Goodfellow first encountered de Beauvoir's work, during the 1960s, she took it as a cue to leave her marriage and live a more open love life, as well as walk out on her job, but she later quipped that the move left her poverty-stricken and isolated as a single parent. 'What you read really does influence your life,' she commented in an interview published in *Daughters of de Beauvoir*. 'The book should carry a health warning.' I quickly discovered that in addition to the increased parental labour and financial stress, there were other pressures. Our jointly owned house was now on the market, and had to be kept immaculately clean and tidy lest our estate agent drop in with a potential buyer. We had accumulated too many possessions as well. Many of these needed to go. Perhaps it was a good period in which to be busy. Perhaps it prevented me from thinking too much about what was missing.

And yet, paradoxically, a lot of what was missing was not at all missed.

While I generally felt good about the decision my ex-partner and I had taken to break up, I couldn't help feeling that there was an element of scandal to it, even in the absence of outright infidelity. I expected to be judged, and so found myself particularly sensitive to the responses of others when I announced the news. No doubt many felt a sense of loss for my five-year-old son. And I did, too, to some extent, but I also wanted to challenge the assumption that staying together 'for the sake of the child' might be such a great idea. Curiously, families in which the parents stay together seem to produce criminals and drug addicts, cynics and romantics, geniuses and well-adjusted entrepreneurs at roughly the same rate as families in which death or separation have played a role. The welfare of children is far more negatively affected by a lack of access to the basics: food, clean water, shelter, affection, stability. Singledom of any kind, however, does counter the normative. It is often read as a rebuff of marriage and domestic coupledom, or, more suspiciously, as a mark of some form of deviance.

On balance, I enjoyed my newfound 'freedom' from the enclosure. But at the same time, perhaps predictably, I had not stopped thinking about the former dean.

'IT WAS POST-INDUSTRIALISM, PERHAPS MORE THAN FEMINISM, that transformed gender roles,' posits Kipnis, writing for the *New York Times*. Increased economic independence has contributed enormously to a decrease in marriage rates, and women with means are far less likely to stay in a relationship like the one my own mother found herself caught in during the 1960s and '70s. But we find ourselves thrust into a period unlike any other in history: it is one which the North American public servant turned Hegelian philosopher Francis Fukuyama has called 'the great disruption'. The triumph of individualism, argues Fukuyama, has led to increases in crime, a lesser role for the church and the breakdown of the traditional family unit. As a result, there is a degree of social, economic and moral turmoil. Fukuyama predicts that while certain positive changes indicative of the new era, such as the 'liberation' of women, cannot be reversed, radical changes to structures such as the traditional family will gradually need to be 'modified' by the new order. It seems that with the rise of neoliberalism in Australia, Europe and the United States, this project is already underway. Is this why marriage has become so popular again with the younger generation, even at the same time as digital hook-up sites like Tinder sign up millions of players? 'We live in sexually interesting times,' writes Kipnis, close to the opening of her book, 'meaning a culture which manages to be simultaneously hyper sexualised and to retain its Puritan underpinnings in precisely equal proportions.'

'Do you think *Against Love* would be a different book if you wrote it now?' I asked her. 'Has the cultural narrative around romantic love changed at all in the last decade or more?'

Kipnis thought this over. 'Well', she said, 'I get the sense that culturally, adultery is far more taboo than it ever has been. I think the people who are married (which is a declining number in the States) are really hunkered down and see any threats or incursions into that territory as far more serious, so the playful tone that I took when I wrote it, I wonder if I would have been able to manage that now.'

ONE OF THE MOST MEMORABLY AFFECTING SECTIONS OF *Against Love* occurs at the opening of the chapter titled 'Domestic Gulags'. Here Kipnis cites ghoulish examples of news stories documenting violence perpetrated against both men and women by their partners in a domestic context. Lovers poison each other, attack one another with axes, or attempt painfully amateur acts of castration.

'You handle these examples with great humour,' I said to Kipnis, 'and yet at the same time, the information you're presenting is devastating'.

'Well, I suppose there are degrees of aggression,' she responded, 'you know, there's emotional violence and low-level emotional violence and I guess that's where recognition comes in, too. In my nightmare scenario, two people stay together yet fail to recognise each other, so there's this covert aggression.'

It seemed I knew this particular nightmare myself.

'I must admit,' I said, 'when I got to the end of reading that section of your book, I wondered: how on earth do any of us survive?'

'Yes, exactly.'

We sat in silence for a little while.

'I wonder about romantic love, under any conditions,' I reflected. 'On the one hand, at the end of reading *Against Love* I was rather convinced by your argument for adultery as a political act, but romantic love is such a profoundly disordering experience in any context. Is it not a political act regardless of whether it's sanctioned and institutionalised, whether it's legal or not?'

'Well,' Kipnis said, with a glimmer in her eye, 'yes!'

TOWARDS THE END OF THE WINTER OF 2013, I FLEW NORTH TO the Kimberley as a guest of their regional writers' festival. My son was having a few days with his father, and it was a rare opportunity for me to have some time to myself, even despite the busy public-speaking schedule linked to the festival appointments. I found myself in a highly positive frame of mind. The skies were blue. The sun was warm. Something about the ancient Kimberley landscape was deeply reassuring. One morning, I took up the offer of road cycling with a few of the locals before daybreak. The landscape held such depth of colour and the roads were all long straight lines, blissfully empty of vehicles.

Pedalling always gives me space for thought. I wondered: when will I let the former dean know how I feel about him, if not now? He was no longer part of the hierarchy at work. And I was no longer committed to another relationship. Perhaps it was too early. I hadn't spent time enough alone. On the other hand, I pondered, perhaps it was too late. He'd already moved interstate. And apart from a friend request on Facebook, which he didn't appear to use regularly, I had heard nothing from him.

During one of the writers' festival events, I was on stage in conversation with another novelist and a local radio journalist. We were talking frankly about writing and belonging, and at the end of the session the interviewer asked us a simple but difficult question.

'What does "home" mean to you?'

'I've moved around a lot,' I explained. 'When I think of home I don't think of a physical or geographical place. Being at home, for me, is about being comfortable in my own mind. It's about being at ease with who I am and what I'm doing and who I am with.'

My voice wavered with emotion. Somewhere in the course of

answering that question, I had made a decision. Later the same day, I sent a message to the former dean.

To my surprise, he replied.

I sent him another message.

Before the day was out, he had replied to that too.

Barely a week later, I was sitting opposite the-man-in-question in a restaurant in Claremont on a school night. He was in town briefly for work, and to tidy up some household loose ends. We shared a table in the only restaurant that was open for business in a neighbourhood neither of us knew well. I don't remember what we talked about, only that, again, he did most of the talking. There were silences but they were not uncomfortable. By the end of the meal, there was a lot left unspoken, but nothing was left misunderstood. He walked me to my car. As we said goodbye he put his arms around me, and I held onto him.

I held onto him.

A CERTAIN KIND OF READER MIGHT INTERPRET MY JOURNEY SO far as a series of failures: the failure to commit, the failure to be faithful, the failure to hold the nuclear family together, to endure. This is not how I understand it myself.

I think that in some ways, being in love is about letting down one's guard. It is about risk and disruption and trespassing bravely into another's way of being. It is illogical and disordered. It disrupts conventional understandings of time and meaning and purpose. It is, as Laura Kipnis puts it in *Against Love*, 'the nearest most of us come to experiencing utopia in our lifetime'.

I remember giving advice to a younger relative some years ago. She was then in her early twenties and having recovered somewhat from a difficult break-up with her first love, she'd started seeing somebody new. She asked me how we know when we meet *the one*. I remember wanting to give her a lecture on the grand narrative of romantic love and how it suited patriarchy and social order for us all to believe in it. I decided, instead, to answer more simply.

'You don't know', I said. 'In my experience, you never really know. There's always going to be an element of doubt.'

Now I wonder whether that is true.

My first six months with the former dean – who I will now call Luis – were spent with the two of us living on separate sides of the country. Our relationship grew rapidly through daily phone-calls and emails and text messages and time spent together on Skype. We met in my city; we met in his. We stole a day or two together interstate when we managed to have our schedules intersect. We talked literature. He kicked ball with my son. We talked politics. We took one another to bed: here and there, and somewhere else again.

'LIKE SOMA IN *BRAVE NEW WORLD*, [LOVE IS] THE PERFECT DRUG', posits Kipnis. '"Euphoric, narcotic, pleasantly hallucinant", as one of the characters describes it. "All the advantages of Christianity and alcohol, none of their defects", quips another.'

In love, the world becomes a playful, tender, life-affirming place. Life is beautiful; nothing seems impossible.

As I finish writing this chapter, I find myself living in a new city, reassessing what I want to be, do, become. Luis and I live in separate apartments within easy walking distance of the other. We find time to see one another every day. I remain the primary carer for my school-aged son; he sees his father, interstate, during school holidays. I sometimes wonder what we ought to wish for in a new relationship as mature adults. Is it possible to 'do' love differently from before? What might we change? What may we discard?

In a recent conversation with my mother, who is now in her late seventies and living on her own, we were reflecting on love and relationships, and she made a reference to that period in her forties when she went, in her words, 'off the rails'.

'You were not off the rails,' I said to her. 'In my mind you were never off the rails.'

'I was in need of affection', she said. 'You can't live in a relationship without affection.'

Perhaps this is the trick, whatever the domestic configuration: privileging the things that matter.

A few years after her husband's death, my friend Maureen fell in love again. 'I can't believe it,' she said of her new relationship. 'All this touching!' I felt so happy for her. It seemed to me exactly what she needed after so many years held, however subtly, at a distance.

For my mother, on the other hand, it is solitude that nourishes. At seventy-eight, she describes the prospect of a new relationship as the last thing she needs.

Another friend, Lee, has a different story. Her experiences of intimate relationships include a string of controlling, dangerous men, as well as experiments in polyamory and the kind of open marriage model followed by Sartre and de Beauvoir. There have been grand adventures, as well as disasters aplenty. Attracted to the notion of non-monogamy since she was a teenager, Lee has thought deeply about the ethics of sexual freedom alongside her desire for commitment. Her interests are not in the notion of faithfulness, but rather, as she puts it, in 'how people negotiate the widely felt conflict between the desire for security and the desire for excitement'. The thing I love about Lee is that she is, above all, curious.

When I ask for her response to Laura Kipnis's *Critical Enquiry* essay, she is thoughtful.

'I should probably declare that I'm quite averse to Marxism. I have a lot of experience with Marxism, having grown up in the Soviet Union,' she says. 'But I do think that monogamy is politicised, I mean, I do agree with Kipnis in that regard. And I'm not against overthrowing any sort of social order but I don't think that without monogamy the order would not exist. I think, to me, when you talk about choices relating to our intimate lives, the main thing is not to do it for ideological reasons, but to do what you want. I think most of the problems that people have when they're not happy in their intimate relationships are because they have gone into it without thinking they have an option.'

'But you are married, right?' I counter.

'I'm a romantic,' she laughs. 'I've been married three times.'

'Why?' I ask.

'I personally don't see any problem with marriage, as long we don't automatically define it as monogamous marriage, or automatically define it as living together if you don't want to live together. To me the idea of marriage sounds very beautiful, because there is the ceremony, and the party. But I've never felt that by the act of marrying, I'm actually doing anything but declaring my love for the person. You can always get divorced. And you can do whatever you like with it, I think. It makes a lot of sense to me that gay people are fighting for the right to be married. If they can enter the institution of marriage that will probably help all of us to interpret it in even more interesting ways. There's a lot of political activism in polyamorous communities, too, where many are also arguing for the right to get married, and I think that these kinds of changes can make marriage even more romantic, rather than conservative.'

'So you are talking then, about changing the institution of marriage from within.'

'Exactly. That's my hope.'

While I understand the political intent of Lee's argument, it is not a strategy I can imagine engaging in myself. Genuine political advancement and change, however, requires multiple strategies. And there is a part of me that rejoices that women like Lee are seeking so consciously and deliberately to initiate change.

The fact remains that the dominant narratives around love and marriage in contemporary culture, as Lee, too, points out, can – and often do – work against us. On top of this, when it comes to romance, many of us seem capable of investing wholeheartedly in fantasies that lack any sense of self-awareness.

WHILE I WAS WORKING ON THIS CHAPTER, I FOUND MYSELF – for a time – quite outside the standard Australian dream narrative of wealth accumulation, career advancement and home ownership. I was renting. I worked from home. My main form of transport was a bicycle. And I found myself settling surprisingly happily into sole parenting. My relationship with Luis remains, in some ways, unconventional: neither of us feel particularly inclined to impose or police prohibitions (which is not, of course, to say that there are none, however subtle, already in operation). At the same time the relationship seems utterly essential. Love has surprised me, again, completely.

I look back on that time when I first stumbled across Laura Kipnis's polemical *Against Love*, and it occurs to me that if ever there were a book that changed my life, it would be that one. Kipnis's focus on errant behaviour called me to attention, but her handling of the topic in a way that privileges paradox enabled me to imagine an alternative way of being – politically, economically, socially, personally. I am against love now, in the less dramatic sense of the term: not just close to it, but bolstered by it. And while I still don't share Flannery O'Connor's belief in the divine, she and I are much more closely aligned on the matter of grace.

CHAPTER
TWO
Play

To be playful is to prioritise movement or diversion, to engage in behaviour characteristically lively or irregular. It is to lean toward the imaginative, sometimes the outright rebellious. The concept has long intrigued me. By way of example, I want to take you back to 1996. I was twenty-six, and sitting in a group – a rough circle – in the mottled shade of a desert gum one searing afternoon in the remote town of Fitzroy Crossing. It was March – late summer – and I was an attendee at a small arts festival. Our group was congregated outside the local arts centre listening to an official give a dry sort of speech. I sat beside my friend Jacqui and on the other side of her was a woman by the name of Rose, whom neither of us knew well at that time. The sun was beginning to sink but it had not lost any of its bite, and sweat trickled freely down my temples, armpits, back. Just as I was beginning to wonder how much longer this heat might go on, and how much longer I, for one, could endure it, a small movement caught my eye. It was Rose picking up her drinking glass. I turned to see her smile and wink at me as she extracted a single ice cube from the glass, reached behind Jacqui's neck and dropped it discretely down the back of her dress. Jacqui jolted to attention and let out a sudden, unbridled squeal as she swiftly re-arranged her clothing to let the icy cube free. The proceedings paused and faltered. Jacqui covered her mouth. I shuddered. I'm sure my own eyes were wide with the sheer audacity of the move, and yet I couldn't help but muffle my laughter. As the official recovered his authority, I thought: how playful and childish, and how bloody lovely, is Rose? We soon became good friends. Whenever I think of her now – years later – I remember that mischievous wink she gave me that first afternoon in Fitzroy Crossing. And it still makes me smile.

Play, of course, is frequently inappropriate. Often it's overtly discouraged. And yet, how awful life can be without it. So many of us find solace and freedom in play, however subtle, and many of us deliberately prioritise forms of work, recreation or friendship that help us to engage in it well beyond our childhood years. Early play theorist Johan Huizinga, whose book *Homo Ludens* (1938) attempts to place play in a cultural and historical context, saw it as a deeply human activity. Like him, I have often wondered about its purpose and meaning, and, in particular, why our opportunities for play seem to markedly diminish once we reach adulthood.

For digital-games designer Miguel Sicart, play is far more than a rules-based leisure activity; he sees it as a way of being, a means for engaging with our environment, and one that has the capacity to re-ontologise, that is, to profoundly alter the way we understand a world we may have thought we already knew. This idea of play as a way of being – and a disruptor – is particularly interesting to consider in relation to its potential influence on individual and communal wellbeing.

MY OWN SERIOUS INTEREST IN PLAY, AND ESPECIALLY IN HOW it contributes to forming a healthy sense of self, dates back to the birth of my son in 2008. I remember being intrigued by a statement in a Western Australian government pamphlet provided by the local area health nurse when my child was a newborn: 'The first and perhaps most important thing to understand about newborn babies is that they do not have any understanding of being a separate person inside their own skin. They have feelings of pleasure when they feed successfully or hear a soothing voice, feelings of pain when they are hungry or frightened – but they don't actually know that fear is what they feel and neither do they understand that there is a "them" to feel it'. I soon discovered that play, sometimes as simple as repeating a vowel sound or imitating another's facial expressions, becomes the primary means through which the human infant begins to develop a sense of subjective being.

Even as my infant turned to toddler, and I made a gradual return to the workforce, my experience of new motherhood was primarily about immersion in play. It was not an aspect of parenting I had really anticipated and so I stumbled into it unwittingly. Roland and I played with light and shadow, we passed objects back and forth, we slotted small pebbles into the cracks between bricks, we upturned buckets of sand, we played with the sound of language, turning familiar words and phrases inside out until only the nonsense of laughter remained. We played in the midst of anything else that happened to be going on. And sometimes, we played at the expense of other things: routines, mealtimes, work.

I remember vividly the ball game we played regularly together when Roland was around fifteen months old. It consisted of throwing a ball down some garden stairs. We lived then on a large block of native bushland in the Perth Hills and so the outdoor play space was a vast, rugged jarrah forest. The game consisted of my son and me standing at the top of the garden stairs, close to the house, from which point he would throw a large, brightly coloured ball. We then watched its trajectory as it bounced and rolled down the slope of the land. It never took the same path twice. Once the ball had stopped moving, usually lodged in a pile of leaves or held against the base of a large tree trunk, I would hold Roland's hand as we negotiated the stairs down from the paved area out into the expanse of bush, a slow journey with a child who has only just learned to walk. Here, we would retrieve the ball and then ascend the stairs hand in hand to stand at the top once more and begin the game again. We both loved this ball game. It felt simple and artful. Each of us settled into the rhythm of it, and through this entered a shared mode of joyful, immersive concentration. I understood that what we were doing was a form of physics experiment, perhaps in the vein of chaos theory, since classical physics has no place for a ball that takes a different trajectory each and every time. What if? was the initial question. And then? It was also a matter of philosophy, for it seemed we could project something, by our own will, and the object would descend this way and that. But, importantly, it was never completely lost to us. We too, could move our bodies through space. We could retrieve the ball. We could throw it again.

The crucial bond formed between infant and mother through playing together and through being immersed in each other's company is something Siri Hustvedt has written about in a number of her works. 'Children must acquire an "I" through a "you"', she writes in *The Shaking Woman* (2009), 'and drawing a line between the two isn't easy because others are *of us*'.

SIRI HUSTVEDT IS BEST KNOWN INTERNATIONALLY AS A WRITER of fiction and to date has published six novels. Like many of her readers, I first came to her work through her bestselling fourth novel, *What I Loved* (2003), widely hailed as that rare thing: a work both intellectually satisfying and compelling. Entranced, I sought out Hustvedt's backlist, which includes a volume of poetry and three collections of essays, and I have read with interest each of her publications since. Many of her key preoccupations are also mine – narrative, identity, art, the relationship between mind and body – and central to so much of her work is the concept of play, a topic she and I are both deeply interested in talking about.

In the days preceding my first meeting with Hustvedt, the most extreme winter weather conditions in more than a century had closed JFK Airport, and a Code Blue had been put in place by New York's Department of Homeless Services, meaning shelters and drop-in centres were required to take in everyone they could: sanctions did not apply. Emergency services and their accompanying sirens were out in abundance on the icy streets and there was widespread closure of schools and other public institutions.

In the midst of these dramatic conditions, I found Hustvedt's home in a row of majestic brownstones in a beautiful part of Brooklyn. Two sets of heavy doors at the entrance to the building sealed off the extremes of the weather and we sat in the quiet downstairs living area, a room that felt lived-in and well loved, and within which the genuine warmth of my host's welcome put me quickly at ease.

Tall and comfortably dressed, Hustvedt had the unhurried demeanour of someone who worked regularly from home and was at ease there, and the quiet self-assurance of a person who has long found purpose through her work.

'I think that so many forms of human endeavour can fall into the field of play', she told me as our conversation began. 'For me intellectual life is also a form of play.'

Hustvedt completed her PhD in literature at Columbia

University, but her disciplinary knowledge is broad-ranging. She has given lectures on art theory at the Prado and New York's Metropolitan Museum of Art. In 2011 she delivered the thirty-ninth annual Freud lecture in Vienna, and she has also spoken on the philosophy of Kierkegaard. In recognition of her contribution to so many fields, she was awarded the Gabarron International Award for Thought and Humanities in 2012.

'I read a lot', she explained modestly. 'I have the time, and I read.'

THE COURSE OF MY CONVERSATION WITH HUSTVEDT OVER TWO afternoons charted some of the century's key thinkers across psychology, neuroscience, education and philosophy. Amongst these, three key figures stood out. We settled, focussed and returned regularly to Sigmund Freud, to DW Winnicott, and to the Russian psychologist Lev Vygotsky. Other key thinkers and scholars made an occasional appearance, but it was the inherently *intersubjective* aspect of play that was at the core of our mutual interest in the topic, and hence of our discussion. I wanted to talk about the question of how crucial play is, not just during childhood, but into and throughout our lives as adults.

'For Winnicott, every human being needs to play,' Hustvedt emphasised.

Donald (DW) Winnicott was an English paediatrician and psychoanalyst who published several books and hundreds of papers, including *Playing and Reality* (1971) and *The Piggle* (1971). In *Playing and Reality*, he warned of the dangerous tendency he had observed in psychoanalytic practice of treating the analyst too much as the authority. He was particularly concerned that patients could be seduced into complying with their analyst's authoritative interpretations, and his solution was an increased emphasis on, indeed a solid argument for, the centrality of play.

A well-known example of Winnicott's approach in his work with children was the spatula game, in which he placed an object commonly found in doctors' consultation rooms – the spatula for depressing the tongue – within easy reach of a child, and waited for him or her to begin to play with it. He noted a period of hesitation and reserve that almost always occurred before the child engaged with the object. Winnicott transferred this idea to the analyst/patient relationship, noting that like a child, the patient also needed to 'discover' the analyst, and become the active agent in engaging the analyst in imaginative play.

On the concept of play as it relates to creativity, Winnicott is perhaps best known for his identification of what he called *potential space*. 'No human being is free from the strain of relating inner and outer reality', he wrote in 1953, proposing that, 'relief from this strain is provided by an intermediate area of experience.' Winnicott named this area potential space and he identified play, creativity and analytical thinking as pertaining to it. The origin of potential space, he argued, was the physical, mental and emotional bond between a mother and her infant.

AS WE TALKED, HUSTVEDT AND I SHARED STORIES OF THE KINDS of play our own and other children we'd observed were involved in as infants and toddlers: a niece who played funerals every day for weeks after attending the funeral of her step-grandfather; a baby who would wake in the night and play contentedly for hours in her cot without so much as attempting to call out for anyone else to come; a pre-schooler's love for playing rough-and-tumble ('You be Rough, and I'll be Tumble!'). Hustvedt related the story of a little boy described in child psychoanalyst Selma Fraiberg's book *The Magic Years* (1959). In the story, the boy's parents, based in the United States, tell him they are planning to fly with him to Europe for a family holiday. 'Everyone was all excited and, you know, the week before they were leaving, they realised that the little boy was full of anxiety, and he was really anxious and mopey and distressed, and they tried to get him to tell them what was going on, and then finally he did, and he said to his parents: "I don't know *how* to fly." He thought his parents were going to take off, and since he couldn't do it, he would be left behind. "I don't know how to fly to Yerp."'

PSYCHOANALYSIS HAS BEEN A LONG-TERM INTEREST FOR Hustvedt. Her first novel, *The Blindfold* (1993), is a study in the disintegration of the self. The central character, Iris Vegan, is a graduate student in New York whose struggles with poverty, illness and loneliness are enacted through a series of dangerously playful engagements with powerful men. Her most radical act of defiance through play occurs when she takes on the identity of a male character from a novella called *The Brutal Boy*, a text she has translated from the German for her professor lover. When the professor leaves town, Iris takes to inhabiting New York's late-night bars as a man in a suit, failing to properly speak and to eat: she is almost completely erased. Iris performs – literally plays – her grief, loss and confusion. The character is a potent precursor for so many of Hustvedt's later characters, for whom Winnicott's 'potential space' is a site of both possibility and danger.

For many years, Hustvedt attended lectures at the New York Psychoanalytic Institute and later became a member of the Mortimer Ostow Neuropsychoanalysis Discussion Group, where she engaged in dialogue about the relationship between contemporary psychoanalysis and neurobiology. The group's members included Jaak Panksepp, an Estonian-born American psychologist who has a special interest in the neural mechanisms of emotion, and who has since become one of Hustvedt's good friends. Hustvedt also worked for eight years as a voluntary creative writing tutor for psychiatric in-patients at The Payne Whitney Clinic at New York Hospital, an act of generosity that can also be read as a kind of experiment, putting into practice, perhaps, some of her accumulated knowledge both as a reader of psychoanalytic theory and as a practising writer.

'Winnicott talks about adults who come to him who are unable to play,' she told me. By adults who are *unable to play*, Winnicott meant people for whom an ability to think imaginatively, creatively and spontaneously seemed to have been profoundly stifled or erased. 'When I was teaching my students in the psychiatric hospital,' Hustvedt continued, 'in a way the most difficult patients to teach were the patients suffering from major depression. Now, the fact that they had already gotten themselves to my classroom means that they were in better shape than other depressed patients who were lying in stupors in their room. There was something that got them there, some kind of will. But still, they were very hard to engage, so that between space that is there between every person and another was decidedly flat.

'Interestingly enough, psychotic patients, all of whom were of course medicated by the time they got to me, had a much greater ability to make verbal play, to have fun with language, including certain – what they call in the business – word salads. Psychotic language has a kind of vivid life and bounce to it that is really notable. It doesn't always make sense, and narrative is very difficult in psychosis, but there is poetic energy in psychosis that can be tapped, sometimes to very startling effects.'

Hustvedt's self-consciously post-9/11 novel, *The Sorrows of an American* (2008), features a narrator who is a psychoanalyst, and his discussion of patients' maladies include people from either end of that spectrum. The psychotic word salads of Mr T – 'Lavinia in Slovenia is slipping into schizophrenia … the whole of life, void and empty noise, boys' – form a lively contrast to the repressed character of Mrs L or the withdrawn Mrs Kavacek, aka Lisa Odland, who locks herself in her house and draws the shutters, permanently damaged by the trauma of early childhood and adolescence. Interestingly, however, even Mrs Kavacek plays. She makes a living producing extraordinary handmade dolls, each based on a real-life person whose life events have some kind of emotional resonance for her. Her creations leave the house in unmarked boxes, sold to collectors via eBay.

Play, in Hustvedt's fiction, is a crucial site of investigation.

'Art is essentially intersubjective,' she surmises. 'It's *always* about the other.'

DURING OUR CONVERSATION, I DISCOVERED THAT HUSTVEDT and I both remained intrigued by the sense of altered consciousness we each experienced for a period as new mothers, a consciousness which was neither separate from nor completely immersed in the emerging consciousness of the child.

'There is overwhelming evidence on neurosynaptic and hormonal changes in both the infant and the mother,' said Hustvedt. 'I think what's interesting is that these are also temporal issues. I remember when Sophie was an infant, I would go to sleep and if she made a noise like this' – Hustvedt mimicked a tiny murmur – 'I woke up. Now, you couldn't wake me up with a squeak! I'm not in that moment. I don't have an infant sleeping in the next room.

I'm just living in a different space. I have a lot of attunements to my husband, you know, but it's grown up, you know, it's different. It's a different kind of "between" space.

'I used to, when I left Sophie during that period of real attachment anxiety that kids have, naturally, I would feel a literal physical tug, you know, if I went on a book tour or something when she was a little kid and I walked out the door. Sometimes she was howling, sometimes not, but I'd get in a cab and I'd just have to get over the ... you know' – Hustvedt mimed turmoil, pulling a face and raising her hands – 'and then I'd get on the plane and I'd think, oh, this is really nice! It wasn't that I was doggedly hanging on to that feeling, it's just that it's a different "between" space.

'What's important to remember is that we all come out of that,' Hustvedt expanded. 'We're all made like that. There are a couple of big lies that go remarkably uncriticised. One is the political theory of the totally autonomous individual, you know, the lonely subject, a male subject usually, wandering around making decisions for himself. Well, fine, there are degrees of autonomy, but those models are always forgetting human development. They just never include it. And certain kinds of static models about how the brain works, or studying the brain in isolation as if it's not this moving, changing organ that develops over time ... it just isn't going to get you anywhere.'

SIRI HUSTVEDT GREW UP IN RURAL MINNESOTA. HER FATHER was an academic who taught Norwegian language and literature at St Olaf College. Her father's parents migrated to the United States in the 1930s, and initially made their living from farming. Hustvedt's mother, Ester, travelled from Norway to marry Lloyd in the early 1950s and stayed home to raise the children, although she later worked as a French instructor. Hustvedt was the eldest of four girls.

While we were talking she remembered fondly an early childhood spent playing with her closest sister, Liv, only nineteen months younger.

'When I was a child,' she laughed, 'I'll never forget, we moved to a house that my parents built outside this little town, this is in the early sixties, and they put in a new refrigerator, and we got the cardboard packaging box. I have very fond memories of that box. We turned it immediately into a house, and a fort and all varieties of that, and we put pillows and blankets in there, and it was a wonderful, wonderful toy. And this very much picks up on Vygotsky, you know? What are we going to do with this refrigerator box? Well, it can be all kinds of things'.

Lev Vygotsky was a Soviet Belarusian psychologist and the founder of a theory of development commonly known as cultural-historical psychology. He saw the emergence of reasoning as dependent on practical activity in a social environment: he was hugely interested in play.

'Imagination is a new formation that is not present in the very young child ... like all functions of consciousness, it originally arises out of action,' wrote Vygotsky in an essay first published in 1933. Vygotsky saw play as both cognitive and affective – intellectual and emotional. He observed the way children seek to transform ordinary everyday objects – a stick becomes a horse – and posited that this kind of active imaginary play is a means for developing abstract thought. He was particularly interested in the relationship between children's imaginary games and reality, and also in the question of rules versus freedom in play. The premise for an imaginary game, for example, is often a reproduction of a real situation. Further, the playing child is always 'a head taller than himself', as though creating a slightly older version of himself through play calls him forward into a future not yet fully knowable but for which he senses the need to prepare.

I have seen Vygotsky's theories played out in the daily life of my son, Roland, who since around three years of age has engaged the two of us in a role-play game we call 'Little Girl'. It's an imaginary game in which I take the role of the little girl, and of her mother, and Roland plays the role of an older boy, Agent, and sometimes of shopkeepers or other strangers who come and go depending on the scene. Little Girl is a bit younger than the real-life Roland, and she is often upset, whereas Agent is several years older. Roland jumps in and out of the role of director: Little Girl is often instructed to cry or get upset if things don't go her way, and she quite regularly misunderstands things or is clumsy or mischievous. Her mother is unerringly patient and is often called in by Agent to explain difficult concepts to the recalcitrant little girl. Agent, too, is patient with Little Girl, and likes to bring her gifts and share things with her, but he is frequently allowed to do adult things – like fly aeroplanes – whereas Little Girl, because she is small, is required to sit and watch.

'In play the child is free, but this is an illusory freedom,' wrote Vygotsky. 'All games with imaginary situations are simultaneously games with rules.' Thus play often requires us to test our bravery a little, to push against or exceed the usual boundaries, to imitate a real-life situation but 'tighten the screws' as we say in storytelling. In the role-play game I engage in with Roland, I can see that he is in some ways both the younger and the older child simultaneously.

Little Girl wants something from the shopkeeper, but he won't give it to her. Or Little Girl wants Agent to wake up but it's too early and he's not ready. Sometimes Agent goes on adventures but Little Girl gets left behind. And then we are playing shopkeepers again and Little Girl wants a present.

'Is it your birthday?' the shopkeeper wants to know.

'No', Little Girl confesses.

'And Mum, she's telling the truth, isn't she Mum?'

'Then there is nothing you can have', says Roland-as-shopkeeper.

'Mum, pretend she gets cross, and then Agent is there. Agent is working for the shopkeeper. And Agent says, "Stop shouting, Little Girl! Stop shouting! Children who shout won't get presents."'

WHAT ABOUT US ADULTS, I WONDER? CAN WE SHIFT IN AND out of play mode – imaginary or otherwise – with the same sense of freedom, and with the same capacity for testing things out, even the dramatically disastrous, illicit or embarrassing things? I think we can, and very often do. This is especially evident when we are at the extreme edge of things, as when we are suddenly in love, but also when we are deeply suffering, as can be the case with grief.

In Siri Hustvedt's most commercially successful novel, *What I Loved* (2003), the narrative centres around the lives of two couples, each bringing up a son. The story maps the development of the children of either couple from infanthood onwards, pondering their differences and similarities alongside their on-again, off-again friendship. After Matthew, one of the boys, dies in an accident at age eleven, there is a profoundly moving scene in which Leo, Matthew's father and the novel's central narrator, describes how he finds comfort in tracing the lines of the many drawings the child has left behind. 'I found the motion of his living hand that way, and once I had started, I couldn't stop.' I read Leo's tracing as a form of play. This incident, along with many others in Hustvedt's work, emphasises the way play – both embodied and intellectual – becomes a way of knowing and experiencing an other.

In the second act of *What I Loved*, Mark, the child who is still living, begins to spend more and more time with Leo, and in doing so he helps him to grieve. Mark, the son who is not Leo's, becomes a kind of doppelgänger or double. When he reaches adolescence, however, Mark changes: he is a good companion one moment, and a lying thief the next. After Bill, Mark's natural father, dies, the book swings into a final act in which Leo's care and concern for Mark becomes a dangerous investment. Mark is closely involved with a drug dealer and well-known figure of the New York art scene, a young man who is eventually convicted of a serious murder in which Mark is implicated. The two young men lead the ageing art historian, Leo, on a strange chase to the American interior. Mark and his friend play with Leo, the way a cat plays with its prey. It is perhaps a form of performance art. They appear in disguises, sometimes as a homosexual couple, sometimes as a man and his son. Leo is forced to question his own motivations. If this is art, what kind is it? Play here takes on a dark, sinister and concerning edge. Where Bill's art, about which Leo is writing, is a playful, handcrafted quest for meaning, Mark's accomplice's art is primarily conceptual, steeped in inventions, jokes, absurdities. It is predicated on cruelty.

One of the most interesting lines in the book is one that draws our attention to the book's title. Mark's stepmother, Violet, witnessing the development of a character for whom emotional connection is a difficult, perhaps profoundly impossible task, reflects on her attachment to the child-cum-adolescent Mark. She had loved him as a boy, but finds herself forced to re-examine that attachment. The small child who frequently misbehaved spent some years doing 'the right thing', but as Violet looks back on that period she wonders whether the 'good' behaviour was itself a kind of role-play. She recalls the 'good' Mark as a kind of automaton. On reflection, Violet asks herself, 'What is it that I loved?'

In other words, was it a form of emptiness all along, that

being I had imagined myself to love? Perhaps love itself is a form of adult play. Like play, it is something we can enact, but it is also a diversion: lively, irregular, elusive.

At the heart of all the playfulness in *What I Loved* is a question about the relationship between love and knowledge. Perhaps because of this, it is also a book about borders. In narrating the story of the two closely connected families across two and a half decades, the central narrator, Leo, is not just straightening out his memories and contemplating the meaning of art, but reflecting on his own connectedness (or otherwise) to others. As with so many of Hustvedt's characters, he is focussed very much on relating inner and outer reality, and therefore on seeking to understand Winnicott's potential space.

IN HIS BOOK *PLAY MATTERS* (2014), MIGUEL SICART TALKS ABOUT play as an act of beauty, precisely because its affordances allow for critical reflection and meaning-making. It is also, he argues, a politically significant activity, because of its capacity to mock reality and produce satire. But one of the more interesting aspects of Sicart's work is his identification of the notion of dark play. The performance of Mark's accomplice in *What I Loved* can be read as an instance of this, particularly if we think about his deliberately manipulative and abusive play with Leo. Here, play itself becomes a form of violent behaviour. In an interesting review of Sicart's *Play Matters*, fellow digital-games scholar Michael deAnda criticises Sicart for not paying enough attention to the boundaries of playful expression: is dark play, for example, a limit case at that border? DeAnda urges us to consider the work of games studies scholars Nina Huntemann and Mia Consalvo who, in their response to violent and misogynistic representations of women in digital gaming, discuss the case of Anita Sarkeesian. Sarkeesian was subject to an extensive sexual harassment campaign including death threats that resembled play acts – for example the 'game' *Beat Up Anita Sarkeesian* – because of her critique of harmful representation and 'play' regarding women in a range of online games. Such an instance is, again, a cruel twist on the border between play and reality, and the 'hiding' of hatred in plain sight.

Dark play has its role, too, in Hustvedt's latest novel, *The Blazing World* (2014). The story spins around a deliberate hoax by a female artist in her sixties named Harry Burden. Harry decides to employ a series of young men as living masks. She creates an exhibition, and then has each young male artist in turn pose at being the lone auteur behind the work. Harry's proposal is that having a 'a cock and a pair of balls' – as she puts it – is the key prerequisite for serious critical and commercial success in the New York art world. In all three of her hoaxes, her theory is proven correct. But the stakes of the game are increasingly high, and when, in the end, the most famous of the three young men denies her involvement in the work, and Harry's attempt at a public unmasking is foiled, she is ridiculed and rejected, convincingly (mis)represented in the public domain as the bitter, hysterical woman whose artwork could never rise above the level of the trivial and the domestic. At the novel's conclusion, Harry dies of cancer, commercially unsuccessful and critically ignored.

'THE OPPOSITE OF PLAY IS NOT WORK, IT'S DEPRESSION', ARGUES American neuroscientist Stuart Brown, whose work sits at the nexus between science and play scholarship. Brown's empirical work with rats in the laboratory supports the notion that play enables risk-taking behaviour and that without the opportunity to pursue such playful modes, we risk not just our individual health, but ultimately our species survival. He describes an experiment in which one group of rats is 'permitted' to play, while another is not. When a cat's collar is dropped into each of their cages, both groups of rats retreat. The scent of a cat is instinctually understood as a threat. But those rats who've been permitted to play eventually poke their noses out of their shelters and assess that the threat of danger is gone. They come out again, and get on with things. The rats who have been denied play, in contrast, never get over the threat. 'They die in their bunkers,' declares Brown.

Linking his empirical work with that of psychologist Mihaly Csikszentmihalyi, Brown identifies play as an altered state. This particular take on Csikszentmihalyi's work interested me when I first came across it in Brown's writing because as a novelist, my own experience of immersion in the creative writing process feels very much like an altered state, or at least a mode of thinking/being that is splintered or detached from other, more normalised or cohesive understandings of purpose, time and selfhood. Significantly, I experience the practice of imaginative writing as both an essential and an inherently *playful* practice. Far from static, it is dynamic, lively and transformative. In and through the doing, my practice moves – paradoxically – both towards and away from knowledge.

WHEN I LEFT HUSTVEDT'S HOUSE AFTER OUR FIRST MEETING, the winter darkness was falling, and my mind was full of thinking about play from a myriad of angles. Luis, who was travelling with me, had just moved us from a downtown Manhattan hotel to a short-stay apartment in the more affordable area of Brooklyn's Bedford-Stuyvesant. He had gone on ahead with the luggage, and

I was yet to navigate my way to the new address. The agreement was that I would get a taxi from near Hustvedt's place, and so I stood for a few minutes on Sixth Avenue but there didn't seem to be any sign of a vacant cab. The weather remained extremely cold, though there was little wind and no snow. I decided to walk. The truth was I needed to walk. The warmth of Hustvedt's welcome, combined with her knowledge and enthusiasm for talking about ideas, had invigorated me. I walked, thinking. I thought about Rudolf Steiner and Maria Montessori and Friedrich Froebel, the way each of these had enthused about the importance of active imaginative play in early childhood, the way in which they each privileged the physical and the tactile, the way in which they conceived of education as first and foremost an exploratory project. Play, for each of these thinkers, was primarily a means of engaging with the world. Ideas such as theirs have been completely sidelined in mainstream education in both Australia and the United States of late, where constant testing and measurement is used to judge teachers and students alike, and literacy and numeracy are held up as the only things that matter, as if any other form of human endeavour is a hindrance to, rather than a means of, enabling these increasingly narrow conceptions of discipline.

As I walked through the New York winter, my fingers were turning numb in my pockets. I stopped at a shop selling handmade wares from Tibet, bought a pair of woollen gloves, and checked my map. When I reached Flatbush Avenue, I turned left. I walked straight past Bergen Street subway station and by the time I reached Atlantic Terminal it was fully dark. I rushed to join a train that purported to stop at the station I was after: Nostrand Avenue. The fact I failed to register was that I'd stepped onto the Long Island Rail Road line, instead of the subway line. Only after the train had pulled away did I realise that my ticket was invalid.

My mobile reception was playing up. When I got off at Nostrand Avenue, I happily escaped the ticket inspector, but I still had a very long walk ahead. As it turned out, I was on the right street, but at the wrong end of it. As I walked along the poorly lit pavement, small gangs of youths were gathered on the corner of each block, and heavily clad alcoholics and druggies muttered to the air as they passed me by.

I kept walking. I was thinking about a German word: *spieltrieb*, which Hustvedt and I were yet to discuss, sometimes translated as play-drive. At the same time, I was thinking about the vulnerability of the body, and counting the numbers down to the new address. One hundred to go ... ninety ... eighty ... seventy ... eventually I reached the other end of the avenue. I recognised Luis standing out the front of the new place, waiting for me. The apartment was practically on top of the K-line subway station: Nostrand Avenue. How easily a little slippage, a slight misreading, can have us drift into unanticipated territory. I thought of the expression *to play it safe*. I thought of the expression *to play into the hands of*. I thought of a novel I'd once read – *The Architect* by John Scott – in which the protagonist is killed by a violent gang in Berlin, ostensibly for his failure to register his own trespass into one of the city's then notorious lawless zones.

Inside the warmth of the new apartment I took off my gloves and coat.

'Oh, honey,' Luis said, pulling me close. 'Your fingers are like ice.'

ON OUR SECOND MEETING, THE DISCUSSION WITH HUSTVEDT commenced with the concept of imaginary friends. 'It used to be that there was some kind of common sense understanding that children with imaginary friends were lacking in social skills,' she told me. 'They were unable to make their own friends so they would invent somebody who was easier to deal with. It seems however that this is just not the case. Often outgoing children will have imaginary friends, so it's not about withdrawal from the world, necessarily.

'I'm very interested in those imaginary friends. I've used a number of them in my books – children in my books have imaginary friends – but also pericosms. Do you know what a pericosm is? Remember the Brontë children had one. It's the invention of a world that lasts over time. A lot of children have what I think of as transient worlds, you know, the worlds of your dolls or your figures, and they can stay for a while, and then they vanish, but this highly activated imaginary world that they return to seems to be a striking precursor of literary worlds. The version of the world that fiction writers make is indeed something like that, even if you set it in a "real" world. It doesn't have to be a fantasy world to "invent" a world in a work of fiction.'

Over the weekend between our first and second meetings, Hustvedt had been to Chicago to do an 'in-conversation' session with the feminist scholar Nancy K Miller at the conference of the Modern Language Association. We talked about this for a while. Miller's academic area of speciality is life writing, and she writes memoir herself. Outside the formal discussion of the conference, she and Hustvedt had spoken briefly about the differences between writing fiction and non-fiction.

Hustvedt reported on their conversation: 'Nancy said, "You know, one of the things that I don't understand is how you can become these other people. I can't do that!" And her comments made a deep impression on me, because, it's always been perfectly clear to me that not everybody is going to choose fiction writing. Fiction is a life calling, right? Not everybody is going to sit down and write about made-up people and have imaginary things happen to them, but the idea that she felt really *cut off* from that activity, you see, this interests me. My sense of this kind of imaginary activity is that it is a human activity, a natural human activity that grows out of a very profound function in human life, which is that we can recall ourselves in the past and imagine ourselves into the future, and we spend a lot of time fantasising as we're growing up.

'I don't know where the line is, then, or if it's just some kind of adult atrophy, but my sense is that it's really not all that different from saying, "Let's pretend that we're taking a ship", as my sister and I used to do, as I told you, you know, we'd have endless disasters as we played, and the aesthetic barrier, or the ability to withdraw at any moment is always there, I mean, you know it's not actually happening. No matter how involved you are, you can withdraw from it. So, I wonder what it is about people who find that kind of activity almost unimaginable.'

In response, I cited a comment I had read by the biologist Robert Fagen, author of *Animal Play Behavior* (1981). Researchers in his field sometimes spend days, weeks and months observing animals at play, and Fagen once reported that what he saw as the most irritating feature of such play was its inaccessibility. 'We feel that something is behind it all', he wrote, 'but we do not know, or have forgotten, how to see it'.

'This is really fascinating', said Hustvedt, ruminating over Fagen's comment. 'There are two ways to look at this. One is that of course we don't have – let's say we're looking at two dogs playing. We don't have access to that form of perception. At the same time, dogs and human beings actually do share quite a bit of neural apparatus. We also share the fact of play. So, there's a lot of criticism in science about anthropomorphising. Scientists, unlike most human beings, are incredibly reluctant to even assign emotions to animals. Now this seems extremely peculiar, since if we look at the limbic system, even in a rat, it has a lot in common with our limbic system. So the question hinges on reflective self-consciousness, and if you don't know that you're feeling pain, do you still feel pain? Well, I think so.

'When we rush around jumping up and down as children, is there some commonality and relationship between our rushing around and doing rough and tumble and animals? I think there is. And I think it's a scientifically valid thing to think about.'

I WAS REMINDED AT THIS POINT OF MY OWN LOVE OF ROAD cycling, the way that the restlessness of the body, the deeply felt need for movement, itself gives birth to the intellect, the imagination, and the play of possibility. It's interesting that the shackling of movement – due to imprisonment, illness, slavery, the burden of responsibility – kills our motivation. No wonder people love driving cars, all the movement with minimal effort: the illusion of release. Through playful physical movement, we can push ourselves – just all of a sudden – towards the uncomfortable, the surprisingly dangerous. I am thinking, in particular, of my love of cycling at speed downhill, the way that sense of freefalling brings both joy – the emptiness of air, the weight of the body taken away from us, the rush of speed – and danger, fear, impending terror.

A few years ago, when I was able to spend long periods road cycling alone on the hills outside of Perth, the joy of careering downhill, speeding up to 70 kilometres an hour on a carbon frame racing bike, and willing myself to lean down, release, let go, provided an extraordinary sense of exhilaration and freedom. Curiously, it also helped me to solve many of the problems I was facing at the time. How often do we have the opportunity to do that in modern life as an adult? Sometimes it seems as though adult life – mortgages, performance measurement at work, competitive parenting – does nothing but corral one in. Extreme forms of play, such as the steep descent, tantalise us with the openness of possibility, the very hint of freefall. Mainstream culture's fascination with extreme sports provides some clues here about our adult yearning for taking risks through play.

In a novel I've been working on while writing this chapter, the protagonist is hinged somewhere between reflective self-consciousness and lack of it. Her narrative continuity – her very existence as a continuous subject – has been damaged by a sudden head injury acquired from a cycling accident, and she drifts, sometimes along the bottom of the river into which her physical body has fallen, and sometimes through impossible ruptures of time and space, resurfacing in fifth-century China, for example, or in a futuristic nether world curiously devoid of risk. The work is already far more experimental than my previous novels, and the experience of creating it has been one of a beautifully immersive and insistent absorption. I think of it as, above all, a playful piece of work, arrived at via a fluid writing process and via physical exercise.

It was both cycling and the manuscript-in-progress that I was thinking of as Hustvedt and I talked about how the body works as a generative source, and about how playful writing, in particular, is generated through an element of physicality: through doing. Hustvedt quoted Einstein: 'He was asked how he worked, and he said, "None of my work involves signs, either mathematical or linguistic. My work is visual, muscular and emotional." And then *later* it's translated into a kind of formula. I thought that was one of the most enlightening ways to talk about what creativity is, because I think it's very much that. It comes from unconscious places. But what's conscious is feeling. And rhythm (which is the muscular part), you know, when you're making a book, you get into these kind of' – Hustvedt moves her body musically for a moment, as if to dance – 'I think these rhythms, even with scientific and intellectual work, are important.

'I also think it's interesting that if you're writing something and it's no fun at all,' Hustvedt confided, 'it's probably bad.' She related the experience of writing her first novel, which at one point contained an extra chapter written with quite a different voice and set in a different time period from the rest of the book. The sheer difficulty of writing that section – more than two decades ago – has stayed with her. 'I hated writing it,' she said. 'I mean, it was a miserable, horrible, wounded, aching experience. I think I was drawing on material from my own life, but it wasn't literally my own life, it was some place that I was unable to go, and I was miserable. I said to my husband, "This is awful".' In the end, she abandoned that section.

'That feeling of wrongness,' she told me, is 'related to some kind of emotional truth. There is no emotional truth with a capital T. What there is, is something in yourself that is answering the text that either feels right or feels wrong.'

The very idea of this took me back to thinking about the working free that comes through pedalling, the leaning forward, the sheer concentration as the road falls and curves, another vehicle passes by, a bird comes in and out of one's peripheral vision, the torso leans forward, and the whole body braces against the wind. I was thinking about descending so fast that the lowest gear has no traction. The legs circle uselessly. The shoulders are low, the spine aligned along the frame. This, I think, feels like courage. It feels almost like flying.

HUSTVEDT'S INTELLECTUAL INTERESTS IN FREUD, IN NEUROSCIENCE, in neuro-psychoanalysis, and hence in the mind/body problem, stem very much from her own lived experience of a disobedient body. She is a long-term sufferer of migraines, an affliction that can painfully warp one's sense of reality, one's sense of self. Further, after the death of her father in 2006, she began to suffer from a strange affliction during public speaking: her body began to shake. Her book *The Shaking Woman* – part memoir, part essay – is the result of that experience. 'The shaking woman felt like me and not like me at the same time,' she wrote. 'From the chin up I was my familiar self. From the neck down, I was a shuddering stranger.'

One of the many theories Hustvedt posited in *The Shaking Woman* was the idea that she might have some form of synaesthesia. She described experiencing powerful emotional responses to colours and lights. 'I seem to translate everything into bodily feelings and sensations,' she wrote. In reflecting on her father's final days of life, she recalled returning home to stay in her childhood bed after a visit to the hospital, and having the distinct sensation that she was becoming her father. 'As I lay there, thinking of my father, I felt the oxygen line in my nostrils and its discomfort, the heaviness of my lame leg, from which a tumour had been removed years before, the pressure in my tightened lungs, and a sudden panicked helplessness that I could not move from the bed on my own but would have to call for help.' Is there such a thing, I wonder, as *too much* empathy?

For Hustvedt, as for early-childhood education and natural science advocates, Friedrich Froebel and Rudolf Steiner, the body is central to play. It can be central, too, to writing. One could say that Hustvedt's fiction is haunted by the body. In *The Blindfold*, for example, the young student, Iris, is disturbed by a photograph taken of her by a budding art photographer, despite her agreement to pose for him. Something strange happens during the session in his studio, some kind of slippage, as if Iris is stripped bare by the power of the photographer's gaze. She descends into a kind of trance. When her photograph is displayed prominently in an exhibition, she finds the image shocking and asks the photographer to remove it, but he refuses. The figure in the photograph both is and is not Iris. The image hanging in the gallery space both is and is not hers. In art, as in fiction, the playfulness at the heart of the project is inherently bound up in questions of representation. Hustvedt's work asks insistently, not just *who am I?* but *where do I begin and end?*

'In one essay, I wrote, *only the open self can feel joy.* And I think this is true, actually. But it's the open self that can be profoundly wounded as well.' While we were contemplating what it means for the self to be resilient, Hustvedt paused for a moment and recalled a favourite line from Winnicott. '"Health is not a flight into sanity. Health tolerates disintegration."' She smiled. 'I think it's the most beautiful line.'

I had to agree. The line rang true for me, too.

AS MY OWN READING AND THINKING AROUND PLAY PROGRESSED, my son grew bigger. He started school. He learned to swim. At home, he took to playing for much lengthier periods on his own, and as we played the Little Girl game less often, he occupied himself instead with his own animated role-plays. From the beginning these were physically demanding affairs. His accomplice was a narrow bamboo stick, a kind of staff, that spun nimbly in his fingers, a weapon against imaginary opponents. Our shared living space became a stage, alive with athletic kicks and turns and spills, and accompanied by sound effects reminiscent of kung-fu movies.

Death was played out. Again, again, the dexterous boy player rose from corpse position, and readied himself once more for body-to-body combat on sturdy legs. This one would never be defeated. This one would always live to fight again.

I ASKED HUSTVEDT ABOUT FREUD, ABOUT THIS NOTION OF the *spieltrieb* which she had written about in her essay, 'Freud's Playground'.

'This is a nice place in which Freud can be linked to contemporary neuroscience,' she said. 'Of course, Freud was a neurologist. And he spent eight years in a lab, you know, taking apart little neurons in eels. So he was a scientist and he never really dropped the scientific hope. Nevertheless, *trieb* is this idea that there are mammalian drives that are moving out into the environment and on to others, and that they can attach themselves in very complicated ways in human beings, in a more complex way than in lower mammals, for example. The *trieb*, which was poorly translated by James Strachey as *instinct*, is not instinct. Instinct is something else in Freud. He did think that there were instincts, and I think, by the way, there are too, but the drives are something else, that is an urge. It is innate, you know. You look at a baby, and this infant has certain urges to go for the other, but also to go for objects, you know, to investigate, to explore.

'I have a physicist friend who is now working in neuroscience,' Hustvedt continued. 'He's the guy who has this dream about two brothers, x and x prime.'

Hustvedt wrote about this episode in *The Shaking Woman*. The physicist had been trying to solve a complicated calculation and he named the central quantities x and x prime. One night he dreamt about twin brothers. 'They were both human actors in the dream but at the same time I knew they were x and x prime,' he said. When he woke up, he knew he had solved the formula. He just got up and wrote it all down.

'But it is important to understand,' Hustvedt told me, 'that these deep things, you know, unconsciousness, sleep, desire, urges, play, fun, all of this is involved in creative work and it crosses all areas of human experience. And that's vital.'

We don't hear enough about the role of the imagination in the sciences. 'Perhaps one of the things that makes it difficult for us in the arts and humanities,' I posited, 'is this perception that the imaginative work we do is inaccessible.'

Hustvedt agreed. 'The imaginary has been feminised. That's really dangerous. If you take these deep bodily metaphors – and I think George Lakoff and Mark Johnson [whose work argues that metaphor can shape our perceptions without our even noticing] were right about those ... not that women are softer than men, that's ridiculous, I mean you touch a man and a woman, you're not going to ...' She pinched her forearm.

'We're very much made of the same stuff,' I observed with a smile.

Hustvedt pulled a face of mock surprise, which made us both laugh.

'I wrote a short essay in a book called *Fifty Shades of Feminism*,' she continued. 'In that I say that there are codes, you know, so the masculine, the feminine. The sciences are masculine, and the novel and the arts are feminine. More and more, you know, most men don't read a lot of novels. As I say in *The Summer Without Men*, if they read novels, they like to have a masculine name on the cover, because then there's something masculine about it.

'If we live in a culture where we are coding the imagination as feminine and the very adjective feminine continues to be a

71

polluting adjective, then I think human beings are in trouble. This is really important, because we mustn't code the imagination as identified with the female sex. When a woman writes fiction, then she's doubly feminised. I notice when I give lectures to scientists, and most of them are still men, I'm masculinised by the very fact that I'm talking about [scientific] material. It doesn't turn you into a man but it's like the discourse is more serious. You know, it's like what you were saying about creative writing not being taken seriously in the academy. It's like ...'

She frowned and shifted her hand, as if to dismiss something. It was one of the few times I'd witnessed her being stuck for words.

'A lot of this isn't even conscious,' she said eventually, and it was on this sombre note that we concluded our discussion.

AFTER I RETURNED HOME TO AUSTRALIA, IN THE MONTHS AFTER visiting Hustvedt, I became increasingly interested in the role of play in research practice right across the humanities and the sciences. I began to speak to experienced researchers from fields as diverse as mathematics, the social sciences, engineering and medicine. I wanted to know more about the role of play and playfulness in their daily work.

I met a physicist, for example, whose chief hobby was ballroom dancing, and who could describe to me a complex problem solved mid-movement on the dance floor. I was taken aback with how enthusiastic the responses of academic colleagues were to my questions about play and playfulness in relation to their work. Many of the researchers I spoke to recognised it as a lifelong practice and as an intrinsic part of what they do when they *do* research. They emphasised the importance of joyful, immersive doing and of play's role in managing what one colleague called 'the apprehensiveness of not knowing'. Colleagues in the creative arts tended to very readily emphasise the role of uncertainty and risk in their practice – 'I never feel there's surety in anything I do,' said a fellow novelist-academic – while those in science-oriented fields tended to voice a greater awareness of the need to balance rules and their absence. 'There is an art to it', explained the dancing physicist in a conversation we had about surety versus uncertainty. 'The art is in balancing the necessity for goal direction … and playing the odds, not necessarily calculated.'

'If it was just straightforward to do something, it wouldn't be very interesting,' a mathematics professor told me. 'It wouldn't lead into interesting answers to a research question,' she said, 'so I think there's always play in what we do.' Perhaps the most surprising response to the question of play was given to me by a colleague in medical research: 'I think it's essential, a bit like sleep, a dream, reading,' he told me. 'It jigs the neurons somehow or other. It's a fascinating thing because there's no escape from the fact that what you're doing is coming from somewhere in your brain that you don't control very well.'

I go on having these conversations with my peers. Frequently, the responses I get inspire me to ask more questions.

BACK IN EARLY 2014, AS MY TIME IN NEW YORK DREW TO A close, the city's Code Blue phase was stepped down, though the temperatures remained bitingly cold. The news channels came up with the term 'extreme weather event' – a phrase they seemed to enjoy repeating endlessly. As it happened, over the course of the same week, my local neighbourhood in Perth was also in a state of emergency. Much of the Perth Hills had been evacuated and my mobile phone had been buzzing with automated emergency warnings: 'There is a possible threat to lives and homes. Conditions are changing. You need to leave the area or prepare to actively defend your home to protect you and your family.' It was high summer in Western Australia, and large sections of the hills that fringe its capital city were on fire. My son, Roland, was safe, visiting his father on the east coast, but while Luis and I struggled to gain traction, walking the icy streets of New York, fifty-seven houses in my local area in Perth's foothills were burnt to the ground. The house Roland and I had emptied out with the help of removalists in the weeks prior, the same house I'd shared with his father for fourteen years, had been sold the month before and was awaiting settlement. It was standing empty when the fires came close. Fortunately for us, the winds that day turned in a different direction and the building was saved. Families we knew who lived closer to my son's primary school were not so lucky. They lost everything they owned.

As Luis and I travelled with a hired driver from Bedford-Stuyvesant to JFK Airport for the return leg of our journey, I watched the suburbs of one of the world's most populous cities flicker by: a patchwork of newly renovated homes, run-down apartment blocks and heavily barred derelict buildings gradually gave way to the light industrial and commercial area of Queens. New and old co-existed as vacant used car lots, brightly lit billboards, empty playing fields and heavily graffitied fences made a motley pattern of grey, black, dull brown, silver. Everything seemed winter-coloured through the back window of the taxi cab, and I thought of the expression *the play of light*.

'I think of play as a way of sorting out the world,' Hustvedt had said to me, days earlier.

I suppose what she had meant by 'sorting out' was that through experimentation and surprise, and through the pushing and extending of boundaries, play teaches us how to make sense of things. I think it teaches us, too, how to be with them. Play supports both testing limits and making do with what we have before us. It collapses the borders between inside and outside, fixed and mutable, self and other. And it can't possibly end at childhood without negatively affecting our ability to survive in a complex and constantly shifting adult world, a world of light *and* dark, hot and cold.

I often think back to a story Hustvedt related to me about a girl she taught at the New York Hospital.

'There was a girl who I worked with who had been neglected and also raped. And you know, this was a long story. It was not an isolated case of rape trauma. It was a whole screwed-up job. And she was so concrete. She could not understand metaphor. There may well be work on this, I don't really know. But this concreteness seemed to me to be connected to a lack of being able to play. She also told me at one point that she had never learned how to jump rope. You know, I said, "Well, that could just be fun." We were talking about jumping rope. She never learned how to do it. And she never learned how to swim. I think that this was just a catalogue of neglect that had shaped one unit, you know, the body-mind into a profoundly unimaginative, concrete, non-metaphorical, finally damaged being. Regaining that at, you know, twelve or thirteen is extremely hard.'

The girl is an extreme case. I don't know if she ever did learn to play. Her story reminds me, above all, of the importance of care. But it also demonstrates just how important it is that we afford ourselves, and each other, the opportunity to play. As children, most of us are granted that opportunity without question. As adults we need to ask: why shouldn't we enable it for ourselves? Why shouldn't we make it genuinely and fully possible, for life?

CHAPTER
THREE
Work

At the age of thirteen, I ventured into my local showground as the annual town carnival workers were setting up their rides and side-show vans. The usually dusty showground paddocks had transformed into a slurry of winter mud after several days of rain and the constant traffic of heavy vehicles. The Dubbo Show was a few days away from opening, but already the newcomers were transforming the area into a makeshift village. At one end great mechanical rides had been unfolded and their operators toyed noisily with generators. The lit signage was garish even before it was connected to the mains. At another end, a modest little sideshow alley had taken shape: vans lifted their canopies to reveal rows of clowns' heads into which children would soon be propelling multi-coloured balls. There were shooting galleries with rows of old-time air rifles, and prizes in the form of huge candy-coloured stuffed animals were being hung from hooks.

I was wearing my best jeans and t-shirt and a sensible pair of shoes, and I felt a mixture of shyness and determination about my newfound project to look for casual work. Aware that running away to join the circus was a thing people did in stories, I suppose my interest in working for the carnival people was a look at whether something like that might be possible for me. The show people spoke rough, even by the standards of my working-class country town, but they had about them a persistent, if coarse, joviality. I sensed in them a determination to make it good, or at least as good as possible under the conditions in which they'd found themselves.

The first few men and women I spoke to shook their heads, but directed me on to another stallholder, then another, and before too long I had found myself a job in one of the food vans that sold hot chips and meat on sticks, cans of soft drink and great messy tangles of fairy floss. A brother and sister, both young adults, were responsible for the van. Jules and Skinny had cousins and aunties and mates peppered throughout the rest of the makeshift village. Jules's teeth were chipped, and her face marked with small scars, but her smile was broad. Skinny carried his limbs loosely, as if rigidity of any sort were alien to him. He had the manner of a small-time larrikin, and I made a note to myself to deal, wherever possible, with his sister.

This was my first formal job, and I was not legal – quite a bit less than the fourteen years and nine months one was supposed to be according to the state. When asked my age I had lied about it, adding a year. The shifts I was granted were ten hours apiece and the van in which I worked was hot and stuffy. It rained a lot those four days. The little lane we faced turned into a muddy creek, but the people still came and either Skinny or Jules handled the hot food while I took the orders and worked out the change. One afternoon there was a lull in the crowds and we leaned against the counter chatting. Skinny challenged me to a race to see who could eat a Dagwood Dog the fastest. I was a vegetarian in those days, but the $5 at stake for eating a single battered sausage on a stick was more than twice what I earned in an hour and there was something about the childish lunacy of Skinny's project that had me enthused. We had to stand back-to-back, Skinny said. I took the Dagwood Dog given me, and it smelled bad, but I'd been working with the smell for a day and a half already and I felt myself somewhat immune. We turned our backs, and at the count of three, I bit into the sausage. Frankly, it was so soft and oily you barely needed to chew. It tasted like damp cloth. I swallowed and took another bite, then another, and another, and when it was down, I knew I'd been fast. I turned swiftly around and there was Skinny, just standing there, his own dog dripping oil down his wrist. Untouched.

'You bastard!' I said.

It seemed like the laughter was nearly killing him. He was a smoker, clearly, the fits and shakes turning periodically into shudders and coughs and then back again to a series of high-pitched, half-strangled guffaws. I had to laugh with him, at least a little bit. My pride depended on it.

'You'll only see the five bucks if you can hold it down for the next hour', he said.

Later, Jules was a little more sympathetic.

'Skinny got ya one, did he? You've gotta watch 'im. He's a cheeky bugger.'

I must have handled the prank reasonably well, because the whole extended family seemed a bit more friendly towards me after that. But I never did see the colour of Skinny's money.

After several days, the Dubbo Show was over and so was the work. I was a little sad to say goodbye. I had enjoyed the extended theatre of the carnival people. There was something about the garish stupidity of the sideshow alley vans and the way people flocked to them that had us all dwelling in a kind of dream, a nether world in which the game of one-upmanship was simple and almost refreshingly frank. At the end of the final day I took my cash in a dark yellow envelope and as I walked home to the other side of town, I thought about Jules and Skinny and their family and regretted, in some ways, that they hadn't asked me to go on with them to the next town.

Part of me was aching, already, to head out into the adult world of work and not come back to childhood, to revel in the pride of earning my own way, to feel the jangle of cash in my pocket and know I'd earned it fair and square, and that any decision about when to spend it and on what was all my own business. I was proud, too, of having mixed with strangers and earned, in a small way, an ounce of what felt like their respect. I felt capable and purposeful. I'd enjoyed myself, and I couldn't wait for my next excursion into the world of work.

More than thirty years after my first and only experience of selling fairy floss, I find myself reflecting philosophically on work: why we do it, what it does for us, what we wouldn't do for it, and that early taste at thirteen seems all the more rose-coloured and other-worldly now. Later, my student years would take me through a range of part-time and casual jobs as a factory worker, barmaid, waitress and bookkeeper. Then I became a casual tutor, and later a TAFE teacher, and finally a lecturer at the university, a job in which I stayed and stayed, until, in the midst of writing this chapter about philosophies of work, I resigned without a parachute. A rash decision, or something a long time coming? It was both.

THE IDEA THAT LABOUR POWER IS A COMMODITY – THAT IS, that we 'own' our capacity to labour and it is therefore within our power to 'sell' it – may seem self-evident to those of us born into market-driven economies, but American philosopher Nancy Holmstrom has made a strong argument that we should look at this assumption closely. In fact, to call labour power a commodity at all, she argues, 'is essentially a legal fiction'. What does this mean? In her recent co-authored book, *Capitalism, For and Against: A Feminist Debate*, Holmstrom explains that the commonly held idea in free market economics is that everyone owns something, even if it is only themselves. Hence the idea that you own your labour power is an ideological assumption. A second assumption under capitalism, she argues, is the idea that agreements based on labour are a voluntary exchange between two 'commodity owners' – a buyer and a seller. But labour power is unlike other commodities because it consists of physical and mental energies, capacities and potentials, and therefore cannot be separated from the labourer to whom these energies and potentials belong. 'Wherever my labour/labour power goes, I have to go too,' Holmstrom emphasises, 'whatever is done to it, is done to me.' Her point is that assumptions about ownership, in relation to labour, are not simple ones. When we start to look closely at the question of how women might best participate in work under capitalism, this question of who owns one's labour becomes more and more philosophically and politically complex.

I WAS BORN IN 1970, WHEN WOMEN'S HOPES FOR FEMINISM were high. The teachers at my co-educational state high school included well-educated, enthusiastic and knowledgeable women. There was the art teacher who refused to shave her legs and introduced us to the feminist edge of contemporary art: Judy Chicago, Cindy Sherman, Tracey Moffatt. There was the conservatively dressed English teacher who, without making any kind of overt statement about it, quietly ensured that half of the novels we read in preparation for our final-year English exams were written by women, many of them Australian. We girls, it was suggested to us then, could do anything. We were post-1965 babies, launched with a sense of the bold and the new. No longer would we have to choose between marriage and career. No longer would we be slaves to childbirth. No longer would we have to wait at home by the phone for some boy to call. We were educated about sex and contraception; we were educated about the absence of women in fields like maths and science and encouraged to buck the trend. We were educated about assertiveness. 'Come on, girls, take a risk!' the art teacher told us. And we loved her for it. 'Bloody lezzo,' the boys reckoned, referencing her hairy legs. 'So?' I'd jeer back. 'So?' though, I shaved my own legs with religious regularity then and was rather proud of them. Yet, I was enthralled by the enthusiasm for and around women's emancipation. Perhaps I really could do anything, I thought. But what, and how, and when?

'You can't just do anything you want,' my mother quipped.

'Yes, I can,' I said, all bravado at fifteen.

'You may think you can, but you actually can't.'

'I can,' I challenged her. 'And I will!'

NANCY HOLMSTROM'S CONTRIBUTION TO *CAPITALISM, FOR and Against: A Feminist Debate* is a fascinating piece of work. 'Has capitalism been good for women?' is the book's central question and, in the tradition of a two-handed debate, Holmstrom and her co-author Ann E Cudd each examine capitalism as both an ideal and as an existing system, with a special eye to the interests of women. Cudd, whose case is positioned first, argues that capitalism has been good for women. It has led to more widespread education, she argues, it has helped us into the paid workforce, and it has increased our standard of living. Acknowledging some of the system's failures, Cudd floats the idea of an ideal form of capitalism – one she christens Enlightened Capitalism, in which women and minorities might play an increasingly representative role in the political system with an eye to monitoring and working to counter the nastier excesses of the financial markets. Cudd argues that such an ideal is something feminists can and should work towards. But Nancy Holmstrom's essay, for the negative, is the far more convincing argument, in my view. While Holmstrom acknowledges that there have been considerable gains made for some women over the past few centuries, her argument is that these gains owe more to industrialisation than to capitalism as a system. Further, they have been drastically uneven. Capitalism, overall, she argues, is not good for women. 'Women are disproportionately among the world's poor,' she points out, and we are disproportionally harmed by the capitalist system due to our childbearing and caregiving roles. Further, feminism stresses 'very different values and understandings' compared to 'those that dominate capitalist culture'. As Holmstrom's essay develops, so does the radical edge of its central passion. It is a call to arms. Capitalism is not essential, she argues, nor is it the only way to organise a culture. We accept capitalism at our peril, Holmstrom warns, concluding vehemently that 'it is time to reject a system where everything has a price and nothing has a value'.

But what is the alternative? Holmstrom's arguments took my reading into new territory: the complex area of political philosophy. Here, one needs to think deeply about questions of genuine human liberation, about hierarchy and interdependence, and, of course, about systems and their effects. There are simple assumptions to examine, too. Like what makes one poor? And what makes one happy? Questions around what meaningful, useful, non-exploitative labour might look like are central here.

BEFORE WE MOVE FORWARD, I WANT TO MOVE, BY EXAMPLE, A little further back, so as to consider generational change for women and their relation to work in my own family. My maternal grandmother, Dorothy, was born in 1901, just a year before women in Australia were awarded the right to vote. She grew up in the shadow of the First World War, and when she finished school she went to work as an assistant in a stenographer's office, a job she did for twelve years. Dorothy was famously good at spelling, and used to challenge my mother when she was first learning to read and write to spell words like Nunjikompita (the name of a small country town in South Australia). My grandmother lived with her own mother until she was thirty-two, and then she married my grandfather, a First World War veteran and a clerk. They moved into their own house in the Adelaide Hills and had four children in ten years. Dorothy did all the domestic labour herself, and was at her busiest as a homemaker during the lean years of the Second World War just after the birth of her fourth child. She cooked and heated her water via a wood stove, laundered by hand and used a kind of ice-chest for a refrigerator. Outside of the home she was heavily involved in voluntary community work: the Red Cross, the Mothers' and Babies' Association, the Anglican Church Mothers' Union, the Adelaide Children's Hospital Auxiliary. She was often the secretary or treasurer or president of such groups. Dorothy was a gregarious and energetic woman who never drove a car, and played tennis and bridge right into her eighties. She was, I see now, outwardly at least, the model female citizen of her era: reproductive, reliable, hard-working and community-minded.

Domesticity and homemaking, during my grandmother's time, were nationhood projects.

Dorothy's youngest child, my mother, Jen, matriculated from high school in 1956 at the age of eighteen, and then trained as a nurse at the Adelaide Children's Hospital. The nurses' union did not have a strong presence during her training. Jen worked six days a week and lived in the nurses' quarters, the door to which was locked by the matron at 10 pm each night. She recalls an era in which the ethics and hierarchies of the Christian church held sway. There was little time for a social life outside of work. After additional training as a midwife, she moved interstate, and in New South Wales she discovered that the nurses' union was stronger. In Sydney in 1960, the pay and conditions for nurses were a marked improvement on those in South Australia, and when Jen took up a job at a country hospital on the central New South Wales coast, she found the nurses' quarters no longer turned into a lock-up at night. My mother told me, happily, that this changed everything, and she quite often stayed out late, sometimes all night. It was around this time that she met and married my father, with whom she would have three children. After becoming a mother, of course, her work options became severely limited. Formal child care was not widely available in country New South Wales at that time, nor was it encouraged, and Jen was mostly engaged in casual and short-term part-time work from then on. In addition, my father regularly applied for transfers in his public service role, and so my mother would resign from whatever local work she'd been involved in as the family moved from one town to the next.

By the time I was at high school, Jen was putting her nursing qualifications to use as the director of a local child-care centre. It was a precarious organisation – an occasional-care centre that took casual bookings and was heavily subsidised by the local RSL club.

Unlike my father's workplace, which I never entered, I remember visiting my mother's workplace regularly. It was a noisy, chaotic place that catered to children from nought to six years old. In the central room, there were children painting and children playing and children variously screaming or laughing or squealing or squashing their lunch between their fingers and calling out for more. There were parents dropping off and picking up on the hour all day long, and at one end of the building there was a nursery lined with cots, in which there were always several little ones sleeping, and through which the noise and chaos of the main room miraculously failed to penetrate. My mother's diverse array of co-workers were some of the warmest and most capable women I have ever met. One was extraordinarily tall and thin; another suffered from dwarfism; another never seemed to stop talking, not even to inhale. They each knew the names and likes and particular anxieties or tactics of every child in the room, even, it seemed to me, those who'd just turned up for the first time five minutes ago. Amidst the noise and the busy physical actions of toddlers and preschoolers the staff were a coherent team, completely in control of the room, without appearing ever to have to struggle to maintain such control. No accident or tantrum could faze them. As a teenager, I had not the slightest interest in small children, whom I found almost uniformly noisy, messy, unreasonable and occasionally completely alien. I had no desire to follow my mother's line of work. And yet it seemed to me even then that my mother's workplace had a rare kind of beauty to it. I admired it as a microcosm – a community constantly reshaping itself in the face of chaos, but somehow always resolutely buoyant.

I am the youngest of my mother's children and by the time I had started university she and her capable co-workers had all lost their jobs. The occasional-care centre was closed due to a failure to meet fire regulations, and at that time nobody in town could find the money required to fund a new fit-out or an appropriate change of venue. The local women, who valued the place highly, rallied hard to find a solution, but to no avail. At fifty-six, in the arly 1990s, my mother was unemployed, and despite spending some years looking, she would not find anything but casual and occasional work as a nanny again. She retired early.

'PRECARITY' IS THE WORD I REMEMBER MOST FROM MY conversations with Nancy Holmstrom when I went to visit her in New York's Chelsea. Precarity's cousin, the word 'precarious', derives from the Latin precārios, which originally meant 'obtained by asking or praying'. It was first used in English as a legal term, in which 'obtained by asking' had undergone a slight change in focus to become 'held through the favour of another'. This introduced the notion that the favour might be withdrawn and so the adjective 'precarious' came to be used for 'depending on chance or caprice' and then, in the 18th century, 'risky'. Sadly, 'precarious' is a term that remains central to any commentary one wants to have now about women and labour.

One of the key questions Holmstrom examines on the topic of labour is: 'Do individuals own themselves and what exactly does this mean?' It's a question that goes to the heart of a worker's vulnerability under capitalism, and it's one that I find particularly intriguing. Holmstrom's interest in work is very much informed by debates around the mind/body problem, an area of philosophy that first captured her interest as a graduate student. The question of the relationship between the mind and the body is a core pre-occupation for philosophy, and new advances in science often raise more questions than answers. Where does the body end and the mind begin, or vice versa? This is a deeply philosophical question, but it is also a political one.

Carrying these problems across to political science, one of Holmstrom's key questions becomes, 'Who am I if I am not my labour or labour power?' Labour power, the capacity to labour, is an inextricable *part* of each person, but they are not identical to it. The idea that labour power can be treated as separate from one's person is not only a conceptual exercise: it also entails an ontological separation of the body from the being, meaning it goes to the question of the nature of being, of who the worker even is. The concept of labour power – decoupled from the person – devalues or literally impersonalises the body/mind, leading to a host of both philosophical and systemic problems for workers without capital, that is, for those who *only* have their labour to live on and to sell.

Before looking more closely at Holmstrom's argument in *Capitalism, For and Against: A Feminist Debate*, I want to have a closer look at the case put forward by Holmstrom's sparring partner in the same book. Ann E Cudd argues, as well as one could, the case for capitalism having been a force for good for women. 'By capitalism,' she writes, 'Marx meant an economic system whose core, defining feature is private ownership of the means of production.' She then outlines several problems with taking Marx's definition of capitalism as both the operative definition and the normative ideal. The first, in her opinion, is that he is describing a system that has never in practice existed. In practice, she argues, in every so-called capitalist nation, tax, regulation and outright public ownership of productive capacities restricts or tampers, to a greater or lesser degree, with private ownership. Universities are, of course, an instance of this kind of government tampering. In Australia, by and large, these are workplaces owned by the state. In addition, Cudd posits, Marx's constant reference to a 'sharp distinction between classes' – that is between owners of capital and others – 'no longer obtains'. On this point, I couldn't agree less, and nor could the author and economist Thomas Piketty, who in his bestseller *Capital in the Twenty-first Century*, published three years after Cudd and Holmstrom's book, presents statistics that demonstrate that income inequality has risen incredibly sharply in the past fifty years, largely around the distinction between those who own or control capital, and those who do not. Sixty per cent of the increase in national income in the United States in the thirty years from 1977 to 2007, for example, says Piketty, went to the top one per cent of earners. While it may no longer be so common to use the word 'class' to describe such a situation, it seems clear that the principle Marx was working on remains firmly in place. Few own significant capital – 'significant' meaning sufficient for it to provide one's living. Most do not. On balance, according to Cudd, while women remain dominated by men in all societies, the massive positive changes in the lives of women and girls in Western democracies in particular over the past two centuries – such as widespread literacy, the right to work and to vote, the right to marry freely – are the result of capitalism's capacity to act as an 'incubator of ideas from technology and marketing' to 'morality and politics'. On this point, I concede, there's an interesting entanglement. It is, however, a risky, and, dare I say, precarious correlation. Correlation does not necessarily mean causation and Cudd's attribution of these advances to capitalism needs to be treated with caution.

One of the most significant differences between Cudd's and Holmstrom's approaches to this debate is the contrast in how they understand several key terms in the four defining conditions of capitalism: 'private ownership of capital; decentralised open markets; free wage labour conditions; and the nondiscrimination constraint'. Defenders of capitalism, such as Cudd, argue that all of us at least own something – that is, ourselves – and they see this self-ownership as the foundation of freedom. Holmstrom, in contrast, zooms in on the words 'ownership' and 'freedom' with a sensible degree of scepticism.

NOT LONG AFTER MY JOB AT THE DUBBO SHOW, AND FOLLOWING on from one or two disastrous shifts at McDonald's and KFC, I found my teenage dream job at a local independent supermarket. I worked there Thursday nights and Saturday mornings as a 'check-out chick' – there was no alternative name given it, that I knew of – and I couldn't believe at first how much better it was than working with poor-grade take-away food. I got to know the regulars quite well and loved dreaming up imaginary life narratives for each customer via the inventory of items in their trolleys. There was one man who only ever came in ten minutes before closing of a Thursday night and who filled his trolley with cans of dog food, two-minute noodles and bottles of Coke. I was the daughter of a health freak who consumed raw parsley in great quantities and sprinkled wheatgerm on her children's toast. Mr Thursday Night's choice of items intrigued me.

'You must have a lot of dogs,' I commented once. The reply was just a grunt.

Mr Thursday Night taught me something about the role of my own body as a female worker in the service industry and it is a lesson I've never forgotten. This was a man with a significant weight problem. Every step and every breath involved determined effort. Serving him took time. Standing at the till, Mr Thursday Night would look me up and down as I processed his items and then he'd keep looking – at my legs, at my breasts – until I became

acutely conscious of the space between us. I was fifteen. My customer always wore the same King Gee shorts and blue Bonds sin-
glet. I wore the required uniform: a white collared blouse and a
short black skirt. There was no counter, as such, just a small ledge.
The bagged items were placed into a facing trolley. Thus, we stood
directly before each other. His mouth hung disconcertingly open.

'Thanks love', he'd say. Or, 'Thanks sweetheart'.

It was thanks to Mr Thursday Night that I began to comprehend the blunt threat behind the male gaze. *You're here for my
pleasure*, said Mr Thursday Night's eyes on me. And it seemed to
me that, if I wished to keep my job, I had no choice but to duti-
fully place the correct change in his outstretched palm and mind
my manners as I wished him goodnight.

I didn't fully understand then something I have now thought
about considerably, and that is that the female body is problematic in public spaces, including the workplace, in a way in which
the relatively normalised male body is not. For those of us born
female, the particular bundle of assets we bring with us to the sale
of our labour complicates the very nature of the exchange.

NANCY HOLMSTROM'S THINKING TAKES US TO THE HEART OF
this complication via the question of self-ownership. Very few
people would sell their labour power if they had viable alternatives; that is, if they were able to subsist in other ways. 'But the
structure of ownership and control of the means of subsistence
makes them not free ... there is no exit,' says Holmstrom. Her
argument rests on Marx's theory of alienation, which underlines
the way in which those of us who are without significant capital
means are coerced into forms of work that alienate us from what it
means to be human. Through labour obligations, the worker loses

quite substantially her ability to direct her own life. Instead, our best energies and efforts are diverted. Marx described alienated labour as forced, not voluntary, and for good reason. The workplace belongs to the owner and by their labour, workers are also adding to the power of those owners – which is power *over them*. In other words, because capitalism is an expanded system not only of production but of reproduction, workers reproduce the relation between themselves and capital: that is, in participating as workers, they manufacture their own alienation.

If one's labour is alienated, argues Holmstrom, it is still possible to be un-alienated in other aspects of life – such as through our hobbies or through creating and maintaining important family, friendship and social connections – but our capacity to do so is compromised and diminished by our experience of alienated labour. 'More importantly,' she says, alienated labour severely 'diminishes the extent to which working people are able to decide upon and to carry out the kind of life they want, a uniquely human capacity'. According to Marx, there are two elements to human nature: freedom and consciousness. 'Alienated labour meets neither one,' says Holmstrom.

Wrapped up in the question of women's self-ownership are hugely controversial beliefs, opinions and assumptions about sexuality, abortion, and the rights of the child, just to name a few. Questions abound: should we be able to rent our bodies for sex, or hire them out for surrogacy? In poor nations, where people-smuggling for the sex trade is rampant, the question might become: how do we stop powerful others from selling us?

In a scholarly article that focusses specifically on sex workers, Holmstrom goes a little deeper into questions around freedom and choice for women. 'What is the prostitute selling?' she asks. Her answer takes into account the important work of sociologist Arlie Hochschild, who has shown how much contemporary work, especially that performed by women, involves emotional labour, in which a worker is required to display or demonstrate a degree of emotional 'service' considered integral to the job. Here, my teenage experience of serving Mr Thursday Night is just the tip of the iceberg. I am reminded, too, of my mother's work as a nurse and child-care worker, and of my grandmother's nation-hood labour via decades of heavy domestic work and volunteerism in the community. For women, as Holmstrom's thinking makes clear, freedom is a perpetually contested concept. In her discussion of sex work, she asks us to consider the way in which all women's bodies are objectified and commodified through capitalism and patriarchy, but she also emphasises that acts and choices are never simply free or unfree. Rather, 'freedom is always relative, on a con-tinuum, in a context'. An act or choice might be more free than the alternatives; it could be an expression of agency and empower-ment at the same time as being 'profoundly unfree because of the paucity of choices'. In the particular case of sex work, it is clear that 'sexual services cannot be separated from the sale (or rent) of the body that supplies those services'. Further, argues Holmstrom, 'only with great effort of dissociation is sex ever purely physical'. The fact that sex workers, especially street sex workers, often suffer from post-traumatic stress disorder, whereas other low-status, dangerous and physically demanding peace-time jobs rarely have that particular effect, is telling, argues Holmstrom. 'The body,' she writes, 'is where we experience pleasure and pain. Indeed it is the original site of emotions.' For these reasons, sex work might be read as the ultimate form of alienation. Indeed, Holmstrom pres-ents it as a kind of limit case and one that enables her to return to and fully underline one of her key philosophical arguments:

The fiction at the heart of capitalist ideology that one can sell parts of one's self without selling oneself, and that doing so is an exercise of freedom rather than domination has led to the commodification of everything that people do not resist in defence of other values, intruding into the most intimate areas of our lives.

Holmstrom's extended argument, across all of her writing, is that Marx's work on alienation needs to be urgently looked at anew, precisely because of the way capitalism has now transformed everything into an 'appendage of the machine'. Labour power, for Holmstrom, remains a legal fiction because it separates from the person as a whole his/her capacity to labour, calls it a thing and says it can be bought and sold by the person. Of course we are not, in fact, just our labour power, but the capitalist apparatus makes it increasingly difficult for many of us to *be* substantially and wilfully active much else beyond. Further, capitalism's incredible growth seems to know no bounds: 'It gets into everything … every aspect of nature, including our bodies, the air, the water, everything.' Thus it becomes harder and harder for many of us to identify our own particular forms of freedom – our position on the spectrum, if you like – and conversely, for us to properly challenge our own particular role in the process of alienation.

WHEN I MET WITH NANCY HOLMSTROM IN 2015 TO TALK about her philosophies of work, I discovered that her interest in the topic could be traced right back to her childhood, and to an early reading of socialism informed by the American scholar Hal Draper.

'My father was from an immigrant family, from Sweden,' Holmstrom began. 'He was two when his father died. His mother had to work as a maid. He quit school – all the kids quit school as soon as they could – at eighth grade. He was a labour organiser and a socialist, and worked at many jobs, which didn't in any way, shape or form meet his intellectual abilities and were always very precarious financially. He had worked in offices or for stores, he worked as a waiter.'

'In what period was he working?' I asked.

'Well, he was born in 1912, and he died in the early seventies, quite young at fifty-nine. So, this is in the forties and fifties and sixties. His last job was as an elevator operator in a fancy building. He was in a union, but it was a terrible union then. Anyway, the precarity, which is a word we use now more commonly because it's more common in developed countries, and the effect on his psyche, you know, the lack of self-confidence, self-respect, satisfaction. It impressed me very strongly.'

'When did you first read Marx?' I asked.

'I think it was in graduate school. And it was just at the time when his early works were translated and they were so appealing, so humanistic. And that drew me to be willing to tackle some of the harder stuff, the later work, *Capital* and all.

'But there was a key article that I read early on that I'm so grateful I read. It was called "Two Souls of Socialism" by Hal Draper. And he was a political activist in the forties. It's sort of an obscure tendency within the history of socialism, that is, you have those who supported the Soviet Union, which I'll call Stalinists, they saw that as socialism. Then you had the Maoists, you had the Trotskyists, but then you had people who were a little more independent of that because they weren't social democrats either. They were anti-capitalists. But they believed that China and Russia were not socialist societies, so they weren't revolutionary socialists, but anti-capitalist socialists who believed in democracy. And Draper was of that tendency, called Third Camp socialists. He made his living as a librarian at the UC Berkeley. And he was a very scholarly, nitpicky type who ended up doing a couple of big books on Marxist theories of revolution but he wrote lots of topical essays, and one of those he wrote was "Two Souls of Socialism". In this essay he described the two souls which were socialism from above, and socialism from below. And socialism from above included the Soviet style or guerrilla army. There were many variants of socialism from above but basically they would be seen as the communist type and then social democrat. Because he put social democrat types there too, you see, they wanted to elect social democrat types who would bring good things to the people. He saw that as a species of socialism from above. Very different from one another – very different – but still, socialism from above. And, on the other hand, socialism from below was the mass of working people trying to take control of their own destiny in workers' councils, in the early times post-revolution in Russia, in Hungary, the Paris commune, you know. Never did they achieve lasting victory, but that was the model. And he put Marx in that category.

'So that appealed to me immensely. And I read that in college. So even before I read Marx, I was predisposed to see Marx in that way. And I certainly found evidence, you know, that's what I found in Marx. I was lucky to have read Draper.

'So then, with feminism and anti-racism there were all these critiques of Marx and Marxists being too gender neutral, just talking about the working class and leaving out that there were women in the workforce and women in the home who were not workers but who were exploited in another way, and I was very sympathetic to that, but I didn't see it as properly a critique of

Marx because he was analysing the capitalist mode of production. I wrote a piece on this. There was a debate among Marxist feminists about how we should understand women's domestic labour. Should it be understood in Marxist terms as exploited in the same way that wage earners are exploited? Or should you understand it as women being exploited by the men in the family? There was a debate about that. And I wrote an article about that.

'When Marx talks about being productive, there's productive in general, you know, when I produce a meal for myself or for others, but productive in capitalist terms is productive of surplus value. So, yes, the housewife isn't productive in that sense, but it doesn't make it sexist, as many feminists charged, because neither are state employees productive of surplus value. There are broader and narrower senses of "productive".

'I felt that some of the early feminist critiques of Marxism were incorrect. But I thought their demand that socialists, whether they call themselves Marxists or not, pay attention to the broader kind of labour, and the many kinds of oppression, was right. Workers come in different races, genders, nationalities. It's too narrow a conception of working-class struggle to only talk about, say, point-of-production exploitation. I think women workers are less likely to make that mistake. They know they need child care. They know they need health care. They know they need better schools, so the integration of feminism with labour struggles, which I think can be called socialist feminism, I think it's crucial. And in places like the United States race always has to be factored in.

'So I guess I'd say that my conception of Marxism was expanded by the writings of feminism and race writers. I would integrate those more with Marxism than I would have when I first came across his work, whether that's a revision of Marxism or whether it's just bringing out the elements that are there, I don't care what you call it. It's an exegetical question.'

'And you think that Marx's ideas are more crucial now than ever before?' I asked.

'I do, because of the ecological crisis. Yes. The analysis of capitalism as a system which is ever expanding to every piece of the globe, to every aspect of nature. It can't stop. I think there's a phrase from *The Communist Manifesto*: "It gets to every corner everywhere."'

AT TWENTY-SEVEN, A FEW YEARS AFTER GRADUATING WITH MY Masters degree, I was offered a continuing academic appointment at one of the largest of the universities in Western Australia. A young university, by world standards, it inclined towards the applied sciences, particularly engineering, but as with many such universities, transformed from institutes of technology in the Dawkins reform of Australian higher education in 1987, this led to the early establishment of creative arts programs, including a well-regarded creative writing program. In the early years of my role, I taught essay and report writing to engineers and computer science students, many of whom could not have been less interested in language and literature, but when a place became available to teach an undergraduate class in fiction, I was thrilled to pick it up. A few years later, I was running one of Australia's longest-established undergraduate creative writing programs. It was a demanding, busy and profoundly rewarding job.

I loved the insights that teaching creative writing provided into the imaginative worlds of students from a whole range of cultural backgrounds, age groups and socio-economic circumstances. It is true that a creative writing lecturer reads work that is often underdeveloped and unsuccessful in its rendering, but I very rarely came across a bad idea. It is seeing a piece of work through, sticking with it to ensure it achieves its best potential, that is the harder part of the art and craft of both doing and teaching creative writing. I loved my work at the chalkface of teaching, and saw many wonderful students really take flight, at first as undergraduates and later as honours and doctoral students, but over time, the demands on my energy and the sheer number of working hours required by the university, alongside the increasingly market-driven management style, took its toll on me. For many years, I had prided myself on working hard, but when the collective project of the workplace with which I identified began to stray too far from my own ideals about what matters and what needs to be defended, questions about why we work, what it does for us, and what we wouldn't do for it began to occupy me, and I started to read more deeply about philosophies of work.

Interestingly, much of the history of philosophy of work is caught up with the question of the work ethic. The influence of Christian doctrines on approaches to work during the middle ages in Europe was extremely powerful. Within that framework, work was understood to be the result of Adam and Eve's expulsion from the Garden of Eden. It's a fascinating history to consider from a feminist perspective: work is a curse, written on (or on account of) the bodies of women. During the post-Reformation period, the view that work was a positive influence came about partly because of the way in which priesthood came to be considered a vocation (one from which women, of course, remain largely excluded), but this emphasis was also, of course, driven by the church's role in social control and its interests in stabilising the structures of power. From this phase of history stemmed the idea, still largely prevalent in today's secular democracies, that work is not just a kind of duty, it is also a service to others. In this sense, the combination of worship and work were long considered the key to a good life.

Max Weber, in *The Protestant Ethic and the Spirit of Capitalism* sees the Calvinist work ethic as 'a strict avoidance of all uninhibited enjoyment'. Similarly, Thomas Carlyle, writing in the 19th century, famously declared that there is 'perennial nobleness and even sacredness in work'. Do we still believe this, I wonder? Interestingly, although I am an atheist, I admit that there remains an aspect of my own approach to work that is still very much caught up in this idea.

Paul Lafargue, who wrote a treatise in 1883 titled *The Right to Be Lazy*, argued strongly for abandoning what he called 'the sacred halo' that had been cast over work by the church, but the fact is that for working-class families like my own, laziness is not and can never be our right. We have no accumulated capital. If we did not work, we would be living in abject poverty.

This puts us in a particularly awkward position when the cultural practices in our chosen workplace begin to challenge our ethics, and the decisions made by colleagues or by line managers disregard some of the principles we hold dear. The question of *what I wouldn't do for work* loomed large for me during the final years of my first university appointment. For a number of years I had advocated for better and more just working conditions for growing numbers of casual academic staff and found no sympathy. I did what I could, as many did, to argue against increased class sizes and increased student fees. Small fires began regularly. A course that ran alongside mine that had been an enormously successful flagship program was suddenly threatened with closure, and then narrowly saved when it was clear that the proper impact of such a closure hadn't been considered. Several ethically complex recommendations I made regarding particular candidates in the postgraduate area I was then directing were rejected by management and overturned, on grounds that seemed not to take into account those ethical considerations. And then, in the twelve months before I resigned, half of my long-term departmental colleagues lost their jobs in a ruthless and counterproductive 'spill and fill' operation in which academic staff across the whole university – with the conspicuous exception of those in management positions – were required to reapply for their own jobs. It was not lost on me that many of the colleagues who lost their jobs were teaching-oriented (read 'service-oriented') women. I am not trying to paint a picture of a particular institution as abhorrent. In fact, large numbers of academics the world over have been resigning, or have been forced into early retirement and confected redundancies over the last decade due to the ever-more overtly market-driven economics of public education policy.

Working life in the university was a far cry from working in a Dagwood Dog stand at the annual Dubbo Show, but although it constitutes what might be described as knowledge work, it is no more immune to exploitation, mismanagement and malpractice than any other line of work. The difference in the case of a university is that many staff have a deeply held belief in the value of knowledge, education and the notion of public good, and they are passionate about passing all of this on. Place this extraordinary degree of intrinsic motivation alongside the fact that gaining and keeping an academic job is highly competitive, and you are beginning to get a sense of the picture. The workplace culture in today's universities depends enormously on this strange combination of collective good will and competition. In addition to the standard teaching, research and administration work that is carefully measured and moderated in annual workload reviews, academic staff undertake all manner of tasks above and beyond that which is measured: writing recommendations and nominations, contributing to professional associations and other external bodies, organising and attending conferences, examining or reviewing for other institutions, contributing to policy, and analysing contemporary debates and developments for the media. A survey conducted in 2013 in the United Kingdom revealed that the majority of academics were then working between fifty-five and seventy hours a week to fulfil these obligations. After almost two decades of dedication to this kind of labour demand, I found it difficult to differentiate my own 'bundle of assets' from those belonging to the institution. What might be left, I wondered, of those other aspects of my life if I walked away?

As the university management steered increasingly towards the hardline economic-rationalist worldview, it became more and more difficult for me to get up in the morning and represent an institution that I felt had begun routinely doing things the wrong way. And there's nothing like feeling you're involved in doing the wrong thing for shredding the pride and the meaning from your labour. The 'sacred halo' fell and gradually it dawned on me that I *could* walk away. Ironically, I had not qualified for any of the redundancy packages that had been floated in those final years because my work performance was too strong. And in the 'spill and fill' operation, I had been successful in retaining my position, a fact that now instilled a sense of guilt because I was taking up a position that could have gone to any one of a number of former colleagues who had lost out. But how could I continue there after all that had happened? I asked myself. And, again, could I afford to walk away? Really? At that time, my son was not yet in full-time school, and my relationship with his father was dissolving into air. It would soon be gone. This placed additional financial pressures on my decision, but it seemed to me that the question of what to do was in large part one of ethics.

FOR THE ROMANTICS, WORK NEEDED TO HAVE MEANING, NOT in relation to God, but for oneself. Here we start to see the idea that an 'authentic' self is one that is self-fashioned, a mythology still deeply embedded in contemporary culture: again, I can see, now, the important role this has long played for me in my own approach to working life. There is the sense that if we have failed to be effective in the workplace, we have failed at the project of selfhood.

But the question of the extent to which meaningful, successful and non-alienated labour is possible in the post-industrial context is a complex one, and even members of that group that Richard Florida, an urban studies scholar, has identified as the creative class – whose work entails a good degree of self-determination and satisfaction, and whom he estimates to be some thirty per cent of the population in developed nations – sits in a complex relation to capital, no less precarious and no better recompensed than anybody else.

As I was thinking once more about the complexities of this question of ethics, I read on and through Nancy Holmstrom to the work she referenced by other women, including Kathi Weeks' book *The Problem with Work*. Passages like this by Weeks disarmed me: 'Why do we work so long and hard? The mystery here is not that we are required to work or that we are expected to devote so much time and energy to its pursuit, but rather that there is not more active resistance to this state of affairs.' Later Weeks writes, 'we often experience and imagine the employment relation – like the marriage relation – not as a social institution but as a unique relationship'. Actually, she argues, it is far from it.

Nancy Holmstrom posits that while capitalism creates the potential for genuine human liberation, it also puts systematic barriers in place. Capitalism may once have been a progressive force in human history, she writes, but it is this no longer. For Holmstrom, 'material inequalities ... are also inequalities of power and freedom and well-being'. Meaningful work can uplift and engage us, she argues, but a negative workplace culture can wreak havoc on our physical, mental and emotional well-being.

In her book, *Cruel Optimism*, American scholar Lauren Berlant outlines the way in which so many of us have an 'affective attachment to what we call the good life' even when the conditions for creating such goodness can no longer be sustained. Cruel optimism allows us to identify why so many people choose not to resist but instead 'ride the wave of the system of attachment they are used to' even when this system – a workplace, an institution – fails them terribly. Writer Marina Warner, whose thinking I profile elsewhere in this book, applies Berlant in her own appraisal of the flailing higher education system in the United Kingdom: 'Cruel optimism afflicts the colleague who agrees to yet another change of policy in the hope that it will be the last one,' she cautions. Like Warner, I had long flattered myself that perhaps by teaching I could make a difference. But my allegiance, as with hers, was with the life of the mind, and not with an approach to public education based increasingly on profit and competition.

At the end of 2013, I had lost my optimism. I applied for every leave entitlement I had, strung them all together, and began the process of trying to imagine for myself a different approach to the question of labour.

ONE OF THE KEY HISTORY LESSONS IN NANCY HOLMSTROM'S essay 'Against Capitalism as a Theory and a Reality' takes us back to 17th-century England, when philosophers were first beginning to discuss the concept of 'self-propriety'. It was a time when old-school feudalism was giving way to the early stages of the Industrial Revolution – later to become full-blown capitalism – and this was creating new tensions between the classes. The disappearance of commons, common land to which ordinary people had hitherto had hereditary rights, was a key concern, as was the issue of slavery. Holmstrom describes a population in which moderates and radicals united against the monarchists, but the philosophical differences between and among the anti-monarchists were pronounced. Among the most radical of groups was a set known as the Diggers or True Levellers, who supported universal male suffrage. The Diggers believed that no one had a right to own someone else's labour: 'neither take hire nor give hire' declared their manifesto. Enclosure of land into private property made everyone who wasn't party to such ownership servants and slaves, they argued. And since those who were buying or selling land had come into ownership 'either by oppression or murder or theft', private property had no moral validity.

Reading this philosophy from an Australian perspective only 230 years after Australia's invasion and colonisation by the British, I realised that my own point of view on self-propriety, at least philosophically, has long aligned very well with that of the Diggers. The connection between property ownership and self-ownership, in the context of labour under capitalism, really came home to me via reading Holmstrom's discussion of the Diggers' manifesto. As one reviewer put it, one of the key strengths of Holmstrom's work is her 'substantive and robust debate of issues that we too often imagine to be settled'. Why let them be settled? Holmstrom seems to ask. Why, indeed.

Sovereignty in Australia remains unsettled, and many Australians like me remain acutely aware of this point. Others cannot admit that it remains an issue, but their hysterical behaviour over borders and asylum seekers suggests otherwise. 'Until England is free and common for all, to work together and eat together,' proclaimed the Diggers, 'England would not be a free land.' Many of us living in secular democracies in the 21st century like to think of ourselves as free. But in a country in which others have the right to exclude any amongst us – from land or from the hours granted us in becoming living beings ('neither take, nor hire nor give') – 'freedom' remains a peculiar word to use.

MY CONVERSATIONS WITH NANCY HOLMSTROM IN PERSON canvassed so many of these issues, but our discussion concluded with a revealing return to the lived experience of precarity. Of each of the female thinkers I have interviewed for this book, Holmstrom is the only one to have successfully forged an academic career in what I call 'Capital P' Philosophy, a discipline in which women have long been 'buried, literally and metaphorically' as scholar Jane Duran puts it in her book on the history of female philosophers in the Western tradition. When Holmstrom retired, in the year before we met, she had been the Chair of Philosophy at Rutgers University in Newark for some years. As we talked about why and how she had become a socialist feminist in a department of philosophy – and why she felt it important to defend that term – she revealed to me several of the uncertainties she herself had to face down during the course of her career.

Holmstrom completed her doctoral thesis on the mind/body problem at the University of Michigan and was then offered a position at the University of Wisconsin, which she took up. 'I did analytic philosophy, metaphysics and philosophy of mind,' she told me. But during her time at Wisconsin, Holmstrom's philosophical focus became more and more political. She had been involved with the civil rights movement, the anti–Vietnam War movement, and with feminism. 'But now, I started thinking about these things philosophically,' she said. She had never studied ethics in philosophy. 'Ethics, then, was very narrow: liberal at best, maybe more conservative. It just didn't interest me.'

As Holmstrom began to publish scholarly works that spoke more to her new interests in politics, particularly Marxism, women's studies and sociology, albeit through the lens of her knowledge of philosophy, problems arose for her at Wisconsin. 'I wrote a couple of things that were very different from what I'd been hired to do, and I wrote, but not huge amounts, and I didn't get tenure. And we didn't have a union. So, I was gone.'

As Holmstrom was telling me this story, I remembered the sight that had faced me a few days earlier as I stood before the central display table in the philosophy section of a major New York bookstore. There I counted thirty-two new-release philosophy books on display. Not one of them was by a female author or focussed on the work of a female philosopher. The image of the table unsettled and saddened me again, as Holmstrom's cat got up from its seat and stretched its legs, and her story continued.

'But then,' she said, 'I got this other pretty good job at Rutgers in Newark.' Things went well, until her application for tenure came up and was again rejected. This time Holmstrom was in a union, and when she compared her own CV with those of her colleagues who had gained tenure in the same round, she decided to lodge a formal grievance. 'My grievance went on for five years,' she told me. 'For two of the five years I was still teaching but for three years I was unemployed.'

As it happened, the birth of Holmstrom's first and only child coincided with her period of grievances and then unemployment. She was forty-two. She took up temporary positions, one at the

University of Hawaii for six months, and another in Pennsylvania, a three-hour commute from home. It was far from easy. The grievance battle was drawn out and complex, and she lost hope of being reinstated. She decided to change careers altogether, and applied to do a course in social work.

'I had been a professor,' she recalled, 'and so I wasn't a mother. And then all of a sudden when I became a mother, I wasn't a professor any more. So that reinforced the idea that you couldn't be both. Being a mother was wonderful in many ways. I chose to have her, but motherhood reinforced the feeling I was no longer a professor.'

'Or that you couldn't get back into academia?'

'Yes, exactly. I really struggled with that, because I did not want her to grow up seeing me depressed and without a job.'

This was a fear I understood well enough myself.

'After all that,' Holmstrom smiled, 'I had a kind of ambivalent relationship to philosophy, in particular, but also to academia.'

'Yes,' I said. 'Of course.'

When her daughter was three, Holmstrom won her job back at Rutgers. In the end, it was proven that Holmstrom had a case for tenure as robust as those of her colleagues who had won it in the same round. The promotions committee had been wrong to knock her back. Suddenly she was a professor again, and later became the chair of the department. Unsurprisingly, though, her ambivalence never really went away. She felt, ever after, an outsider to philosophy, and an outsider to professorship too.

WITHIN A FEW MONTHS OF MEETING WITH NANCY HOLMSTROM, my mind full of political philosophy, I resigned from my workplace of seventeen years. And perhaps in line with the strangely impersonal manner in which the university was being managed at the time, I never did receive a formal reply, nor any acknowledgment of the value of the labour I had invested in my work at that institution. Some weeks later, on the appropriate date, my salary was discontinued. Kathi Weeks was right, I thought. Though I had loved and laboured hard, under an illusion of loyalty and joint purpose, and perhaps a fifth of my lifetime had passed by during that endeavour, ours had never been a unique relationship. Looking back at it now, something about the experience of that seventeen years seems illusory: as if, like the showground life of my teenage years, it had existed in a parallel realm.

As I discovered after the leap, at the age of forty-four, freedom is indeed a state one should approach with all the wits one can muster. During those first months, I woke regularly at night, ill at ease about my uncertain financial future and the impact this could have on my son, who I was then parenting unassisted in a city I barely knew. On a good day, without formal work, even while acknowledging that my savings balance was heading liberally south and that there was a ticking-clock aspect to being 'outside' the system, I felt remarkably good. There was space and time to breathe, to contemplate, to be. I did not regret my actions. Mostly, I settled in to work, on my own terms, on the writing of this book: finally, perhaps, a project *outside* capitalism? Well: yes and no. Somewhere in the transformation into book form – into the object you're scanning (whether digitally or on paper) it too becomes a form of surplus value. Holmstrom, via Marx, is right. It could be that *nothing* is outside.

Perhaps the real freedom and beauty of being 'out of work', as I found myself in 2015, was that it enabled me to think of myself as something other than a 'bundle of assets and preferences' abstracted from all the other important things that go to make up who I am. And yet the question pressed on me still: *Who am I if not my labour?* For myself, even with the time and space granted me to contemplate it, I still do not know the answer, but I'm grateful to Nancy Holmstrom and others, including Marx, for laying down the thinking that makes that question possible.

Reading in the field of political economy has been helpful for the opportunity it has provided me to properly consider my own position in relation to the broader economic field: to be clear-sighted about the limited nature of the choices I face, honest about the real question of what, outside of money, I might find fulfilling and purposeful about work, and to feel properly armed, at least intellectually, to negotiate the challenge of erecting defences against the encroachment of the market in so many aspects of my daily life. I have been forced, too, to interrogate some long-standing, and deeply buried, fears I have about change, precarity, and poverty. As a result of all of this, I took what turned out for me to be a hugely positive leap, and gained a better sense of perspective and control.

I THINK THE ASPECT OF MY READING OF NANCY HOLMSTROM'S work that has been most provocative relates to the question of the bigger picture: the philosophical principles on which the capitalist system is built. These go beyond questions of how we as individuals might consider our own circumstances or craft our own approaches to the realities of work. For, as the Diggers well knew, the sale of one's labour at all is not philosophically separable from the idea of private property ownership. The challenge of imagining a viable alternative to capitalism – and therefore to the whole notion of private ownership – remains. In my opinion, Nancy Holmstrom is right on this: there are few challenges more urgent.

The majority of us, including life forms other than humans, are terribly vulnerable to a system designed to increase the fortunes of the rich and powerful and to expand incessantly at the expense of all else.

'The challenge to come up with an alternative is not just mine,' Holmstrom writes. 'We all need to unleash our imaginations and collectively work out what such an alternative would look like.' In the daring intelligence and deep moral urgency of Holmstrom's challenge, I find hope. Perhaps the biggest threat to our collective future is that, through fear, we fail to dream big enough to enable something genuinely different. Perhaps it is *only* this that prevents us from taking the larger, more radical collective leap.

CHAPTER
FOUR
Fear

Once, while browsing the collection in the Singapore National Library, I stumbled across a collection of women's poetry that included a piece by the Indian feminist Kamala Das. I was intrigued by a line from one of her poems, which I wrote down in my notebook as: '*Fear is a woman's place.*' In the context of Das's larger poem, my memory suggests that the line was not an assertion, so much as a moment of illumination for the poem's narrator, but I wrote it down in my notebook, perhaps incorrectly, because it was an idea that I found shocking, and I have carried it with me for some years, returning to it now and again to re-assess my position on it. As sometimes happens during a whimsical browsing of the library shelves, I did not take down the fuller reference, and despite looking, have not been able to find the original again, but the line has stayed with me. 'Fear is a woman's place.' I still find myself mentally turning it over from time to time, wanting to refute it, and finally dismiss it, but then asking myself, again, 'Is it? But … is it?'

IT COULD BE SAID THAT FEAR IS EVER PRESENT FOR HUMANS OF either gender; that it is, indeed, common to all of us. In classical philosophy, there is the regularly told story of philosopher Michel de Montaigne, for example, who lived for many years in constant fear of death. His fear intensified during his thirties, when he suffered a series of bereavements. His closest friend and confidant, Étienne de La Boétie, died from the plague in 1563, a loss from which it is said Montaigne never fully recovered. Étienne's death was followed by the death of Montaigne's father, from gallstones, and then a younger brother by freak accident. Montaigne was right to suggest that fear undermines our rationality, that 'there is no emotion which more readily ravishes our judgement from its proper seat'. The more Montaigne thought about death the more he feared it, and the less rational about it he became. Then one day, during an excursion on his horse, he suffered a near-death experience. In a closely avoided collision with another horseman, he fell and hit his head, knocking himself out. Onlookers described how dramatically he behaved on coming back to consciousness – clawing at his chest, and vomiting blood – but his own memory of the incident was more serene. He described floating on clouds and hovering in a state of heightened pleasure. Later, as he recuperated, he realised he'd come to terms with his worst fear. 'Don't bother your head about it,' he advised others. The more we try to control things, he reasoned, the less control we actually have. What we need to do is relinquish control, and try and better understand ourselves.

This advice Montaigne provides about relinquishing control is, of course, born of wisdom. But, while Montaigne's fear of death was not nothing, I feel it needs to be put in context. Montaigne was a member of the ruling class in 16th-century France. He was an intelligent, well-educated man, heir to a massive country estate, and had at his constant service an obliging wife and numerous servants and employees. Alongside the running of his agricultural estate, he held positions of power in local politics. He was a man, in other words, with plenty of experience in control.

For women and children, our experience of fear is often complicated by a distinct lack of control over our immediate life circumstances. Further, the dominant narratives about fear that circulate in our culture often seem designed specifically for us: they can and do work to keep us in a relatively powerless place. The #MeToo movement, which gained momentum on social media during 2017, has gone some way to demonstrate this. Alongside death, women often quite reasonably fear harassment, threats, physical violence and rape right throughout our lives. While a number of scholarly studies carried out during the 1980s suggested that women's fear of crime was exaggerated, more recent research has tended to acknowledge that the reality of sexual violence is a core component of 'being' female. Taking into account the fact that a significant percentage of rape, domestic violence and sexual harassment cases still go completely unreported, it's now generally acknowledged that women's fears about crime actually tally surprisingly well with the risks we face. According to the latest statistics in Australia, more than one woman dies at the hand of a current or former partner in our country every week; one woman in three has experienced physical violence since the age of fifteen; one in five has experienced sexual violence. Girls are almost twice as likely as boys to be the subjects of sexual abuse. In addition, many of us quite reasonably feel vulnerable in public spaces, fearing anything from objectification at one end of the spectrum through to physical violence at the other. Large numbers of women fail to participate in urban outdoor recreation, for example, because of gendered constructions of public space. Such constructions encourage us to read public space as freely accessible to men at any time, but only accessible to women under particular conditions, or alongside an element of judgment or risk. In this way, geographies of fear have taught us not to be comfortable in outdoor public spaces, and we limit our movements accordingly, often sticking to the private and the domestic realm, where we tend to feel more at ease.

The interesting thing about fear is how complicit we can be in both constructing it and in how severely it influences us, as Montaigne's story does amply demonstrate. This is so even when we can see its negative effect upon us, even when we can see that powerful institutions and conservative cultural practices – governments, marriage, the cosmetics industry – benefit from keeping us in its grip. How then, do we escape from fear's long shadow? Is it enough for us to take Montaigne's advice and better understand fear by better understanding ourselves? Or do we all need to find the courage to do more than that, to step out from the shadows and speak up, to bring down the whole goddamn house?

In this chapter, I take a particular interest in women, fear and violence. Is fear a woman's place? I suspect the answer is no, but also, yes.

'TO LIVE IS TO BE IN A STATE OF CHANGE, TO BE UNDER SIEGE from a variety of sources,' writes philosophy scholar Noëlle McAfee in her appraisal of the thinking of influential French philosopher, Julia Kristeva. I first came across Kristeva's writing at the age of nineteen. The essay in question was titled 'Stabat Mater' after a hymn about the Virgin Mary's agony during the crucifixion of Christ. The hymn begins 'Stabat mater dolorosa' – meaning 'Stood the mother, full of grief'. I still remember vividly the portrait

Kristeva paints of the maternal in that essay. Through childbearing, labour and maternity, boundaries between mother and infant are blurred, never to be fully re-established, she argues. 'I plant my feet firmly on the ground in order to carry him, safe, stable,' she writes of her experience with her infant son, 'while he dances in my neck, floats in my hair, looks right and left for a soft shoulder, slips on the breast ... and finally flies up from my navel in his dream, borne by my hands. My son.' I had, at the time I read this essay, still almost two decades to live before I would become a mother myself, but I recognised my own already-leaky female body in Kristeva's writing, as well as my profound relation to the body of my own mother.

Kristeva has an abiding interest in what we call subjectivity. She and her contemporaries were early advocates of the term 'subjectivity' as an alternative to conventional understandings of the 'self'. This is because of the way the term 'self' has tended to be used and understood, historically. 'Self' supposes a being who is fully aware, guided by reason and intellect and able to act autonomously. Such a self is his or her own master, and subject to no one or nothing else. The term 'subjectivity' turns this notion on its head. Those who use it believe the Western tradition has been utterly mistaken about how we come to be who we are. The experience of subjectivity is not sealed off from the kinds of phenomena that shape us: culture, context, relationships and language. Rather, we are subject to such phenomena. We emerge in the folds of such relations, in ways that we can never fully comprehend, and our process of doing so continues as long as we live. Nevertheless, for Kristeva, the subject is never disconnected from his or her biology: the body is ever present. It is not possible for the subject to float away from it.

Kristeva's essay on the maternal is and remains a radical

reworking of how we come to understand the maternal subject. The text was presented in the form of columns – sometimes one, sometimes two – so that the reading experience itself was discontinuous, as if dismantled from within as one column competed over another for the reader's attention. Kristeva uses the occasional left-hand column to reflect poetically on her personal experience of pregnancy, childbirth and breastfeeding, in which infant and mother are in and of each other, body and mind, and in no way autonomous. In the right-hand column, in a more prosaic fashion, she discusses conventional Western representations of maternity, particularly the notion of the maternal love of the Virgin Mary as a means for dealing with fears of mortality. The virgin mother is a fantasy, she argues, that is at the root of dominant representations of motherhood, calling for the sublimation of women's desires, and for our asceticism, sacrifice and suffering. It was a chilling thing for a young woman not yet twenty to read and to understand this essay for the first time, and I have had an abiding interest in and respect for Kristeva's way of thinking ever since.

Kristeva's key work on the topic of fear is a book titled *Powers of Horror*, first published in English translation in 1982. In it, Kristeva writes about her own experience as a child of feeling nausea and revulsion whenever her parents served her milk upon the surface of which there had formed a skin. Simply the sight of it, never mind her lips having to actually come in contact with it, sent the young Julia reeling. Kristeva extends her discussion of things that have the power to repulse us in this deeply felt, bodily way to considerations of blood, pus, faeces, vomit and the human corpse. What is it, she wonders, about these abject things? It seems they have power over us. But how?

Her proposal is that we are horrified by them because of the way they confront us with the notion of the border – the border between self and other, or between that which we feel we can contain, and that which is utterly uncontainable. '"I" want none of that element,' she writes, of the skin on the milk. '"I" do not want to assimilate it. "I" expel it.' This notion of expelling that which we strongly reject through fear forms the basis of her influential thinking on 'the abject', a concept I will explicate more fully later. It is an idea I'm keen to think about more deeply in relation to women, fear and violence.

BEFORE I RETURN TO KRISTEVA, I WANT TO LOOK AT THE STORY of Rosie Batty, an activist well known in Australia for her work on family violence. Batty is a former Australian of the Year and a passionate campaigner. In 2015, a year after the death of her only child, she published her autobiography, A Mother's Story. It is a very difficult book to read. I read it in a single day, and felt I understood precisely those passages in which she talked about the close relationship she'd developed with her son, Luke. They were predominantly a family of two. It's as small as a family can be. I also felt a great sense of grief in reading of the slow demise over a decade or more of Batty's one-time partner Greg Anderson, the father of Luke. Anderson suffered from schizophrenia, and the description of his declining health corresponded with my own experience of a close friend's struggle with the same illness. My friend Jo, whose story I discuss in more detail in a later chapter, was never violent towards me, but in other ways her decline echoed Anderson's in every way. Over time, Greg Anderson lost everyhing he had: jobs, friends, shelter, and eventually, his family and his life.

My childhood experience of the worst years of my father's alcoholism further coloured my reading of Batty's story. I was confronted with a deep sense of recognition whenever she described feeling unsafe in her own home. Batty's son, Luke, witnessed her being violently attacked by his father several times, and in conversation with a psychologist he once confessed, 'I tried to stop him. I tried to pull him off Mum, but I was too little.' I recognised Luke's pain, along with the sense of shame and helplessness inherent in his statement. At this point in reading the book, and at many others, I found myself having to put *A Mother's Story* down. I couldn't sit still. I walked in circles around the house sobbing. *A Mother's Story* is deeply, deeply sad. But each time, after a moment when I felt I simply couldn't continue reading, I led myself back to it. I picked it up again, and continued.

Despite repeated attempts to have Anderson's increasingly serious emotional and physical violence recognised by the family court system, and to have his access to her and her son limited by court orders, Batty had to rely almost completely on her own wits in her attempt to keep herself and her family safe. Anderson regularly turned up unannounced at her home and later stood on the boundaries during her son's weekly sporting events, at times in clear contravention of court orders. Batty believed that Anderson would not attack in a public place. She was wrong.

On an otherwise ordinary weekday afternoon in February, in front of many other families and children, Anderson approached eleven-year-old Luke during cricket training and struck him in the head with a bat. Then he pulled out a knife and stabbed him to death. Batty was standing fifty metres away at the time of the incident. She happened to have her back turned. A child witness to the violence, aged eight, ran from the cricket nets calling, 'The dad hit the boy! The dad hit the boy!' There was chaos and confusion and in the immediate aftermath, Batty was shielded, initially, from the truth. When the police arrived, Anderson approached them aggressively, brandishing the same knife with which he'd just murdered his son. The officers shot him, and he died in hospital later that night.

SOME OF THE MOST AFFECTING PARTS OF BATTY'S AUTOBIOGRAPHY are those passages, long before Luke's death, in which she describes violence towards her that is not carried through with impact. They are affecting in part because we know – via paratextual content such as the back-cover blurb – what will happen to Luke and to Rosie in the end. But there's something else going on, too, and again, Kristeva's ideas can help us to make sense of it all. Several times Batty describes Anderson switching quickly from relatively normal behaviour to a violence that threatens but fails to enact physical damage. In front of Luke, he picks up a large vase and takes aim at Rosie with it, but falls just short of throwing it. At another time, he aims a kick at her head, but crucially falls just short of contact. The effect is to hurl Rosie into and then suspend her in a kind of imaginary, nether world, beyond that which Kristeva would call the symbolic (reason, logic or the dominant reality). Did she imagine it? Did something just happen? Is it all in her head?

Kristeva says abjection is above all ambiguity, because 'while releasing a hold, it does not radically cut off the subject' from that which threatens it. 'On the contrary, abjection acknowledges [the subject] to be in perpetual danger.' Thus, says Kristeva, a subject like Batty is as if braided or woven through with the other's loathing. She is wholly altered by her fear, and that fear itself is a 'fluid haze' and an 'hallucinatory, ghostly glimmer' both unapproachable and intimate.

Kristeva's concept of abjection has been drawn upon to

explain the horror genre in film and literature, particularly the way in which the female body or other symbolic references to the feminine becomes sites of horror in such narratives. One of the most oft-cited examples in science fiction is the film *Alien* (1979), in which forced impregnation, bodily dismemberment and the chameleon-like nature of the alien can be read as deeply unsettling encounters with the abject maternal body. Film scholar Barbara Creed's reading of Kristeva is that it is femininity itself that has been historically constructed as monstrous. According to Creed, women have been consistently 'constructed as "biological freaks" whose bodies represent a fearful and threatening form of sexuality'. This monstrosity in difference can be traced as far back as Aristotle, who stated that 'Woman is literally a monster: a failed and botched male who is only born female due to an excess of moisture and of coldness during the process of conception.' I think Kristeva's ideas can go a long way to helping us to understand men's fear of women and particularly their fear of women who may be capable of wielding any real power. Misogyny, too, can be understood in terms of Kristeva's notion of abjection. Woman is violently rejected by the misogynist in order for him to assert himself as 'I' and 'not that' – his 'gut reaction' to women and to the maternal is essentially a deeply felt panic about borders.

THERE ARE SOME INTERESTING COMPARISONS TO MAKE between fear of violence on an intimate scale and fear of violence on a massive, global scale. Both are to do with potential abuses of power; both are interesting to look at in Kristeva's terms. In thinking through contemporary applications of Kristeva's work on the abject, I began to consider the career of veteran peace activist, Helen Caldicott. What role, I wondered, had fear played in motivating Caldicott to shift from ordinary citizen to intrepid anti-nuclear lobbyist? What role did fear continue to play in her work? Whereas Rosie Batty is only a few years into her journey of speaking out, Caldicott has been a full-time activist for more than forty years. She became active as a public speaker during the early 1970s, when I was still a toddler. By then a specialist paediatrician in Adelaide, and married with three children, she added an increasingly busy schedule as spokesperson for the anti-nuclear movement to her calendar. She played a significant role in Australia's anti-uranium movement at that time, and was instrumental in convincing the Whitlam government to take the French to the International Court of Justice at The Hague over the issue of nuclear testing in the Pacific. The Australian anti-nuclear lobby of that period ran a highly successful grassroots campaign, the likes of which political activists ever since have aspired to re-enact. The fact that now, more than forty years later, Australia remains one of the few developed nations to have remained free of both nuclear power and nuclear arms, is a legacy of the work done by Caldicott and her peers during the 1970s.

During the 1980s, Caldicott followed her husband, a medical specialist, to the United States, where she too secured a good professional appointment. Caldicott practised out of Boston Children's Hospital's Medical Center and taught paediatrics at Harvard Medical School. Here, she began to speak with and motivate fellow physicians about the medical implications of nuclear weapons, the stupidity of the nuclear arms race and the burgeoning dangers of the nuclear power industry. She became the president of Physicians for Social Responsibility (PSR), a member organisation of some 23 000 medical doctors at its peak, and was later instrumental in forming its sister organisation, International Physicians for the Prevention of Nuclear War.

Caldicott's true gift was in public speaking, and while the Cold War continued, her speaking schedule gained momentum across the United States. From 1980 to 1984 she spoke at colleges and demonstrations across the nation, and dominated United States television news and talk shows, gaining as much airtime during the campaign to freeze nuclear weapons proliferation as did the United States president at the time, Ronald Reagan.

Interestingly, like Montaigne, Helen Caldicott has spent much of her life suffering from a palpable fear of death. In her autobiography, *A Passionate Life*, she traces this fear to an incident she suffered as a toddler, when her parents left her briefly with carers in an institution. She developed a severe infection, accompanied by fever, and has a powerful memory of being held down forcefully by an anaesthetist before being given an anaesthetic. 'I remember the hair on his hands,' she told me, relating her story. She was convinced that her parents had abandoned her to death.

Caldicott's fear of death was compounded when, as a young adult, she read the novel *On the Beach* by Nevil Shute. The true horror – and lesson – of Shute's novel creeps up slowly on the reader. There has been a war, known in the book as the Short War, which lasted only thirty-seven days. As a result, the whole of the northern hemisphere is unable to communicate, and the book's protagonists are the war's survivors, carrying on as best they can with daily life in Australia while a radioactive cloud is sweeping south towards them, poisoning everything in its wake. The people of the book must face not just their own impending deaths, but the creeping annihilation of everyone and everything they know.

For Caldicott, the representation of her home town in such an horrific – and yet entirely possible – post-apocalyptic scenario was deeply disturbing. 'The image of the people of Melbourne giving cyanide to their babies as the radioactive fallout was about to strike has stayed with me all my life', she would write, decades later.

'I guess I was frightened,' Caldicott told me, reflecting on the Cold War years during our first meeting. 'I've always been frightened.'

A KEY DIFFERENCE BETWEEN BATTY AND CALDICOTT AS agitators and activists is that Caldicott's arguments about the dangers of the arms race and nuclear proliferation are largely based on fears regarding future possibilities: further accidents, conflicts, incidents of military aggression. Like my son's fears of our apartment building catching fire, which resurface every time the evacuation alarm sounds, they are not unfounded. In fact, they are firmly based on logic, experience, history, knowledge and probability. We have seen this can happen; we know it is possible. Similarly, images of the horrors of Hiroshima and Nagasaki remain vivid for many of us. Caldicott's extensive research on the military–industrial complex, and on the medical and environmental consequences of accidents such as that at Fukushima, have produced a weighty and disturbing body of knowledge. Yet, because so many of Caldicott's predictions and sound warnings are speculative, they are constantly at risk of being dismissed. Rosie Batty, on the other hand, is narrating an intimate experience of fear that has already reached an impossibly dark outcome. For Batty, the unthinkable has already happened. Her mission is to stop it happening to others.

The other significant difference, as mentioned earlier, is that the fears of which Batty and Caldicott regularly speak in public are of different scales. Batty addresses personal violence either threatened or perpetrated by our intimate partners; Caldicott addresses larger-scale violence openly sanctioned by the state. It seems one is easier for us to understand and assimilate than the other.

FEAR CAN BE A POWERFUL MOTIVATOR. HELEN CALDICOTT'S most famous public address is one which has become known as the 'bombing run' speech and it is of interest here because of the way it effectively employs the genre of horror, and therefore Kristeva's notion of the abject. The speech was given to large audiences across the United States during the 1980s. It began with Caldicott asking the audience to imagine a missile approaching their home city, a missile which was about to release a nuclear bomb. She then provided a very full description of what might happen next. What would the explosion sound like? How many people in how great a radius would be instantly incinerated? How far would the toxins spread? What would the injuries sustained on the bodies of the survivors look like, feel like, smell like? Caldicott listed potential answers to these questions in detail, using the precise, specialist language of the medical profession. What would be the likely effects of the radioactive chemicals on bodies, animal and human? How would such chemicals affect the surrounding air, water and soil, and for how long? The images of abjection conjured go well beyond the skin on top of a cup of milk. Caldicott's 'bombing run' speech was hugely effective, but not without controversy. It confronted audience members at the very border of meaning – beyond religion, morality, law – at a place where death keeps house. People regularly left her public appearances in tears.

When I spoke with Caldicott in the late spring of 2015, her 'bombing run' speeches were a thing of the past, but she was quick to agree that the prospect of an apocalyptic future remains a fearful topic, and she defended her use of fear as legitimate and necessary.

'Fear is a totally appropriate response to danger and if you're chased by a bull, the adrenal gland, which is just above the kidney, pumps out adrenalin. Your blood pressure goes up, your blood sugar level goes up and you can jump a fence six feet high if necessary to escape. It's that adrenal response to fear that has allowed us to survive.'

'It must be an awfully difficult line to negotiate as a political motivator', I responded. 'On the one hand you're trying to get across information in order to mobilise, but on the other hand the facts terrify people.'

Caldicott seemed not in the least bit surprised by my line of thinking. For her, the dangers of a nuclear future remain real and urgent.

'People need to be terrified,' she said bluntly. Of her strategy, she said, 'I work to change lives,' so that those who attend, 'don't just go out and say, "That's an interesting lecture, pass the cornflakes". Often people come up to me and say, "I heard you talk at Colgate College thirty years ago, now that's why I work for the *New York Times*". I hear that story again and again. So, their lives are changed. Otherwise, why do it? I'm trying to induce a cure and the only cure is through education, as Thomas Jefferson said, "An informed democracy will behave in a responsible fashion."'

I can see the logic of Caldicott's strategy, but I'm not sure I could routinely deliver such a speech myself. At what point, I wonder, does the use of fear as a motivator backfire? Can it backfire? Fear is above all a powerful emotion and the forms of expression it takes in us and through us are not necessarily easy to predict or control.

A HISTORY OF PHILOSOPHIES OF FEAR MIGHT ITSELF OFFER AN interesting lesson in gender politics. Thomas Hobbes, for example, proposed that fear is utterly central to man. According to Hobbes, a violent death is the thing we all fear the most. Hence fear is a strongly determining power, both socially and in terms of the individual. 'The original of all great and lasting societies,' he wrote, 'consisted not in the mutual good will men had towards each other but in the mutual fear they had of each other.' His argument is that without an authority (such as a head of state or a monarch) to wield power, and hence order, over us, we are in a perpetual state of war: man against man. Fear, then, is both the principal cause of war, and the principal means for attaining and maintaining the peace we associate with civility. The fact that Hobbes employed the word 'man' to stand in for all of humanity was in some ways simply characteristic of the fact that he was writing in the 17th century. On the other hand, it seems to me that in addition to accepted usage, he simply wasn't taking women into account; his understanding of the role and power of violence is constructed on the assumption that only men matter, particularly in terms of maintaining civil order. Paradoxically, it is this same assumption that makes it so difficult for women to enter into political dialogue about violence and militarisation at all. Helen Caldicott's experience of public life is a case in point. She has been extensively ridiculed in the media and online, and over a long period. Most recently the high-profile British columnist George Monbiot launched an attack on her reputation in the *Guardian* over what he saw as incorrect information she'd quoted on the death toll of the Chernobyl nuclear accident. Helen defended herself on live television, and was backed up by a number of other environmental-science journalists, including Jim Green writing for the Green Left Weekly. The disagreement turned on a larger debate among scientists about the health effects of low-level ionising radiation, but Caldicott's interpretation of the numbers remains a valid one. It's notable, too, that in recent years television journalists have lightly belittled Caldicott's expertise by introducing her as a grandmother, a term she described to me as 'a label used to work against you'. Rosie Batty has also had to endure highly visible public-domain attacks, particularly from former leader of the opposition in Australia, Mark Latham, who sought to discredit her for alleged financial misconduct in relation to a charity she'd set up in her son's name. Latham's claims were also widely discredited, but Batty was deeply rattled by them: 'It's been a difficult few days, trying to understand why someone wants to attack you so much and try to accuse you of things that are so not true,' she wrote on the Luke Batty Foundation Facebook page at the time. 'It has dragged me down ... I feel violated.' In light of attacks like these, it is not suprising that speaking up and speaking out is seen as a risk by many women, one we are often reluctant to take.

DURING A DISCUSSION OF DOMINATION AND POWER I HAD while sitting with Helen Caldicott in her garden in rural New South Wales, our conversation turned to the connection between sex and violence.

'When I was very young,' she recalled, 'I said to Dad, "Why do men rape women when they conquer a territory? What have the women had to do with it?" Well, now I ask, why do they show porno films to men when they take off in their planes from aircraft carriers to kill people?' Alarming as it is, this practice of using pornography to encourage aggressive behaviour in the military has been documented in several instances internationally, as outlined in a recent article by political science scholar Sheila Jeffreys.

Caldicott was firm: 'There's a very big connection between sex and violence'.

It's a topic she is hoping to write more about.

'I've read some research by a woman in California who is doing work on hormones and their effect on behaviour,' she continued. 'She noticed that when there was confrontation in the lab the men would go into their own room and slam the door and fume. And the next morning the women would come and clean the benches and make the coffee and try and produce cohesion and fix it. She tested the hormones and what happened was with that confrontation the men's testosterone went sky high, but the women's oxytocin went up. Oxytocin is related to lactation. It's the nurturing hormone.'

I read up on this issue when I returned home and although I couldn't find the exact study Caldicott was referring to, I certainly found studies evidencing a relationship between increased oxytocin and more pronounced maternal behaviour, and plenty of scholarly research going on in the field of gender and violence, although here the issues are quite complex. One recent study cites a significant amount of literature that confirms substantial sex differences in hormonal responses to social conflict and aggressive behaviour. Statistically, too, it is clear that there is a higher incidence of violence among men than among women. And yet, a recent article by Debra Niehoff which investigates neurobiological research into men and violence concludes, interestingly, that while there are parts of the brain we might usefully label 'male' and 'female' – and these do react differently to various stress factors – different individuals are made up of different combinations of 'male' and 'female' brain characteristics. Niehoff warns against oversimplifying brain patterns based on sex differences. Essentially, she says, all of our brains are 'intersex' and it is misleading to suggest that men's brains are at all 'hardwired' for violence. Environmental and cultural influences count for an awful lot.

'Really,' Caldicott asked me, in the midst of our backyard conversation, 'why the hell do we glorify war? Why is there a man on a horse in every square in Europe? So many of the "great" people in history are killers. What's that about? I don't know.'

It's a fair question to ponder.

DISTURBINGLY, PERHAPS, THE OPENING FEW SENTENCES OF JULIA Kristeva's *Powers of Horror* have a poetry about them. The book begins:

> There looms, within abjection, one of those violent, dark
> revolts of being, that seems to emanate from an exorbitant
> outside or inside, ejected beyond the scope of the possible,
> the tolerable, the thinkable. It lies there quite close, but it
> cannot be assimilated. It beseeches, worries and fascinates
> desire, which nevertheless does not let itself be seduced.
> Apprehensive, desire turns aside; sickened, it rejects.

All of Kristeva's work is deeply informed by psychoanalytic ideas, particularly Sigmund Freud's, but in my opinion she goes further than Freud ever did in thinking through the nature of subjectivity. Kristeva has a capacity for empathy that I'm not sure Freud even considered important to this kind of work. Kristeva constantly imagines herself into the heart of the matter. 'Not me', she writes, contemplating the notion of the abject and its relation to the thinking subject. 'Not that. But not nothing, either. A "something" that I do not recognise as a thing. A weight of meaninglessness, about which there is nothing insignificant, and which crushes me.' Kristeva's ideas have political promise because of the way she calls upon us to rethink our own subjectivity and therefore make possible a more conciliatory and open relationship with others. We, each of us, need to examine the perpetual play between inside and outside, a constant, and perhaps constantly surprising, process. This is so even – or perhaps especially – in the face of that thing that horrifies us most.

I EXPERIENCED A SURPRISE LESSON IN BORDERS AND ABJECTION while I was writing this chapter. I was on a crowded bus, returning home from a neighbouring suburb when, under the gaze of twenty or more onlookers, I seemed to become someone else. It was a brief transformation, a sudden and unwanted entrapment, accompanied by an awful sense of vertigo.

It was a Friday evening, and my son, Roland, and I had taken the bus to Carlton to choose a book each at one of our favourite bookstores. His was a reward for progressing well with his daily reading at home, and mine was, well, a consolation perhaps. I was feeling fragile. After extended browsing, my son settled on a garish Lego Star Wars number with a free Han Solo mini-figure. I chose a new collection of essays by Rebecca Solnit.

Earlier that week, I'd suffered a small accident after a routine trip to the dentist involving a local anaesthetic. The dental procedure itself was straightforward, but afterwards I failed to wait long enough for the anaesthetic to wear off. Some hours after my appointment, and at home, I resolved to prepare myself a late lunch. I toasted some crusty olive bread and ate it with cheese and tomato and a handful of green salad. I ate it hurriedly, absentmindedly, conscious that it was almost time to pick up Roland from school. Later, my lower lip felt odd. When I glanced in the mirror just before leaving home, I realised it was slightly swollen. There was nothing much to do. Only on my bicycle, pedalling down the busy arterial road, did I notice blood. The vague numbness of the receding effect of the anaesthetic was being gradually replaced with the throbbing of a fresh wound.

It turned out that my mouth was quite severely lacerated and swollen. I had chewed over both my lower lip and cheek. Over the next few hours, the swelling increased. The whole site tingled and ached. By the next morning there was a vibrant display of blue and red bruising, and I both looked and felt like I had been punched savagely in the face.

After leaving the bookshop that Friday night, Roland and I boarded the 207 bus back east along Johnston Street to take the ten-minute ride home and I was overcome with tiredness. My face was throbbing. It was 6 pm and the bus was almost full. We sat in the last couple of empty seats, those facing side-on towards the front and meant for the elderly and disabled. As is often the case, there were no other children on the bus and the eyes of many of the passengers fell on Roland, who was asking permission to take out his book. I gave him a nod and he spent the rest of the trip home engaged in an imaginary narrative that involved flying the little Star Wars mini-figure about in the air, verbalising his imaginary game in the form of short pieces of dialogue and imitating gunfire. I was vaguely disturbed by the violence of his play narrative, but grateful he was amusing himself. I leaned my head back against the window and closed my eyes.

When I opened them, I caught a dozen or more fellow commuters suddenly glancing away from me, their body language slightly tense, and I realised that my son and I had created a little set piece. I suppose the movement of his play had caught their attention, and then their gazes had fallen on my damaged face.

Our circumstances were being assessed, assumptions were being made, conclusions drawn. One woman in her sixties standing just across from us gave me a smile I took to be an understanding one, but precisely what it was that she thought she had understood, I could not be sure.

The people on the bus were not to know that I grew up in a household in which alcohol-related violence was a very regular threat. It was generally not me who was beaten. It was my mother. But, as Kristeva makes clear, and as I understand now that I am a parent myself, the distinction between a mother and her children is mutable. It is sometimes difficult to know where one ends and the other begins. The act of those fellow commuters averting their gazes *en masse* caused an immediate sensation of falling. I struggled to maintain my own sense of continuity. A whole set of eerily familiar commentaries floated through my own mind, judgments that were made of my mother thirty years ago, lines overheard in bars, comments that are still being made of women in such circumstances now: *She should have kept her mouth shut. Why can't she walk away for the child's sake? Someone had to pull her into line. She had it coming, didn't she? She's a wild one, that one. Why doesn't she leave?*

I was not who they thought I was. But also, I was her precisely. I was the ghost of the beaten woman. She was alive in me.

I straightened my back. I looked blankly out the window. I did not shift my gaze for the rest of the journey. Frankly, I couldn't wait to get my son and myself off that bus. As the journey continued, I felt more and more faint, less and less myself. Perception buckled. I began to sweat.

THINKING BACK TO THAT INCIDENT, SOME MONTHS LATER, I

am reminded of feminist philosopher Ann Cahill's description of power as a force not solely punishing and authoritative, but also subtle, persuasive and creative. It is a force that is capable of influencing actions on the level of desire and identity, says Cahill, and for this reason it should not be surprising that the body becomes for it a privileged site.

It's taken some time for me to process my thoughts about what happened on that otherwise ordinary bus journey. The point is that something happened – several things actually. The first thing was that my fellow passengers noticed that my face was wounded and most of them, having registered that I had noticed their gaze, looked away. The second thing was that my childhood experience of violence in the home marked me, invisibly, but as surely as the bruised and the lacerated lip, and it was this 'other' kind of marking that drove my own reaction to the passengers and their turning away. That experience was disconnected, as it happens, from the wound I wore on my face, but it *could* have been connected, and it appalled me that the best my fellow commuters could muster between them was one brief, sympathetic smile. The third thing that happened was that, recognising that I might have been misunderstood, I responded to my own body's 'abject speech' with a sense of horror. In a moment of giddying transformation, it seemed to me that the wound stood in for me. 'It lies there quite close, but it cannot be assimilated,' wrote Kristeva. I felt as if my experience of childhood family violence had ruptured and bloomed on my adult face almost thirty years after bearing witness to it. It was speaking on my behalf. And I was erased by it.

When I say to myself and others that I am not a fearful person, what do I think I mean? The truth is that I have long been fearful of intimate male violence, of becoming the so-called beaten woman, the woman whose personal horror everybody knows about, but about which nobody will speak. She is trapped, this woman. She is trapped and tormented and there is no way out. Further, she is publicly humiliated. She is shamed, even by something as subtle as a looking away.

If my rendering in language of the scene on the bus seems inadequate, I cannot help it. Thinking about it still conjures for me a heady mix of anger and shock, an automatic flow of tears, but also a sense of dissociation. In my memory of the events, I occupy my own perspective, but also, at times, the perspective of those others on the bus, for I have been them too at different times. Frankly, who amongst us hasn't ever looked away? A wound is abhorrent to look at. It is blood and pus and bruising, a gesture towards the human corpse we will all one day become. A victim – right in the midst of a crisis that has marked her – is hard to look at, too. Sometimes, looking back to my experience on the bus, I am neither myself nor the others. Sometimes I am hovering in the air, up towards the ceiling of the crowded vehicle, both there and not there, and my vulnerability is everything. And it is strangely beautiful.

In *Powers of Horror*, Kristeva writes of 'a sublime point at which the abject collapses in a burst of beauty that overwhelms us and that "cancels our existence"'. I wonder, now, if that's a little bit like what happened.

IN FACT, MY PHYSICALITY RETURNED. I BOWED MY HEAD. MY sense of vertigo continued. Our bus stop arrived and then I took my son's hand and shuffled through the back exit. Tears fell the full length of the several blocks home.

'Are you all right, Mum?' asked Roland.

I was grateful for his question and I wanted to answer him

honestly, but he was still so young, and I didn't know where to start. I remained disoriented, stripped back, raw.

'It's just that my face hurts,' I said, wiping away my tears. And in this fashion, I let silence stand in once more for the unspeakable. We stumbled home.

The sense of having fallen through and into another mode of being – a shadowy, alternative mode, in which I had glimpsed the awesome persistence of fear and violence – took some days to dissipate. Curiously, it was the silent communal acceptance of the matter – including my own quick denial to my son that anything at all had happened – that frightened me the most. It frightens me still.

When I say that I am not a fearful person, again, that fear has no hold over me, who ought to take that as the truth?

IN HER ESSAY 'THE PHENOMENOLOGY OF FEAR' ANN CAHILL writes about the social production of the female body and the threat of rape. Interestingly, she says, even the bodies of women who have never been raped or directly threatened with rape are 'likely to carry themselves in such a way as to express the truths and values of rape culture'. This, in hindsight, goes some way towards explaining both Rosie Batty's inability to recognise herself, for many years, as a victim of family violence – a fact she acknowledges on reflection in her memoir – as well as to my own inability to speak back to the people on the bus, to counter and properly call out the actual and potential damage done by their collective passivity.

The social production of the female body is an interesting phenomenon to keep in mind when trying to make sense of Rosie Batty's experience. In the final decade of his life, the self narrative of Batty's former partner Greg Anderson became increasingly schizophrenic. He was attracted to many different religious traditions, retreating regularly for months at a time to a Catholic monastery in New South Wales, as well as spending significant time with devotees in traditions as disparate as the Hare Krishna and Jesus Christ of Latter Day Saints sects. One day, when Luke was still a baby, Rosie criticised Anderson for getting the infant up from bed and perching him in his bouncinette in a precarious spot atop books and folders on the kitchen table. Anderson turned silent, and then seethed. 'Woman follows man, man follows God,' he declared. 'If man follows woman, it leads him to the devil.' Rosie tackled him on it. 'What?' she replied. 'What do you mean? As a woman, I cannot have a direct link to God?'

Later, Anderson's aggression and paranoia could be triggered by any hint that his son had shared his mother's bed – something that happened regularly, in fact, as Rosie and Luke often found comfort in co-sleeping. Or it could be triggered by the idea that a woman other than the boy's mother had been looking after him. Once, on an access visit, Anderson phoned Rosie to say that he had noticed an 'offensive smell' about the boy and demanded to know whether a babysitter – a woman – had been looking after Luke the previous night.

Batty also describes Anderson's relationship to sex as furtive and aggressive, often laced with shame. Never officially a couple, in the conventional sense, the two never lived together, and sex between them was characterised by Anderson's very occasional visits to Rosie's bed. These visits were so covert and sudden that Rosie would be woken from sleep, and afterwards be left alone again to wonder whether anything had actually happened between them. In those early years, she was frequently puzzled by the nature of the relationship. As time went on, however, it was as if Anderson sought out religious tracts that served to confirm his own view of sexual intimacy: that it was ungodly, improper and unclean. Sexual relations, it seemed, were Anderson's version of the skin on the top of the milk. Women, by association, repulsed him, and his semi-monastic retreats into solitude seemed, as much as anything, an attempt to cleanse himself of his desire. After Luke was conceived, sexual intimacy between Rosie and Anderson ceased altogether.

Kristeva, in the tradition of psychoanalysis, reads a psychotic person as someone who is in such a narcissistic state that they are incapable of following ordinary logic or orderly cultural paradigms. It's not difficult to read into Anderson's self-narrative an increasingly deep-seated fear and hatred of women. Rosie Batty is not just herself. She is standing in for something else: a conflicted representation of the maternal Virgin Mary and the monstrous feminine, both. Anderson feels he must dominate and control such a thing, despite his inability to manage even his own basic needs for shelter and routine.

In February 2014, when I first heard the news of an eleven-year-old boy's murder at his father's hands during cricket practice, I understood immediately that it was an act of aggression directed primarily at the mother of that child. I felt for Rosie Batty, deep in the pit of my gut, even though I did not yet know her name. My reaction was not unusual among women I know.

AT A PUBLIC FORUM DURING THE 25TH CHICAGO HUMANI-TIES Festival, a member of the audience asked guest speaker, Julia Kristeva, about her opinion from a psychoanalytic point of view of the kinds of violence being enacted across the United States in the form of school shootings, usually perpetrated by young men.

'I'm very much concerned with this,' said Kristeva, who had earlier in the session made a cogent argument for the continued relevance of psychoanalysis to politics and culture, criticising many fellow analysts for not being engaged with contemporary politics enough. 'You are maybe familiar with the Kantian notion of radical evil,' she continued.

Kant's notion probably needs some explanation here. Philosophy scholar Claudia Card says that, according to Kant, 'we become radically evil when we subordinate the moral law to our own self interest'. But one of the problems with Kant's approach is that he fails to properly discriminate between acts like murder, and other, more petty acts of immorality, like small-scale theft. His work has been widely criticised for leaving the real source of radical evil too mysterious. Surely it can't be all so perfectly logical and reasonable as Kant makes out? Philosopher Hannah Arendt, in her treatise on totalitarianism, picks up where Kant left off. And here we come closer to Julia Kristeva's work on abjection and horror. Across our entire Western philosophical tradition, argues Arendt, 'we cannot conceive of "radical evil" ... We actually have nothing to fall back on in order to understand a phenomenon that nevertheless confronts us with its overpowering reality and breaks down all the standards we know,' she writes.

'Hannah Arendt took this notion of radical evil,' continued Kristeva, in answer to the question asked of her in Chicago, 'and said when some people decide to take the life of other people, the killing, the murder is radical evil. How is it that some people can reach such a situation? Many religions consider this a sin, but at other times they utilise it in order to fight another religion. For us psychologists and psychoanalysts, this state of mind is due to the fact, and I will speak in Freudian terms, that we have two mental components, two essential mental components. One is the erotic component – excitation, in the sense of procreation, of love, of sexual intercourse, of tenderness. The other one is violence and this violence is called by Freud the death wish. When the identity of an adolescent is well built, and when the need to believe is satisfied, the death wish is integrated. "I will be aggressive in order to achieve some ideal. And my ideals will prevent me from being cruel, because my ideals, if they are in the frame of love, will prevent me from destroying other human lives." But there are situations where the psychic apparatus has not satisfied the ideal wish and we see a falling into pieces, a sort of dismantling. "I don't know who I am." There is nobody in the place of the ego. We can describe this as schizophrenic or paranoid. It is a psychotic experience and the ego is abolished and overwhelmed by violence which is experienced either like a void, a sort of hallucination – "I don't know where I am" – or by pleasure from the violence itself. And in this situation people go to a sort of obscurity in which they can kill their similars.'

Kristeva concluded her answer by referring to an example of a terrorist attack in the south of France, in which a number of war veterans who'd fought in Afghanistan as well as several Jewish children were killed by an adolescent man under the influence of religious extremism. We need to reach out to such adolescents, argued Kristeva, and work with their families and communities to detect the first signs of their destruction of identity so as to prevent these young men from becoming victims themselves. We need to do this, she argued, even when those with political power are unwilling to give us space to do so. We need to insist on compassionate action, rather than recoil in collective fear.

WHEN I LIVED IN THE HILLS OUTSIDE PERTH, I TOOK TO CYCLING a 30-kilometre circuit once a week. The route took in a group of challenging ascents, along with several long, easy stretches, bordered by paddocks containing sheep and cattle. Sometimes the surface of the road offered up interesting sights: the flattened carcass of a fox; a large snake soaking up the sun. There were few vehicles. I enjoyed the ride, but I always had on my mind a particular hill that marked the distinctive feature of my route.

I can still remember the first time I pedalled down Liberton Road in Wooroloo on my new carbon-fibre frame. I was still getting used to riding such a lightweight model. It's the kind of bicycle that at speeds over 50km/hr makes you feel as if you're flying. Except you are not. You remain on the ground on an ordinary road with all the standard traffic hazards coming to greet you: uneven road surfaces and debris, speeding vehicles, blind corners, unexpected pedestrians and stray animals. The Liberton Road descent had a bit of a curve about it, preventing me from seeing exactly what I was up against a little further down the road. Australian Tour de France champion Cadel Evans once said that the sport of cycling is the sport of suffering, but he has also been known to say that it's all about the descent. A road cyclist learns to descend by building up a certain degree of technical skill. You need to know your bike, to feel comfortable with your gearing and your brakes, to know which way and when to shift your weight or lean. Beyond that, what you need to do is let go of your fear. I couldn't. Not completely. I don't think I ever ceased to be frightened of both the approach and the descent itself on Liberton Road, but one day, on the way down, I thought of the line from Kamala Das's poem.

Fuck fear, I thought. Women need courage. We need courage to endure childbirth. We need courage in the workplace. We need courage to go out on the street. Sometimes we need courage to lie in our own beds at night. I determined to descend the Liberton Road hill at absolute maximum speed. And to my surprise, I managed it. And then I learned to chase the feeling. I learned to properly fly. Over time, descending Liberton Road hill became an addictive pleasure, the sense of which began to stay with me. I found I could close my eyes anywhere and at any time of day, and call up the feeling of flight and freedom, taking strength from it. I still believe that the courage I found that year to leave my long-term partner, to plant the seeds of positive change in a number of areas in my life, was all because of my change in attitude to the descent on Liberton Road. Embracing the descent has deepened a long-term commitment to cycling, but it has also taught me something profound about capability. Oddly, I feel as if it goes on teaching me.

THERE'S A BEAUTIFUL PASSAGE IN ONE OF JULIA KRISTEVA'S later works in which she writes of putting her theory into practice. She is working as a psychoanalyst with a small boy by the name of Paul who has not yet come to language. He should be talking already but for some reason he is not. Kristeva teaches him to speak by first teaching him to sing. There is something about the connection between the imaginary realm of song and the verbal speaking voice that fits beautifully with the way Kristeva categorises us humans as, above all, *speaking subjects*. I can see Kristeva as she crouches down low with the child and begins to make a sound that is not yet symbolic or linguistic. She is working with the non-verbal: sound, melody, rhythm. Somehow the child's body/mind understands the musical diction – the imaginary (or in Kristeva's terms semiotic) roots – the grain of the voice, the emotive spaces of song, and he gradually begins to respond. Kristeva and Paul make up songs together, and he learns to find pleasure in his own voice. It is as if she sings his courage out, and through this, brings him more fully into the possibility of being.

At the Australian of the Year Awards in January 2015, Rosie Batty stood up to accept her award with a shock of recognition. She felt unlike the other outstanding citizens shortlisted for the award – a more 'productive' neuroscientist, a well-known actress an adoption campaigner– and as she stepped forward she remembered precisely why she had come to be there. The unthinkable had happened to her and at the very moment she stood at the podium she felt this sharply and was overcome with sadness. She could barely talk. 'The only reason I am standing here holding this trophy and receiving this ovation is because I have endured the kind of tragedy that makes people recoil,' she would write later, reflecting on the incident. Conscious of the audience in front of her on the day, and of the media beaming her voice and image around the country, she fought through her teary silence and opened her mouth to speak.

In Helen Caldicott's case, at the age of eighty, there remains a sense of disappointment about the lack of progress on global weapons disarmament on her watch. 'We nearly got there,' she told me, referring to that time when she was president of Physicians for Social Responsibility and a genuine and lasting agreement to end the global nuclear arms race seemed possible. Instead, as I write this, military tensions between China and the United States, as well as between the United States and North Korea, remain serious, and fears around the potential of President Donald Trump's widely observed narcissism to ignite serious conflict are legitimate. Caldicott, meanwhile, keeps speaking out. In the week before we met, she had given expert evidence at the South Australian Nuclear Fuel Cycle Royal Commission; within a few months she would give speeches in San Francisco, Berlin, St Louis and Auckland.

While talking with Helen Caldicott, I was in awe of the drive and stamina behind her long-term commitment to speaking out in the public domain, despite repeated attempts by the pro-nuclear lobby to discredit and belittle her. This called to mind Marina Warner's commentary on the different ways speech by men and speech by women are received in our culture: the former's inclination to speak his mind, and to do so with confidence, is so often regarded with respect, while the latter's is treated as a sign of excessive stridency, or a tendency to prattle. Nevertheless, some women, thank goodness, will insist on being taken seriously in public life. Caldicott is one of these.

With this in mind, particularly given her four and a half decades of service, I asked Caldicott whether she thinks of herself as a woman of courage.

'Other people say I've got courage.'

'You don't feel brave?'

'No, I've never felt brave, never.'

She described to me a scenario she had often encountered after delivering a lecture in the United States. People would group around to talk to her afterwards, she said, floating ideas and strategies. 'Sometimes a man would say something and I might say, "That's a good idea. You should run for the Congress." He would stick his chest out and say, "Yeah." But if I said it to a woman in a similar situation, she'd literally take two steps back and say, "Who, me?"'

'It's interesting isn't it?' I responded. 'I'm only just coming to realise now that in working life, and in everything I do, really, I don't have to step back.'

'Now why did you think you ever had to step back? See, that's the obvious question.'

'Yes, that's right.'

143

'Do you know?' she asked.

'Well, probably just a lack of confidence,' I fumbled. 'I think the problem in part is that I have read that lack of confidence as a weakness in myself rather than reading it as something that's actually been culturally constructed.'

'It *is* a weakness in yourself. *It is.*'

'But it's also a taught practice.'

'Why a lack of confidence? *Why* don't you feel confident in yourself?'

I couldn't answer her question then. Retrospectively, I suspect I have been cautious all along of stepping too stridently forward because of a fear of belittlement and ridicule, as well as overt and covert male threat.

ONE OF THE EXERCISES I ENGAGED IN AS PART OF MY preparation for meeting Helen Caldicott was to follow the instructions on a simple teaching exercise she advocates in the 'Resources' section of her website (Fig. 1). The exercise is titled the 'Trident Nuclear-Armed Submarines Demonstration' and involves printing twenty-four copies of a crudely hand-drawn graphic. The graphic itself is endearingly simple: eight undeniably phallic missiles coloured in black on a white background. Each represents one warhead. If you print twenty-four copies and tape them up on the walls around a room or along an empty corridor, as I did, you have a visual representation of the 192 warheads on just one Trident submarine.

I recommend the exercise. It's a staggering and affecting visual representation of the sheer scale and stupidity of the military–industrial complex. The United States Navy owns fourteen submarines armed in this way, and four in the same class are owned

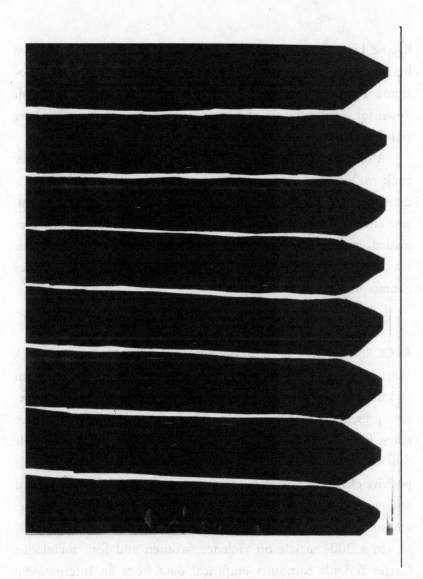

Figure 1.
'The Trident Nuclear-Armed Submarines Demonstration.'
Helen Caldicott.

Source: Helen Caldicott

by the United Kingdom. Just one of these black warheads is a hundred times more powerful than the bomb dropped on Hiroshima. Pin them up along the length of a wall you're facing and sit down for a few minutes and look at them. Just look at the sheer number of them.

After leaving Caldicott's place, and during the long journey back to Melbourne, I would remember the image of 192 Trident warheads taped up on my office wall. Thick black phalluses, row after row after row. Do they really have all those submarines loaded, and on standby, every minute of every day, I wondered? It's just posturing, no? Like a kick at the head that never makes contact, right?

ACCORDING TO MID-20TH-CENTURY GERMAN PHILOSOPHER Martin Heidegger, one can lose all sight of one's possibilities in and through fear. 'The temporality of fear,' he writes, 'is an expectant, present-making forgetting.' One of the key lessons I have taken from both Helen Caldicott and Rosie Batty, despite their different approaches to and experiences of fear, is the idea that positive change desperately requires more women to step forward and engage with politics: to speak up and speak out, to organise, and to agitate for positive change.

In a 2004 article on violence, women and fear, sociologist Carrie Yodanis combines empirical data from an International Crime Victims Survey with statistics from the United Nations to support the proposition that 'in order to stop men's use and women's experiences of violence on the personal level, structures of gender inequality at the societal level must change'. It is a theory feminist commentators have espoused for at least a century. Yodanis's article proves empirically that countries in which women enjoy higher educational, occupational and political status are also ones with a reduced incidence of violence. Or, to put it differently, fear and violence both decrease as women participate more fully in civil society.

Heidegger's emphasis on temporality stresses, wisely, the nowness of fear. If fear is our overarching mood or emotion, he argues, we focus our attention too heavily on whatever we perceive to be the present threat. Hence, fear can become our entire way of being, restricting any alternative future from ever properly forming, and simultaneously preventing us from learning anything meaningful from the past. In other words, a world we fear too markedly can never feel like home. It is my conclusion that fear is complex, and it is a deeply human instinct, but it is not and should never be accepted as our holding place.

JULIA KRISTEVA REMAINS ONE OF FRANCE'S MOST CELEBRATED public intellectuals, appearing regularly on television, and invited often to speak both in Europe and internationally. Her project has consistantly sought to elucidate how thought and sexuality are intertwined. In this sense, the subject, as far as Kristeva understands it, is always immersed in the social. As a *speaking subject* she is always being political. Kristeva's work on the maternal and on the abject has influenced many thinkers, including many feminists. She remains, for me, an inherently hopeful philosopher. It's interesting that this hopefulness is what I am left with, even though so much of the work she has produced has stemmed from the dark depths of infinite abjection, the barely tolerable, the unthinkable. The direction of her philosophy has been, in some ways, precisely the opposite of the likes of Heidegger. From that which cannot be assimilated, she has effectively produced a political consciousness that is *open* to the other. Kristeva's thinking helps us to recognise the powers of horror, and through this recognition, to engage with our worst fears rather than retreat from them. And it is apparent through the powerful public advocacy work of women like Helen Caldicott and Rosie Batty, this is precisely what is needed in the world we are confronted with now.

CHAPTER
FIVE
Wonder

When I was small the Pacific Ocean, where it met the wild and windswept beaches of Australia's mid-east coast, was the chief energy in my world and in the world of my family. The beachfront was broad and long, the surf a constantly restless body of water full of rips and breakaways, changeable hour by hour. Our family would spill out of my father's VW station wagon daily, each of us immediately charged or somehow expanded by the sea air and the space. My parents and older sister liked to walk and their figures would recede far into the distance while my brother and I loitered and drifted on the shoreline, constructing complex dug-outs and castles in the sand, and chasing each other along the water's edge. We lived, then, in a house with no television or internet and our childhood story worlds were rich with fantastic, adventurous yarns of humans and animals pitted against the unpredictable elements: storms, tides, the struggle to find shelter from the wind.

For my brother and me, still emerging from the dream-state of early childhood, the ocean was a source of both wonder and fear. We learned to stay afloat and later to swim in water that regularly sought to drag our bodies down, to consume us, tossing us to the surface only when it was ready and we had been exposed as pathetic things, punished for our need for air. It gave us what we called the Washing Machine Treatment, reminding us constantly of our smallness and insignificance in the broader world. On good days, the surf kept us buoyant and carted us along like champions, gifting us with speed. It was a giver and bearer of creatures and treasures, both frightening and awesome. We became collectors of curiosities, large and small, foreign and familiar – clothes, shoes, smoothed glass, shells, driftwood. It all came home with us, crowding into the family station wagon with our mess of salt-encrusted limbs and the wet and deliriously happy family dog.

Even at that age, I knew that somewhere across that ocean we adored was The Rest of the World. I would stare into the broad horizon and wonder about all the things I was yet to discover, or that were yet to discover me. When I started kindergarten I relished learning in the local three-room school, in which every child and family were known to one another. But I somehow associated knowledge with the great beyond. The only thing separating our school from Old Bar Beach was a straggly strip of Crown land dotted with coastal heath. If you took off at lunchtime (strictly forbidden), you could scoot along the sandy track at the base of the school oval in minutes, and then you were right there: facing the vast empty blue horizon, wondering.

TO WONDER IS TO MARVEL. IT ALLOWS THE POSSIBILITY OF BEING openly amazed by knowledge or the very possibility of knowledge. Children, in particular, cannot seem to help it. 'Why don't we see two things with our two eyes?' asked the children at the experimental Malting House School in Cambridge in 1924. 'Why do ladies not have beards? Why can't we see the stars in the day time?' Almost a century later, I record a similar list of queries asked of me by my son, including the simple and provocative – 'What is life for?' – voiced over a breakfast of oats and full-cream milk one autumn morning when he was six.

Perhaps some of us are more inclined to wonder about things than others. A smaller number again take to the task of wondering with such seriousness that it gives the act a paradoxical sense of purpose. Certainly, British author and scholar Marina Warner is an example of the latter. 'Alice *falls* down the rabbit hole,' she writes in her essay on the topic of curiosity, 'but after that she wants actively to know what's happening around her.' Of course, women, in particular, have a tendency to fall, or rather, to be marked as having fallen. And gender plays a particular role in wonder as we know it. It is no accident that Lewis Carroll decided Alice should be a girl protagonist, for example, as I shall come to discuss later. But first, let me articulate a few questions of my own: What does it mean to wonder? How does something become wonderful to us? And is our sense of wonder central to our capacity to change who we are?

There are few contemporary thinkers more curious about wonder than Marina Warner. The first of her essays to strike a chord with me was itself a collection of curiosities. Titled 'Out of an Old Toy Chest', it begins with reference to Charles Baudelaire's essay on childhood toys, specifically their capacity to spark and enliven the childhood imagination, and yet also to profoundly disappoint us, to remind us abruptly of our own mortality the moment our imagined narratives for them lose their sense of vitality. 'But where is the soul?' asked Baudelaire of his own childhood playthings. Where indeed? echoes Warner in her essay. Here, her commentary on the children's books *Pinocchio* and *The Velveteen Rabbit* works as a tantalising preface to a more complex discussion of the whole question of make-believe. The essay amply demonstrates Warner's scholarly capacity for research, and for artfully written prose, but in reading her essay I recognised a fellow traveller's deep-seated interest in the nature of the imagination. In 'Out of an Old Toy Chest' Warner discovers things. She picks up such things (ideas, objects, ideas about objects) and sets them before us, holding them up to the light until all their potential colours glimmer and glint with possibility.

The experience of reading 'Out of an Old Toy Chest' set me off on a quest to read more extensively and fully into Marina Warner's body of work, a collection that fuses classicism and popular culture, journalism, history, memoir, literary criticism and fiction. She has published more than twenty sole-authored books to date, along with many more essays, articles and reviews. Throughout my reading of her work I have been intrigued by her inclination to marry the well-equipped scholarly researcher's quest for knowledge with a genuine capacity to marvel. Like those of the children at the Malting House School, which she has written about in her work, Warner's questions disarm and intrigue: 'Is it possible to be curious by mistake?' she asks. Her abiding theme circles fairly constantly around the topic of make-believe. 'How and why does the fantastic keep surfacing in us?' she ponders. And, 'What might stories and convictions – both marvellous and true – do both *for* us, and *to* us?'

DURING THE ENGLISH SUMMER OF 2014, HAVING TRAVELLED halfway around the world, I found my way to Warner's modest double-storey terrace at the end of a quiet cul-de-sac in London's Kentish Town. Her tiny English garden extending in an L shape from the front of the house was an attractive mess of late summer flowers. When I rang the doorbell, it took several minutes before

I heard footsteps descending the stairs and hall inside, and just as I was beginning to reconsider the address, Warner opened the door. She was a slight woman in her late sixties, and gracious in her welcome. She had been expecting me.

We entered a hallway crowded with interesting objects: mostly artworks and books. Just by the front door was a long and very thick plait of rope, something reminiscent of a 19th-century sailing ship, except surely too beautiful to be merely functional. The piece was set in a long glass frame. Later I would discover it is a part of a series by Warner's son, the sculptor Conrad Shawcross: a meditation on the passing of time.

In the kitchen upstairs, Warner served us tea in delicate cups – her latest op shop discovery. We talked briefly about tea and about our shared experience of teaching creative writing in a university setting, and then, to begin our discussion proper – to talk about wonder – she led me along another crowded hallway and up a second flight of stairs to her study. Heavily populated with towers of books, the generous room led to a small terrace overlooking the front garden. It was a beautiful and relaxed setting. There was sunshine and a light breeze and as Warner began to talk her deep-seated curiosity and intelligence, along with the sheer breadth of her knowledge, impressed me once more, as has happened so often while reading her books.

MARINA WARNER WAS BORN IN LONDON IN 1946 AND SPENT her early childhood in Egypt, where her father ran a Cairo bookshop. As an adult, she would identify her father as Creole but when she was a child he and his family seemed to her more English than the English, a characteristic no doubt influenced and sharpened by having 'descended from a long line of Empire servants' who were active as plantation owners in the Caribbean. Warner's mother was Italian and Catholic – the marriage approved of by the extended British family, reports Warner, because Italian women were reputedly 'beautiful and voluptuous' and conscious of their 'obligations towards men and children'. Cairo had a reputation for being the cultural capital of the Arab Middle East during the 1950s and a childhood spent in an expatriate bookshop there at that time no doubt lent itself more than most to stumbling across mythologies and curiosities. When the family prepared to return to England, via Belgium, Marina was sent ahead to St Mary's School in Ascot, a Catholic boarding school. She later studied French and Italian at Lady Margaret Hall at Oxford, and began publishing her writing while still a student. She graduated in 1967 and as a journalist posted several influential articles from war-torn Vietnam – although she says her shyness with people made journalism challenging. Nevertheless, she still credits that early career choice with sparking a lifelong interest in going out into the world as an observer.

An early and deep interest in gender inspired Marina Warner's first major publications, which focussed on iconic heroines and the myths and cults surrounding them. While still in her twenties, she published her first biography, of the late 19th-century Chinese empress, Tzu-Hsi (*The Dragon Empress*, 1972). This was followed by a cultural biography of the Virgin Mary (*Alone of All Her Sex*, 1976), and then an extensive work on Joan of Arc (*Joan of Arc: The Image of Female Heroism*, 1981). Warner cites the work of anthropologist Shirley Ardener as a key early influence on her writing. Ardener's work, first published in the 1960s, demonstrated the way in which so many ethnological records completely excluded women's experiences, perhaps because women were not accessible to visiting male anthropologists or, more often, because their knowledge and opinions were simply not considered meaningful, and were therefore not sought in the first place. Ardener identified women and children as muted groups because of their structural absence from the historical cultural record. This struck a deep chord with the young Warner, who set herself the task of retrieving, or as she says, 'overhearing' such voices.

'I became very interested, very committed to this idea of women's voices, and I found that you can sort of pick up echoes of female interests, female anxieties, in fairytales. Hope is a very strong element that drives fairytales. These are stories of largely oppressed individuals or oppressed groups. Some of them are male, but a lot of them are women, and the stories are stories of a possible way out through resourcefulness, or through cunning and high spirits.'

Warner's 1994 Reith Lecture series focussed on the monstrous in myth and fairytale and the ways in which the monstrous haunts the contemporary imagination. She later extended her focus on myth and mythology with books on fear, phantasms, metamorphosis and transformation. In the wake of the events of 11 September 2001, Warner began work on a major book celebrating *The Arabian Nights*, published as *Stranger Magic* in 2011.

The premise of the *Nights*, of course, is that Scheherazade is the latest in a long list of wives to a sultan who has made a habit of killing his women. Along with her sister, Scheherazade devises a plot to tell a string of enchanting stories to her husband, each instalment beginning in the evening and finishing on a cliffhanger at dawn. The sultan's desire to know what happens next thus prevents him from immediately having his latest wife killed. 'The technique of the book and the technique carried by the figure of Scheherazade is one of opening the sultan's mind. He's emblematic of the ignorant person: the ignorant, lock-in, raging man who wants to kill all he doesn't understand,' Warner told an interviewer for *The Rumpus*. 'She's telling stories to save her life,' she said to me. 'So survival is the actual manifest problem.'

I want to come back to Scheherazade later, for this business about oppression and hope is central to women's experiences of wonder.

'WONDER IS THE FIRST OF THE PASSIONS, ACCORDING TO some thinkers', said Warner in the gentle light of Kentish Town's late summer and in response to the first of my questions about how wonder might be best understood.

'*I wonder* means *I ask* or *I enquire* or *I wish to investigate*, but I'm also struck by wonder, when I'm, as it were, struck speechless by awe and astonishment. So there are these two poles.

'For me, there's a definite gender implication as there is for all the virtues and vices. You can pretty much line them up on one side and the other. It's changed a bit since feminist gains and activity, but still, you know, what's assertive, confident speech in a man is strident, shrill, excessive, indignation in a woman. In a woman, it's called gossip and garrulousness. In a man it becomes eloquence and pre-eminence, confidence.

'And with curiosity it is exactly the same: curiosity is a scientific virtue on the male side; on the female side it tends to be identified as the sin of Eve. The problem with Bluebeard's last wife is very complex: the fairytale is about a serial killer and the victory is given to the young woman who overcomes him by the end, the last of his wives who manages not to be killed and succeeds in bringing him down. In that sense, it's a kind of parallel to Scheherazade in the *Arabian Nights*: the serial killer of women is confounded by a woman. There are some versions of the Bluebeard story where the last bride is a trickster, but that angle has generally been lost, and she's presented as a passive heroine who is rescued by her brothers. The fairytale, after it was published very widely, became a moral lesson for women not to disobey their husbands and not to show curiosity, fatal curiosity like Eve; it's a warning not to use the key to go into the bloody chamber.

'So the story sort of flipped over upside down in terms of its moral. When Walter Crane, who was a socialist and a rather marvellous upholder of good causes, illustrated it, I think at the beginning of the 20th century, he put a tableau of Eve eating the apple behind Bluebeard's wife using the key. So even he saw her action as disobedience. There's an element of play, an element of irony, perhaps. But nevertheless, curiosity on the whole was seen as a female weakness from the classics onwards. There's a treatise by Plutarch on curiosity which follows one he wrote on garrulousness and both of them are labelled women's vices. He was developing a strand in ancient Greek philosophy that the Creator's works were the Creator's works and that therefore it was hubristic, beyond the reach of human beings, to enquire too far into this perfect system. But there was a countervailing trend as well, because great works of classical science on the nature of things were also produced in which philosophers definitely try to understand the mysteries within us.' She paused for a moment.

'Have you seen my essay on curiosity?'

I HAVE.

'"Curiouser and curiouser", cries Alice, when she finds herself "opening out like the largest telescope that ever was!"' the essay begins, quoting directly from Lewis Carroll. 'With her feet disappearing beneath her and her neck stretching till it strikes the roof, she takes the tiny golden key and opens the little door to Wonderland.'

In this essay, titled 'Contradictory Curiosities', Warner identifies and expands upon several key characteristics of curiosity. The first is that curiosity involves rupture – of accepted standards, of cordoned-off or taboo subjects, of known experience. The second is that it involves agency, and it is here that she poses the question of whether one can be curious by mistake. The answer is no, argues Warner. Someone who is curious has agency. Questions drive some of the best dramatic narratives forward but at the centre of those questions is a narrative agent: the curious, often tormented, central character or subject. Her third key point is that curiosity is a form of resistance. It's almost as if the more a curious character is stifled by convention, by the establishment, by patriarchy, the more curious she becomes. Because of this, curiosity can turn up some unexpected and wholly transformative results. Finally, and perhaps most intriguingly, says Warner, at the core of the curious experience is enigma. It cannot be otherwise.

'Alice, of course, is the great questioner', Warner told me. 'She's a sort of reluctant questioner. When she's in Wonderland she keeps not understanding what's going on and asking very fundamental questions. The adults don't want to explain, you know: "A thing is a thing"; "A word is what you want it to mean".

'She's a figure of the writer or the questor, somebody who doesn't assume they know things.'

'It's interesting that she's a young girl,' I prompted, 'given the point you were just making about curiosity as a culturally gendered characteristic.'

According to Warner, it is in fact, no accident. The casting of a young girl in the role of the curious and reluctant explorer was a decision on Carroll's part intended to mock a tradition that saw curiosity as a vice young girls were prone to indulging. Warner sees Carroll's curious collection of poetic animals in the Alice books as a deliberate nod towards the natural history tradition and the scientific quest to catalogue and to know.

In her essay on the topic, she paints a portrait of Lewis Carroll as a man who belonged to an era in which science had begun to challenge quite radically our ideas about what it means to be human.

What is the flipside of wonder? Is it disappointment? I admit that disappointment was what I felt when I discovered as an adult, and via reading Warner's work, that Lewis Carroll had taken hundreds and hundreds of photographs of naked girls. Little Alices, all: catalogued, collected, and in some way possessed. And she, Alice, one of the few girl protagonists to ever be permitted a genuinely interesting adventure.

'Yes,' Warner frowned at the mention of Carroll's photographic collection. 'Well, by the standards of today he definitely would be in jail. It was all so systematic, which is also characteristic of paedophilia. He photographed hundreds of children – boys too. Alice wasn't by any means alone.'

WHEN I WAS SEVEN, LIKE ALICE, I EXPERIENCED A RATHER surprising rupture: our family suddenly packed up and moved to a regional town several hundred kilometres inland. The shift propelled me backwards, *away* from the coast, *away* from the world waiting for me beyond the ocean horizon. Lying in bed in the new house in the whispery quiet of Australia's semi-arid wheat fields, I grieved deeply for the night-time sound of the surf, a fierce, dependable beat that had helped me to sleep since I was an infant. Everything familiar to me, until then, had become familiar to the backdrop of the Pacific Ocean's great, regular pounding rhythm. Surely this new landscape to which we'd been transported, a world without that constant watery heartbeat, could *only* be desolate and hopeless.

In the Central West New South Wales town of Dubbo, during the decade I lived there with my family, the area's main business was agriculture, specifically wheat and sheep. The town was the regional centre for a number of state government offices. My father worked in such an office, for a regulatory body then called the New South Wales Forestry Commission. He managed the region's state forests east to the Warrumbungles, north to the Pilliga, and west to Broken Hill. He was frequently out bush. But when he was home, we knew it.

The decade from the late 1970s onwards was a tumultuous period for our family and during that time I shifted from dreamy, imaginative child to rebellious, anti-authoritarian teenager. In my mind, our house in Ronald Street, Dubbo is central to all that took place then. A solid, double-brick house with red-tiled roof, the original building dated from the late 1920s, and was the oldest in our street. It was built with wide verandahs on three sides, in a country Australian tradition of that period, but over time all but the verandah facing the street were closed in. Here, my father placed a single armchair. It was his. The rest of our suburban block was mostly taken up by cheap, identical 'fibro' houses that had apparently arrived *en masse* in the 1960s in the form of state housing. Further up the hill was a Royal Australian Air Force base and it was populated with similar architecture: resolutely square domestic boxes painted in a range of pastel colours.

My father's alcoholism reached its most desperate phase in the Ronald Street house. I didn't have words then for a concept like patriarchy; I only knew my own quarter-acre block, the family within it. I wondered at my mother's capacity to endure the unpredictable storms born of my father's rage. Her patient endurance, not without occasional expressions of resistance, was the closest thing to the miraculous our agnostic household could have witnessed. The effect of my father's unpredictability on me during those years was that I learned to tread carefully, to speak carefully, to focus on the virtues of silence, alongside considerable attention to the gendered art of gentle placation in the domestic space. This has had a lasting impact on me.

During the semi-arid Australian summers the house in Ronald Street was hot all day and night. Relief came in the form of cool evening breezes, which you could only enjoy if you left the building. Sometimes my brother and I slept on narrow army stretchers under the Hills Hoist, gazing at the night sky through mosquito nets. Through this gauzed vista we saw shooting stars with such regularity that they continued to fall behind closed lids, a stellar backdrop to the fragile landscapes of our dreams.

It was from that house, aged eleven, that I covertly phoned the police for help late one Sunday afternoon. They came, and I opened the front door to them even as, at the far end of the house, the din continued. I was in fear for my mother's life that day. I tried as best I could to explain the situation to the two officers in neatly pressed sky-blue shirts, these adults twice my height, standing there on the front verandah with holstered guns at their hips.

'Are you the owner of the premises?' they asked me.

'No,' I said, struggling with the relevance of the question as my father's barely coherent shouting continued from the back of the house.

'Who is the owner?'

'My dad.'

'Is he at home? Can you get him to come to the door?'

Yes, he was home, but did they seriously expect me to approach him on my own? Did they want *me* dead? I stood there with the big grey wooden door open, looking at the two strangers, incapable of forming an answer to their question.

'I'm sorry, but without the owner's permission, we're unable to enter the house.'

Minutes later I was watching, confused, as the two police officers returned to their vehicle in the fading dusk light. They folded themselves neatly back into their seats, fastened their belts, and drove away. Then I closed the door on a dark hallway. My father's anger raged, unabated.

I don't remember exactly what happened next, or how the balance of the day and evening ended, but I know that I never phoned the police from my father's house again. This incident changed me. It changed the way I saw the world and the place of myself and my mother within it. I know that the way the New South Wales police respond to domestic violence call-outs has changed enormously since I was a child, but at that time the response given me at the Ronald Street doorstep was standard practice, and the message I read from it was clear and long lasting: he has the right.

I think I retreated then, double-time, to the world of the imagination. Wonder nurtured me. It saw me through my bewilderment and beyond it. It led me, perhaps miraculously, towards a richer, more subtle form of resistance and, eventually, understanding.

SOMETIMES WE READERS STUMBLE UPON A PIECE OF WRITING that disarms us, that seems to simultaneously strip away our knowledge or understanding *and* compound it. The philosopher and theologian Thomas Aquinas posited that fear and wonder are two sides of the same coin. The suddenness of wonder's revelation can be a kind of shock, he said, for it reveals to us something about the depth of our ignorance. This sense of lack brings us face to face with fear. Yet, paradoxically, the flush of recognition – of not knowing – that accompanies a moment of wonder can also serve to motivate us, to nudge us to begin a journey towards knowledge. In this way, although it may startle us, wonder is also a cause of pleasure. Looking back, the source of my own determination to find hope through or beyond the dark decade of the worst of my father's violence is mysterious to me. How did I not lose my sense of wonder altogether? 'Hope,' writes theologian Sophia Vasalou in *Wonder: A Grammar*, is 'a form … of vulnerability, though a vulnerability that constitutes an achievement, asserted in the face of possible despair'.

I have experienced the feeling of being disarmed more than once while reading Marina Warner. Immersed in *Signs and Wonders: Essays on Literature and Culture* (2002), for example, I was deeply affected by her essay, 'Saint Paul: Let Women Keep Silent'.

Of all the saints whose lives were chronicled and held up as examples during Warner's years at St Mary's School, Saint Paul seems to have had the most enduring and pervasive influence. The girls saw him as an adventurer, a real historical figure whose journeys were dramatic, transformative and purposeful, encompassing shipwreck and famine, imprisonment and near-death experience. Warner and her friends admired his heroics, and took to heart many of his teachings. She reports lying in bed at night and dreaming up for herself a future in which she is 'intrepid, unstoppable, self-willed'. At the same time, however, it was from and through the doctrines of Saint Paul that the behaviours of women and girls subject to the institution of Catholicism were shaped and disciplined. The virtue of silence was firmly impressed upon them, for example, along with the benefits of patient endurance. I recognised this pattern. Some of the writings attributed to Saint Paul have since been used as an argument against the ordination of women: 'Let the women learn in silence with all subjection', he wrote. Warner underlines the political implications of his call for silence among women: powerlessness, lack of agency, disenfranchisement.

She also contemplates the complex role of the nuns in shaping her own and others' expectations about their future. There was a noticeboard, for example, in one of the school's hallways where the successes of former boarders were announced. Such successes included marrying an Italian, and then bearing him a son. In the essay, Warner describes standing close beside one of the nuns she admired as they read together the noticeboard's latest announcements. Beside her, the older woman's body simply quivered at the news of a former student's good marriage. Here is wonder written on the body: the raised eyebrows, the open mouth, a forgetful relaxation or subtle alertness in our carriage. Warner's teacher's joy was contagious: she couldn't help but feel it too.

When I remind Warner of this scene as described in her essay on St Paul, she smiled in agreement. 'What a strange role the nuns played, and in fact the whole discourse of Catholicism played, in your sense of how to be, and what you aspired to become,' I posited.

'Yes, well, I mean ... the paradox,' she said. 'I didn't really realise it until much later in my life, probably when I was writing that essay or around that time, that the nuns – and they seemed themselves unaware of it – held up for us a number of female heroines, mostly martyrs, but one of them was Mary Ward, who was the founder of my school's order. Mary Ward was a truly remarkable woman who decided that women should be educated, and she wanted to found an order of female Jesuits. She suffered a double whammy – she was imprisoned by the Pope for overreaching ambition, and she was persecuted as a Catholic in England by Elizabeth. Yet, although we were told endlessly about the virtues of the school's founder, we were also asked, always, to be modest, and *above all* not to assert ourselves. And, of course, to obey, and the people we were meant to obey were our fathers, and then our husbands.

'Subjection, subordination, the entirely virtuous was inculcated by women who themselves had chosen lives of independent, intellectual courage. I couldn't see the contradiction then, but I can see it now.'

'Some of this must never leave you,' I marvelled.

'Of course, it was entirely formative. I went to boarding school at nine, and left when I was sixteen. I've never got away from it, but I have managed to think it through. I'm not a Catholic any more, but I do have sensations of guilt. In a way, my writing has been a very long therapy upon myself, which I think in a sense is a success.'

We both laughed gently at the idea of such a practice. It is not unfamiliar.

MY TEENAGE YEARS ARRIVED IN THE HOUSE IN RONALD STREET. I developed a penchant for self-absorption and experimented wholeheartedly with the art of noncompliance. Looking back, I do not like the person I was then. I was distracted, disloyal, and often dishonest. I excelled academically, but found it difficult to conform to the institutional rules and regulations of the local high school. I sought out transgression in all its forms, made friends of the town's punks and queers and misfits and felt profoundly grateful for their company. I experimented with alcohol and drugs, moving quickly through a brief enchantment with self-annihilation towards a cautious respect for the various manners in which intoxicants influenced perception. I climbed clandestinely out of my bedroom window at night, undertook bold and mostly successful campaigns to score drugs and alcohol for my friends, and hooned raucously along the backstreets in stolen cars with like-minded reprobates. I was curious. 'Why conform at all?' I often wondered. 'How do people do it?'

My father's house remained my father's house. He forced my elder sister out of home at sixteen. She was taken in by family friends back on the mid-north coast, where she finished her final years at school. Meanwhile, my brother discovered motorcycles.

I struggled with how to be.

These were the years in which I remained loyal to my love of trees, particularly of climbing them. I climbed trees well into high school, beyond the point most other children had stopped. At sixteen, my favourite pastime was to skip school for the day and spend the hours clandestinely perched up a tree in a stranger's back garden with a book. I scouted all of south Dubbo for suitable trees in sheltered backyards left vacant by the working week. I liked the way the heightened vantage point in the crook of a bough could lift you out of things, changing, however slightly, the way you perceived the world beneath. How many days could you take off school and still score enough of a grade to get you into university? It was a dare I set myself, a line I walked.

Sometimes at night, as my father raged, I escaped to the park at the end of the street, climbed the highest tree and slept precariously in its uppermost branches. Beneath me, come closing time, the local drinkers shuffled home. One of them once pissed against the trunk of the tree I inhabited, oblivious to my presence. It still amuses me all these decades later that it didn't ever occur to the gentleman to look up.

Most of the boys at school avoided me, during those years, for my skin was almost constantly blemished due to acne. I didn't mind so much about the boys' aversion to me. They didn't interest me. But their schoolyard banter could be ruthless. I still remember the students in my year coming up with a list of pop songs, one to match each individual, as we approached graduation. Somebody made sure I overheard the one being contemplated for me: it was by the English band The Monks, and titled 'Nice Legs, Shame About Her Face'. If you listen carefully to the lyrics, the song is intended as a joke on men who think like that, but I doubt this was the spirit in which my classmates chose it for me. The news of their choice of song both wounded me and redoubled my hope for some means of escape, not just from Ronald Street, but from the town itself. I didn't know then, of course, that cruelty is in no way confined to particular neighbourhoods.

In 1986, as my final year at high school was about to come into view, there was an accident. My older brother was involved in a serious collision on his motorcycle just outside the town's main shopping centre. The collision caused him extensive neurological as well as physical damage. He was flown to Sydney by air ambulance the same day, and would spend the next two years in rehabilitation wards.

I still remember walking into the emergency room at Dubbo Base Hospital to see him before he was transferred. Nic was deep in a coma and yet when I entered the room he knew it. The two of us were as close in that moment as we'd ever been.

'Hey, Nic,' I said.

'Hey,' he replied in the same casual tone.

I stood beside him, laid a hand on his lightly covered body, felt his heat. He'd taken the Washing Machine Treatment, but we were so, so far from the ocean, both of us. It would take a long time for him to be at all able again. He would have to learn, almost from the beginning, how one puts together a sentence. He would have to learn, over again, to walk.

Not so long after Nic's accident, I too left Dubbo, albeit under less dramatic circumstances than either of my siblings. Within hours of completing my final high school exam, I was on the afternoon train towards the capital: Sydney. I would await news of a university place while couch-surfing through the summer in a drug-infused share house in Stanmore. I had with me some Antipodean literature – Janet Frame's *Owls Do Cry*, Jessica Anderson's *Tirra Lirra by the River*, Tim Winton's *An Open Swimmer* – and with these in tow I commenced a journey that I hoped would finally re-unite me with The Rest of the World.

WARNER AND I FINISHED OUR TEA.

'Wonder is a kind of enchantment, yes?'

'That's right,' she said.

'It's the charm in storytelling, isn't it?'

'Wonder *is* enchantment. And the enchanted object is inside the text or the painting or the opera or whatever, the wonder is *in* it. There are evoked the effects of enchantment, the effects of wonder, but there's also the wonder that you feel on the outside. So, there's a symbiosis between the enchantment performed or described, and the charm, the state that it puts you in. And that state is really deeply interesting, because it's neither belief nor suspension of disbelief. I mean, I've tried endlessly to get at this.

'I don't believe in fairies, but it doesn't lead me to suspend my belief in fairytales. I just don't believe in fairies. But I am caught up in something. And what is that something? Well, it's hard to define.

'I think that one of the reasons that one is caught up in this pleasure in childhood is that it is about escaping the conditions that constrain us. I mean, a lot of fairytales in which there is a happy ending are looking at circumstances that are full of suffering, but always (or usually) in the context that there is an alternative. It's positing some sort of hope. The story is marvelling that, *My God, something could be different*. And that is why, I think, very strong enchantments take place in an opera like *The Magic Flute*. Mozart is a great artist of reality.

'Now, I don't know about Shakespeare or Mozart and their state of belief, but I think for us, there's a central aspect of this kind of wonder literature which is emphatically something that we don't have to believe in. There's a great pleasure in that, there's a freedom. Because it's not a religious system, and it's not a moral system. It's actually got a lightness, and sometimes there's sheer immorality.

'Fairytales can be completely immoral worlds. And there's luck and blessing. You might have a completely hopeless son who falls over his clothes because he's too lazy to lift his long tunic and keeps tripping up, a completely idle good-for-nothing like Aladdin, but he gets rewarded. So, fairytale is an immoral place. Delinquency is a place literature can go. It's pleasurably transgressive.'

WARNER'S ABIDING INTEREST IN THE VOICES OF WOMEN, AND in the silencing and oppression of our sex, has remained consistent throughout her career, and while the critical reception of her work has largely been tremendously positive, it is interesting to note the gendered nature of some of the more dismissive commentary. Journalist Nicholas Wroe, for example, begins a character portrait published in the *Guardian* in 2000 by declaring that Warner was rumoured to be 'the prettiest undergraduate of her generation' at Oxford during the 1960s. He then quotes from a review of her book on fairytales *From the Beast to the Blonde*, published by historian Noel Malcolm, also in the *Guardian*: 'Once upon a time, there was a very clever girl called Warner,' wrote Malcolm, 'who read lots and lots of books. Every book seemed to connect up with every other book, and they all told her something about images of womanhood in cultural history.' It's impossible to imagine a man of Marina Warner's stature and accomplishment being infantilised, objectified and belittled in quite the same way. Indeed, it seems sadly ironic that the very cultural traditions regarding women who dare to speak out that Warner has worked so hard to expose in her writing still circulate vigorously enough in contemporary culture to trip her up in supposedly serious reviews of that very work.

Warner has spent much of her career working independently of the academy, despite the quite scholarly nature of much of her work. I admire this about her. When I told her this, she confesses that the challenge of earning a living entirely from her writing over the course of several decades eventually became too difficult. Many of her books have been both critically and commercially successful, and she has garnered a string of visiting fellowships, awards and honorary doctorates, but when she became unwell and was unable to write for an extended period in the early 2000s, it had a significant effect on her livelihood. Like many freelance writers, she found herself without a safety net. In 2004, she took up an invitation to join the staff of the Department of Literature, Film and Theatre studies at the University of Essex, an institution known for its free-thinking, emancipatory values, and she began to teach both graduate and undergraduate students in creative writing. She would keep that appointment for the next ten years.

At the time of our meeting, Warner was only just emerging from a protracted dispute with the University of Essex over workload expectations and ideological differences. The dispute had led to a very public resignation. Not long afterwards, she published two essays in the *London Review of Books*.

The second of these, 'Learning My Lesson', moves from the particular example of neoliberal, commercialised management practices at the University of Essex to philosophical questions about the purpose of knowledge. Warner compares the university to other public assets, such as national parks: places created for the good of all citizens, and aligns her philosophy of teaching and of education with Seamus Heaney's philosophy of poetry. Heaney has asserted that, 'we go to poetry to be forwarded within ourselves', expanding that our immersion in literature provides a kind of 'foreknowing' in and through which we recognise something we actually knew but couldn't before now properly reach, never mind articulate. 'Good knowledge,' writes Warner, 'requires inquiry on your part, your absorbed attention – and to be attentive to the point of self-forgetfulness also lightens discontents. So curiosity must be met by responsiveness – by listening, not silence.' Warner favours difficult knowledge, and that form of learning that leads not so much to a solution but to a set of further questions. She quotes philosopher Bernard Williams, who has labelled this kind of learning 'honestly difficult'. It is not the kind of learning, or the kind of knowledge, that flourishes in a culture of fear and compliance. 'Something has gone wrong with the way the universities are being run,' she concludes.

Some of these points go to the heart of the question of

wonder, and in particular, to the question of its purpose. For Aristotle, wonder was merely a source of motivation, a state that compels us, usefully, towards knowledge, but that ultimately can and should come to an end. 'All men [sic] begin by wondering that things are as they are,' he wrote, but they 'must end in the contrary and, according to the proverb, the better state, as is the case … when men learn the cause'. Understood this way, wonder dissolves behind us, like a bridge we willingly burn; it is weakened and then disposed of by a successful quest for progress (conquest). This is, in my view, a lesser understanding of the richness (endless) wonder might offer us, over and over again.

IN EARLY 1988, I WAS ACCEPTED INTO AN UNDERGRADUATE university program in the coastal, industrial city of Wollongong, 500 kilometres from home. I commenced in their School of Creative Arts, and like many full-time students, my day-to-day existence was precarious from then until I graduated, six years later, mainly due to poverty. And yet I was free from Ronald Street and from the high school environment in which I'd struggled to fully invest my understanding. I was, I suppose, emerging, at last, and there was much to discover. I took direction from and shelter in art and literature and music and poetry: Tracey Moffatt, Bill Henson, Barbara Kruger, Laurie Anderson, Italo Calvino, Margaret Atwood, early Peter Carey, and the overtly political and experimental work of the Sydney Women's Film Group and the Sydney Women Writers' Workshop. I remember copying out by hand and carrying with me Ania Walwicz's short prose poem, 'Little Red Riding Hood':

> I always had such a good time, good time, good time girl.
> Each and every day from morning to night. Each and every

twenty-four hours I wanted to wake up, wake up. I was so
lively, so livewire tense, such a highly pitched little. I was red,
so red so red. I was a tomato. I was on the lookout for the
wolf. Want some sweeties, mister? I bought a red dress myself.
I bought the wolf. Want some sweeties, mister? I bought a red
dress for myself. I bought a hood for myself. Get me a hood.
I bought a knife.

I look back on my love for this prose poem and I am shocked by
its call to violence, but for my late-teenage self carrying it around
was not about a literal intention to knife someone. The poem gave
me metaphorical armament. The poem gave me courage. I suppose I expected and anticipated violence from men and was surprised, over time, to discover that one could experience daily life
without necessarily having to be confronted by it quite so directly,
so incessantly, as I had expected upon first leaving home. It would
take many years for me to get used to this discovery, and to trust
men more fully, particularly intimate partners. I suppose a peace-
ful domestic life is something I am still getting used to, in my way.
Thirty years later, part of me believes I may yet turn out to regret
having put down the hood and the knife.

At university, I was drawn to learning, and especially to the
disciplines of film and literary studies. I fell in love and was loved
in return by a young Catholic boy from Sydney's northern suburbs: gentle, poetic, companionable. I took fewer drugs. I drank
less. I made good and lasting friendships with a genuinely diverse
group of peers, and with several of my lecturers and tutors. And
gradually, as the hours I spent in the university library began to
eclipse all others, I discovered that perhaps I could write fiction:
this was a new source of wonder to me. I gained confidence.

Even despite the gradual demise of the more liberal aspects of university education, identified correctly by Warner in her essay, and a period of reform which coincided approximately with my commencement as an undergraduate in Australia during the late 1980s, university changed me profoundly. There was the shock of the new, the carrying of intellectual and creative experience in and through the body, the blending of wonder and other emotions, the very possibility of new knowledge. I fell in love with all of these things. I am in love with them still.

WHEN I ASKED MARINA WARNER ABOUT HER ESSAY ON botanical artist Maria Sibylla Merian, titled 'Hatching', we entered into an enlightening discussion about knowledge and creativity and the relationship between art and science. Maria Merian's work crystallises so much of what is at stake in each of these spheres. She was a pioneer in observing the world fully and attentively, creating insightful botanical drawings that influenced scientific knowledge.

A native of Germany, Merian married young, but the marriage failed and after a stint living with a religious sect, she refused to return to live with her husband, sailing instead to the Dutch Caribbean colony of Suriname in 1699 at the age of fifty-two. Merian travelled not with a male companion, but rather with her young adult daughter. She had made a lifelong study of insects and her trip to Suriname was part of a quest to discover another kind of spinning insect, something to substitute or perhaps to rival silk. Merian's sketches had a significant impact on understandings of the life cycle amongst her natural science contemporaries. The folio of biological drawings that resulted from her two-year study in Suriname was titled *Metamorphosis Insectorum Surinamensium* and was published in 1705. According to Warner, it is one of the

Figure 2.
Plate XXVII from *Metamorphosis insectorum Surinamensium*.
Maria Sybilla Merian (1647–1717).

Source: Wikimedia Commons

earliest instances in which the term 'metamorphosis' was used in connection with insect life cycles. Merian's work enabled many to look anew at the prevailing view of natural development, which still relied on Aristotle's notion that it was the purpose of generative life change to aim towards greater and greater perfection. On the contrary, Merian's documentation of some rather beautiful caterpillars showed how they might transform into very ugly butterflies. Further, her sketches disrupt the very idea of the contained, consistent and solipsistic (self-reliant) being. Warner's writing on her work emphasises Merian's role in demonstrating how dissimilarity, interdependency and reciprocity permeate the way an entity develops.

'There were elements of her selection and arrangement that were already creative narratives,' Warner told me during our discussion. 'And by creating these narratives she couldn't prevent our engagement with her images on metaphorical lines. We can't help but see in metamorphosis and change something further than the animal's amazing capacity. She so often includes rotting, and the life cycle. She traps on a single page the idea of the life cycle, and the life cycle has repercussions in meaning. You can't stifle them. And I suppose metamorphosis is a good word when looking at this problem of the literal and the figural co-existing. Because metamorphosis is the word Merian chose and it continued to be used in this scientific context. Maybe she and her contemporaries could have invented another word. Metamorphosis was a mythological word.'

When I looked up the etymology of the word 'metamorphosis', I discovered what Warner meant. This term, now so central to the language of biology, has been lifted directly from its home in classical mythology, where it is very much to do with *magical* transformation. As such, metamorphosis is an idea that runs counter to the Judaeo-Christian tradition of a unique, consistent sense of self. We can look at its co-option by science as an example of the strong but often fraught link between wonder as a form of bewitchment – a magical, quasi-religious experience – and wonder as a means through which to seek greater, fuller knowledge and understanding.

Examining Maria Merian, I have found myself reassessing the place of the botanical drawing in the greater scheme of things. I am struck by the way in which Merian's sketches demonstrate metamorphosis not only as narrative, but as a process of becoming that arises through a particular ecology. In the world of the plant, the insect; in the world of the insect, the plant. As Warner helps us to appreciate, Merian's was an unflinching gaze. Her close scrutiny takes in insect devastation and intra-species massacres: savage incidents in nature that she makes no attempt to gloss over or beautify. Warner argues that Merian's capacity to look and 'look hard' is central to the *wonder* of her artwork. Through this exact attention, her work becomes both poetry *and* knowledge, art *and* science.

The connection between wonder and seeing can be traced a long way back. The Ancient Greek term *thaumazein* (to wonder) is related to the verb 'to see', a connection evident in the common expression 'a wonder to behold'. It is found, too, in the corresponding term in Latin, *admiratio*, the root of which (*mir*) is also linked to sight. Almost a century after the first publication of Merian's Surinamese sketches, the poets William Wordsworth and Samuel Taylor Coleridge would ponder the task of 'awakening the mind' from the lethargy of habit and custom by directing us to look towards 'the loveliness and the wonders of the world around us'. This call to look differently at the ordinary was a hallmark of the Romantics, encouraging us to orient ourselves towards a quasi-spiritual gaze that might reveal 'the miraculousness of the common' as Ralph Waldo Emerson put it. Sophie Vasalou traces a tangled back-and-forth line from this strain of aesthetic wonder to the scientific wonder that dominated the natural sciences right through the 17th and 18th centuries. This entanglement was to have a long cultural life, she argues, 'leaving a paper trail through the work of many of the philosophers' including early 20th-century thinkers such as Maurice Merleau-Ponty and Henri Bergson.

More recently, literary studies scholar Philip Fisher in *Wonder, the Rainbow and the Aesthetics of Rare Experiences* (2003) laments wonder's status as 'the most neglected of primary aesthetic experiences within modernity'. Renewed interest in the history and philosophy of the emotions has sparked some interest in the position of wonder, but as Sophie Vasalou has argued, wonder 'emerges as an emotion unlike others in every way'. Its neglect by contemporary theorists, she argues, is perhaps precisely because 'it is too slippery to be responsibly handled'.

I BEGAN THIS CHAPTER WITH REFERENCE TO THE QUESTIONS asked by the Malting House children. 'Why do ladies not have beards?' Any parent can attest to childish wonder as a source of both amusement and, sometimes, profound discomfort. My son, aged nine as I conclude this chapter, is still full of questions. Many of them, befitting his stage of development, have taken a turn towards the macabre: 'Would you rather die of drowning or of having your head chopped off?'

'Which superpower would you prefer to have?' he quizzed me on the way to school one morning recently.

'Oh, I don't know,' I said. 'What about you? Which superpower would you choose?'

'The power of the shapeshifter,' Roland replied without hesitation, 'so I could take any form'.

Later the same week he declared, 'I'd like to have a go at being a girl. Also a bird, and a cat.'

I take some comfort in my son's openness to imaginative play that sets aside, albeit temporarily, the traditionally masculine tendency to war, conflict, goodies, baddies, and endless forms of weaponry that are so regularly present in various role-play games in our small shared living space. I want to encourage this more in him, to draw this tendency out, to support it wherever it takes seed.

Destruction, extermination and annihilation are the goals of combat myths, argues Warner. 'The association of magical power with weapons of destruction, not with philosophical wisdom, is problematic,' she writes in an essay on the topic published in 2002. 'Do the current mega-hits at the box office reflect anxieties and dreams, or do they shape them?' Of course, the real answer is impossible to know, but her question certainly caused me to ponder the ways in which a tendency towards dualism (and the duel) robs us of the possibilities of more imaginative responses to the myriad challenges we face.

It seems to me that wonder – and hence transformation – has always been central to my desire to both write and read fiction. If I could answer my son's question again, I would say that my superpower of choice is the narrative imagination. Importantly, though, it is a narrative imagination that is not disconnected from knowledge. As I have argued elsewhere, the urge to write something substantial in a way that requires imaginative effort, to shift ideas from fleeting feelings or impressions towards a more fully realised and complex creative work such as a novel, requires a certain disease, often a rather deep-seated sense of dissatisfaction: anger, confusion, disbelief, disapproval, or just an inkling, a subtle desire, for things to be, in whatever way, *other than this*. In this sense, fiction comes from the question of why. It comes from the question of how. It comes, therefore, from the embedded, lived experience of knowing intimately those circumstances that hold us down, that pressure us, that prevent us from taking flight. It comes, for me, from the hope that Warner has identified as being crucial to the fairytale, a hope born of resourcefulness, a hope that makes the very idea of transformation possible.

The Australian novelist Kim Scott, in response to the question of why he writes, has spoken of the pleasure of absorption – of 'getting lost in the making of things' – and this too, can be thought about as a practice steeped in wonder, for wonder paradoxically encapsulates what 18th-century philosopher Adam Smith called 'an emotion or movement of the spirits' that 'exhibits all the painfulness of disorientation' even as it has us 'float' or 'glide' with 'effortless facility' along what he calls the imagination's 'natural career'.

WHEN WARNER AND I MET FOR OUR SECOND DISCUSSION OF the topic of wonder, I reported to her the fashion among the buskers around Piccadilly Circus and the National Gallery in London. At the time, the squares were full of figures in fantasy costumes inspired by Tolkien or *Star Wars* characters that magically hovered a metre or two above the ground. They formed a kind of living statue, their hats upturned nearby to collect donations by coin.

'Are they on a stand?' Warner wanted to know.

'They must be, but it's not visible.'

'Interesting. Well, they are living statues, yes. And I suppose the most famous progeny of the character of curiosities, in a way, is Madame Tussauds.'

Our conversation turned to the topic of wonder as a skill, and to the long tradition in stagecraft of designing props and aids that instil in the audience a sense of awe and wonder. It is a tradition that goes a long way back.

'We have this expression *deus ex machina*,' explained Warner, 'and that refers to the descent of the god or goddess in Greek tragedy. Medea at the end of Euripides' play goes to heaven, you know, she flies off the stage in a dragon-drawn chariot. So that was probably imitated in some way, we don't know exactly how. And in the ancient world in Egypt, you know, they were already creating *automata* – statues that moved, statues that spoke for ordinary religious purposes, you know, to create oracles for the priests to go inside, sometimes just as part of a cluster of mechanical wonders.'

Warner outlined the history of the water clock or clepsydra, as an example of an early scientific instrument that was designed to invoke a sense of wonder. This artefact has been dated to 338 BC in Persia, but there are examples of intricate water clock designs across ancient Babylon, India, China and the Greco-Roman period. In the medieval Islamic world, the polymath al-Jazari invented one of the most complex clepsydra ever documented. Developed in 1206, it included automata – five musicians, two falcons – and a complex system of pulleys and weights inside the structure. An inscription above the opening doors at the top of the clock reminded onlookers to revel in the glory of God.

Given the sweep of our discussion towards *deus ex machina*, I brought up the subject of the flying machine. The topic of flight is one about which Warner has written an evocative chapter in *Stranger Magic*.

'Unexpectedly, there's rather little flying in the classic body of

European fairytales,' Warner observed. 'I mean, it isn't a feature of "Red Riding Hood" or "Snow White" or "Cinderella". There are witches who fly, and there are amazing journeys and, of course, objects fly. There's a certain amount of uncanny activity, but the tradition now, that all fantasy involves easy flight, has become completely endemic, especially in film. In all of the latest fantasy films there are amazing scenes of flight (in *Avatar*, in *The Golden Compass*) because it can be simulated so well on screen. This is a post-*Arabian Nights* fantasy, because in the *Nights* the narrative delights in its own ability to move anywhere, and it does so, airborne.'

'We have the expression "flights of fancy"', I suggested, 'and there's a sense that dreaming about flying brings with it a fluidity, an opening up of perspective.'

'In *The Arabian Nights*,' said Warner, 'the characters really are flying. They don't always need wings, and there's no attempt at constructing complex flying machines. Flight simply happens. The jinn fly and magical objects levitate. The carpet, which doesn't have such a profile in the original text, has become the principal motif of the *Nights* in the West (alongside Aladdin's lamp). When I first gave a lecture about this, in Munich, and I suggested that the flying carpet was an intuition of aerodynamics that was far more accurate than Leonardo's ornithopter, you know, his bird-winged contraption ...'

'It seems clumsy in comparison, doesn't it?'

'Yes! But the Munich audience was absolutely resistant!'

'Oh, really?'

'Yes, afterwards they came up to me and said, "Preposterous!"'

For some reason we both find the offence implied in this reaction enormously amusing. Is it because it seems to demonstrate, at some basic level, a shocking failure of the imagination?

MUCH OF THE LITERATURE THAT PRIVILEGES WONDER HAS BEEN read as being against empiricism. Warner has argued that this should not necessarily be the case.

'When Rousseau and Locke, the two great thinkers about education in the 18th century, condemned fairytales and myths and so forth as foolish fantasies and as nonsense, they wanted children to study the real world. They wanted children to go out and look at spiders' webs and flowers and rainbows and actually be involved in the phenomena of nature that was observable, that was empirical. They thought that demons and goblins were the kinds of nonsense that nurses and foolish ignorant old women described to children to control and frighten them. In their own way, in a humanitarian way they had good intentions; they wanted to stop using stories to terrorise the young.

'Sophisticated, post-Enlightenment cultures of human beings are expected to proceed empirically. I see myself as part of the Enlightenment tradition, but my argument has always been that we are simply a myth-making species in the same way that we are a language species, and our languages are metaphorical. We have a limited empirical language: a door is a door. But a metaphor of a door has a vast range of meaning. And that's really the way that our minds communicate and are structured, and so my argument has always been: let's find out about these imaginative structures and then, once we understand them better, then we can't destroy them or expurgate them, but maybe we can think about them in ways that help rather than in ways that hinder.'

In a contemplative moment, Warner told me, 'I feel, personally, that if religion could remain metaphysical it would be fine. I don't share Richard Dawkins' dislike of transcendental systems. I mean, I love Renaissance astrology. I think it's an incredibly beautiful testament to the extraordinary inventiveness and imagination of the people of the past. I don't believe a word of it, but it's a marvellous creation. They believed it, or some of them believed it. But we're in a different position from that now.'

FACED WITH THE 'OPEN SEA OF ENDLESS QUESTIONING, strangeness and possibility' that is wonder, it is perhaps not surprising that some have posited that wonder, like seasickness, is a passion to be endured. But as the nuns in Warner's convent school demonstrated, framed by the work of Saint Paul, women have too often been actively and systematically discouraged from dipping a single toe into such an open sea. Questioning is not for the faint-hearted, nor it seems, is it to be too actively encouraged in those with nothing left to lose (witness, most recently, for example, the banning of the media from Australian refugee detention centres). As I finish writing this chapter, I remain deeply encouraged by Marina Warner and her thinking, by her capacity to go out into the world – of knowledge, of history, of mythology, of popular culture – and open it up to an examination that is in turns scholarly and imaginative, empathic and hopeful. I can't help but think that her long therapy on herself – her writing – has also been of immense benefit to others. It is telling that Warner's motivation began with a commitment to retrieving or 'overhearing' the voices of women, from *Alice in Wonderland* to Maria Merian, from Joan of Arc to the powerful and enchanting Scheherazade. For it remains the case that many women, like Scheherazade, are dreaming in order to find a way to live. Should certain structures restrict and confound us, we must not consider them utterly intractable. I began this chapter with the question of whether our capacity for wonder can actually change who we are. The answer, of course, is yes. Yes.

CHAPTER
SIX
Friendship

The importance of friendship to feminist philosopher Rosi Braidotti can be captured in an anecdote she tells about leaving her family's village in Italy, against her will, as a fifteen year old. Born in the decade immediately following the end of the Second World War, Braidotti spent her childhood in a small town not far from the northern Italian border. The extended network of friends and family was large, and she and her friends roamed freely on their bicycles from an early age. Braidotti's grandfather was a leader in the anti-fascist movement, and politics was very often the topic of conversation amongst the adults in her world; perhaps because of this, her early memories include a deep-seated sense of life as a collective project. In Braidotti's fifteenth year, her father's supply business failed and he was suddenly bankrupt. He felt a great sense of shame about his circumstances, and so her parents made an abrupt decision to take up the offer of assisted passage to Australia. When the migration plan was announced, the children were in shock. Braidotti told her parents, 'You've got to be kidding me. I'm not coming.'

'They said, "Well you can stay, we go",' she told me. 'It was that sort of situation, because they were desperate. My beloved uncle offered to take me in and I could have just worked and studied. One year older, at sixteen, I could have made decisions, but at fifteen I was just in limbo. And I was too attached: I loved my brother and sister dearly. I'm the eldest. So, with tears in my eyes and my entire world crumbling – as it can when you're at that age – I went along, but the last night in the city, I still have that picture. It was as hilarious as it was dramatic. We went around with all of my friends – the group, the little gang – saying goodbye to the different places in the town, singing and drinking, and they literally threw me onto the train. It was going from my town to Genoa to take the boat, because we are in 1970 and the Suez is closed, so the boat has to go from Genoa all around Africa, to take us there. We thought it was the end of the world.

'And now everybody wants to go to Australia, as you know. But I mean, in Italy in 1970, the idea of Australia was not a cool thing. It was a very different world. What I love is that unity with those friends. I think my trauma was also their trauma. We became aware of migration. It united us in so many ways.'

The same group of friends are still in contact almost fifty years later.

THE OFFICE FOR THE CENTRE FOR THE HUMANITIES AT UTRECHT University, which Rosi Braidotti has directed for some years now, is on the ground floor of a 14th-century canal house. A trio of huge windows overlook the street. I passed by these windows each time I came to meet with her in the spring of 2016, and each time I glanced in at her sitting at her large desk. She would look up and wave at me the moment before I pressed the buzzer at the door. It seems a very Dutch thing, this going about your day in a manner that is fully visible to others. I have always liked looking in at

Dutch interiors. There is a beautiful sense of openness glimpsed when strolling past canal houses in cities like Amsterdam and Haarlem, where rows and rows of carefully decorated rooms glow with the warmth of domestic life, but I know from my father that there is an aspect to the display that is deliberately demonstrative, too. He chose to move away from his homeland as a young adult, and would make only one trip back during his lifetime. He did not miss the petit bourgeois aspects of Dutch life. Braidotti, for her part, wasn't so keen on the big windows either, and reported that she was looking forward to moving to an office upstairs.

In person, Rosi Braidotti is a commanding character, but she carries her authority in a manner that suggests comfort and ease with her recognised skills, rather than a vain pleasure in an intelligence few of us can equal. Paradoxically, she is also someone who seems almost surprised by the success of her career: as if it happened by accident. She left Australia many decades ago, but still speaks English with an Australian accent.

'When I look back on all of my life, I must say it has this sense of unreality, like there's a plot going through it. Like you think, "How did that happen?"'

TODAY, ROSI BRAIDOTTI IS ONE OF EUROPE'S BEST-KNOWN feminist philosophers. When she was awarded a knighthood by Queen Beatrice of the Netherlands in 2005, she was honoured not just for her contribution to philosophy, but for her achievement in working to connect feminist thinkers across Europe in a range of formal and informal networks. Her former student, literature scholar Moira Fradinger, introducing her at Yale for the 2017 Tanner Lectures, described her as notable for her capacity to 'transform the lives of those around her' and for her 'contagious joy in sharing, in thinking *with*' others. I think Fradinger's introduction is a fitting one, especially to a discussion of Braidotti's approach to friendship, for it illustrates feminism's deep-seated commitment to, as Braidotti puts it, 'rethinking the living processes of existence, literally the spaces between the mental and the physical, the theoretical and the experiential'.

I first read Braidotti's work as a doctoral student. Her first book, *Patterns of Dissonance*, was published in 1991. I joined her readership with the second, *Nomadic Subjects*, published in 1994. The groundwork for this book arose, clearly, out of Braidotti's own experience of migration, for after only ten years in Australia, she was uprooted again, this time to France. By the time she reached the Netherlands to take up the position in Utrecht in 1988, it was the fourth time she'd moved countries. Each of these moves involved significant cultural, geographic and linguistic shifts. Not surprisingly, her focus in *Nomadic Subjects* is on the notion of movement in the contemporary context. 'The motivation to explore nomadic subjectivity,' she writes, 'comes from the conviction that in times of accelerating changes, many traditional points of reference and age-old habits of thought are being re-composed. We need to learn to think differently about the kind of subjects we have already become and the processes of deep-seated transformation we are undergoing.'

Like the philosopher Gilles Deleuze, who was one of her professors at the Sorbonne during the 1970s and has had a significant influence on her thinking, Braidotti uses the term 'subject' rather than 'self', and by extension, 'subjectivity' to speak about the concept of identity (as does Julia Kristeva, discussed earlier). This is because the way in which Braidotti and her contemporaries think about *who we are* and *how we become who we are* disconnects radically from the classical ideal in Western philosophy,

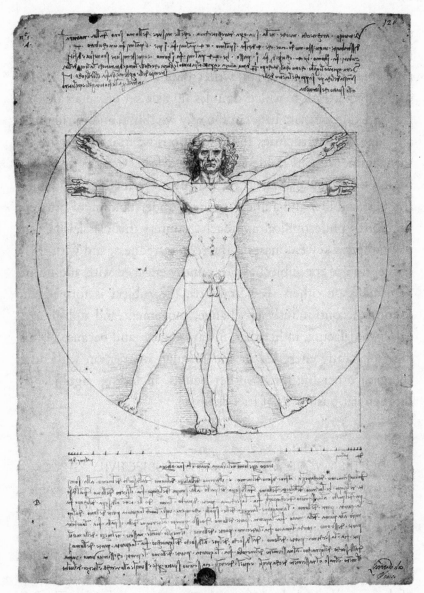

Figure 3.
'Vitruvian Man', c. 1440. Leonardo da Vinci.

Source: Wikimedia Commons.

stemming back to Leonardo da Vinci's Vitruvian Man. In classical terms, the self was understood as a contained, unitary and autonomous being. Vitruvian Man, writes Braidotti, represents 'an ideal of bodily perfection' which doubles up as a set of values that are embedded in our language, in the way we think, and in the social and ideological structures and institutions we inhabit and that, in turn, influence and moderate our behaviour. Caught up in this notion of Vitruvian Man is the pursuit of individual and collective perfectibility and a linear, rational understanding of progress. Braidotti's philosophical approach counters this classicism. One of Braidotti's key emphases is interconnectedness, and with this a conception of the subject as profoundly engaged with and deeply dependent on others. For Braidotti, the subject is formed and re-formed continuously by change, movement and upheaval. It is outward-facing, rather than inward-facing, and because of this, it is constantly energised in and through interaction with other energies, other life forces, other beings, including, significantly, through various forms of friendship.

BRAIDOTTI'S WORK ON NOMADIC SUBJECTIVITY STRUCK A chord with many readers worldwide, and went on to become a twenty-year project, leading to two further books: *Metamorphoses* (2002), exploring the cultural politics of the nomadic subject, and *Transpositions* (2006), exploring the ethical implications. Her approach to subjectivity develops over the course of all three of these works, and also informs her more recent books, *The Posthuman* (2013) and *Posthuman Glossary* (2018). One of her key points is that relations between oneself and an other – as between friends – have too often been understood as a binary: difference versus sameness. She argues instead for difference as positivity.

Friendship becomes a 'play of complexity'. With this kind of emphasis, it is no longer useful to think of ourselves as 'an expression of in-depth interiority'; we are instead 'opening out to the possible encounter of the "outside"'. The imagination plays a crucial role in enabling this whole process but the key involves allowing ourselves to see the extent to which the process of identity formation is in a constant state of flux, in large part because of the way such a process is collective. Braidotti calls this constant state of flux 'becoming' – a term first applied in this way to the subject by Gilles Deleuze.

These ideas can be confronting to consider in a world that still appeals daily to our sense of ourselves as autonomous individuals with a stable, essential identity in the classical Western philosophical sense. Ever-present advertisements that capitalise on the pressure to succeed, that push cosmetics and bank loans, just to name a couple, seek to reinforce our sense of ourselves as unique and self-directed. 'It's all about you', beams a billboard advertisement for a university I pass regularly in inner Melbourne. Braidotti's philosophy challenges these ideas, but importantly, she doesn't do so to dismay us. On the contrary she does so, she says, as a matter of urgency, to bring us to our senses about the complex circumstances we find ourselves in globally and locally, here-and-now. For Braidotti, understanding these circumstances, and our own complex state of flux within them, is a responsibility we cannot afford to shirk. She asks her readers to be worthy of the present, and argues that one of the ways we can do this is to gain a greater understanding of the way in which we are, all of us, interconnected, not just to other humans but to other beings, other forms of life.

In this chapter, I consider what Braidotti has to say about friendship in and through her ideas about the subject: a notion of identity that is nomadic, moveable, relational and dependent. I am keen to share her work because there is a positivity and a compassion to her thinking that is deeply life affirming.

THINKING ABOUT FRIENDSHIP THROUGH THE LENS OF BRAIDOTTI'S philosophy has caused me to reflect on a time during my early twenties when I was enveloped in and enlivened by an energetic friendship that changed my way of being in ways I am still trying to understand. I have kept a postcard-sized pastel drawing from that time, on the back of which is a written message from my friend Jo:

Dear Julienne

Thank you for havin' me. This picture is for you because you know what trains are like and how to really enjoy a rockpool. Thank you for your support … I admire what you do and ummmmm … well ummmm … I love you …

Lub and luff
Jo

Even more than twenty years later, something about Jo's reference to the shared material experiences of rockpools on the New South Wales south coast, and to riding the trains that ran in that area at the time – from within which we both loved to stand in the carriage entrance and wedge a door open with a foot to feel the rush of sea air – still has a resonance for me. I have written elsewhere about my friendship with Jo, but I have not fully finished (and may never finish) appreciating all there is to understand about the to-and-fro of it, the elemental force or positive vitality Rosi Braidotti calls zoe, which is at the heart of it all.

The French term *mon semblable* (my friend or my likeness) implies that our friends are in some way similar (*semblable*) to us; my friend might be seen as another version of my self. But in Braidotti's terms, a lively, immersive friendship, such as that occupied by Jo and me, has more to it than this. I am particularly interested in exploring the way in which my friendship with Jo could be said to have been built on Braidotti's notion of the 'joyfully discontinuous subject'. I want, also, to discuss and unpack more fully her notion of embracing the space between self and other as a source of vitality rather than viewing it as one that threatens us with loss or lack.

MY FRIEND JO AND I MET AT UNIVERSITY IN 1989, WHERE WE were both enrolled in creative arts degrees. We met among fellow writers, musicians, visual artists and actors. I was eighteen and she was twenty. The world of ideas was just opening up to us, and it was wondrous and complicated and interesting.

What I remember most about the early years of our friendship was that I wanted to be more like her. I wanted my voice to be more like Jo's, the warmth she could carry in it, the way she tilted her head and asked you a question you might never have thought to ask yourself. And I liked the way she disarmed people, whether strangers or friends, with her concern for their well-being, her interest in their hopes and small frustrations. Jo made friends quickly and widely. There was also the way she spoke constantly about the future, so full of confidence and nutty, ambitious plans.

After university, Jo and I moved physically apart, across states and continents in a kind of improvised, unpredictable dance. She wanted to travel overseas. I wanted to see Australia. I kept studying. She took a gap year. While I won myself a postgraduate scholarship, Jo bought a round-the-world ticket. When we were together, we talked and talked, but over distance our intimacy was etched in the form of old-fashioned letters, handwritten and then sent by email, stuffed into undersized envelopes, pushing the limits of postage stamps and incorporating all manner of small detritus (feathers, collages and sketches, bus tickets, newspaper articles, postcards).

26 September 1991

Dear Julienne

My main current activity is looking for somewhere to live in Glasgow. I found London to be extremely depressing. Without going on too much about it, I had a very adverse reaction to the place, despite the fact that it was really good to spend time with my grandmother. So, I decided to come up to Scotland, to see what the future holds for me here.

So far things are going pretty well, in that I have managed to find work. I'm working in the mornings doing secretarial stuff at Scottish Breweries and in the afternoons as from next week will be working in the Student Union at the Art School here. This I am really excited about, because I will be fulfilling my ambition, which had its origin in Wollongong, to be a tea lady!

Tonight we were watching the news and I thought of you because I really wanted to be able to be sitting across the table from you and say, 'Fuck, there is so much going on at the moment' – Serbia/Croatia/USA pseudo disarmament (a bit dodgy, do you reckon so?)/hostage releases/Israel-Palestine

stuff/disgruntled Romanian miners/the whole breakdown of
Communism bizzo – so much it's amazing. I really feel like
having a good meaty rave with you about it all. I loved the
way we could get stuck into politics and issues together and
for it to be a non-competitive thing – I loved it because we
seemed to just really enjoy getting our teeth into it all.

Anyway, time for me to zzzzz until morning.

Lubb, lubb
Jo.

It was while we were still at university that I first watched Jo fall
for the wrong men. There was M, a mutual friend. He and Jo
shared a house together for a while, and they were close, but M
was not interested in Jo romantically. He went out with other
women. Meanwhile, Jo was always trying, with constantly falter-
ing confidence, to prompt him to reciprocate her desire for a more
physical relationship.

Only a year or so into our friendship, I was sharply affected by
Jo's descent into an extended episode of psychosis. I wasn't there
when she was put into a police van and transferred to a psych ward
in Campbelltown, but I was terribly concerned for her well-being
and her lack of agency, and I couldn't help feeling proud of her
when she escaped from custody a few days later.

'She always escaped', her father would tell journalists at the
Australian, so many years later. Jo had been diagnosed as a schizophrenic at sixteen. Of the Campbelltown incident, her father
remembered telling doctors she would get out of the ward. '"Oh,
no, it's maximum security, there's no way", they said, and within
four hours of that conversation she was out. Pretty much as I was
driving home.'

Jo later joked with me that she was aiming to write a travel guide to the world's mental health institutions.

'A travel guide or an exit handbook?'

We laughed.

When she travelled overseas, she fell in love with other men. Nothing ever quite worked out. My observation, over time, was that her relapses often followed on the back of some kind of romantic rejection. I sometimes wonder whether if just one of her romantic interests had loved her properly back, even for a short time, would things have turned out differently?

2 December 1991

Dear Julienne,

Your wonderful Frill-Necked Lizard postcard arrived this morning and as usual you are spot on when you talk about what defines a place to a person or people collectively. Dis is something I have been ponderin about a bit myself recently:

> But the problems are many if we want to determine
> the profound reality of all the subtle shadings of our
> attachment to a chosen spot. For a phenomenologist,
> these shadings must be taken as the first rough outlines
> of a psychological phenomenon. The shading is not an
> additional, superficial colouring. We should therefore
> have to say how we inhabit our vital space, in accord
> with all the dialectics of life ... (Gaston Bachelard)

And dat was one of the quotes used on a catalogue from a group exhibition which D. was involved in and which I saw in the States. (Remember mention of this strange and interesting man? Broke my heart, but by god I'm glad of it.)

One of the main questions I get asked here, apart from where is my kangaroo, is 'Why did you choose to come to Glasgow?' 'I've got no idea,' I say. I don't know why I'm here, Julienne ... I know that I wanted to travel to learn ... to learn how to live ... to get a bit of perspective on Australia ... but I don't know why it is that I chose this particular place of all the spots to come to ... there are logistical reasons such as for the time being I had to plonk myself somewhere English-speaking in order to find work ... but apart from that ... [Your house in] Domville Road, Otford, resides permanently behind my left ear. Every day I always see it and the verandah and the trees inside my head ... and quite regularly recently I feel pangs of what could be called homesickness. I miss you. I miss our conversations.

Jo

Philosopher Friedrich Nietzsche, in *The Gay Science*, compares the art of learning to love to listening to a piece of music. We play and replay such a piece until the melody is thoroughly known, and when it dawns on us that we would miss it if it were lacking, we can be said to have learned to love. I've carried this notion of Nietzsche's around with me for some years now, and while it still has for me a residual beauty, considering it again now, many years after Jo's death, and so close to the full and immersive reading I have done of Rosi Braidotti's philosophy, I realise that it no longer resonates with me. It is, for one, too melancholic. In addition, its focus is too heavily on lack. I'll come back to Braidotti's thoughts on lack shortly, but for now, I want to take you to Lander Street, in Sydney's Darlington, circa 1993.

Jo had been hospitalised again in Glasgow and was able to fly home to Australia only on the condition that she be accompanied

197

by a psychiatric nurse. Once here, her doctors had instructed her to stay on monthly injections of anti-psychotics. She didn't do that. She hated their effect on her creativity.

It is fair to say that I engineered us a share house in Lander Street in part to get my brother out of a bad arrangement in Leichhardt, and in part to provide Jo with a loving environment after her return from overseas. The house was a double-storey terrace painted the slightly sickly apricot colour favoured by renovators in the 1980s. At the beginning, Jo took the front room upstairs. I took the room behind that, which had a little Juliet balcony overlooking the courtyard at the back, and my brother took the front room off the hallway downstairs.

In the little kitchen at the back of the house, Jo and I drank cup after cup of tea and talked for hours. We could talk art or politics. We could talk music or literature. We could gossip about friends. We could talk frankly about matters of the heart. Jo was a good listener. She took an interest. And occasionally she would pull out her guitar and sing.

She slotted back into her old job with a nut importer in Bondi. When I phoned her at work, she would joke, 'Yes, we're all nutty here.' In those days, Jo spent a good deal of her pay on taxis. She was suffering from sciatica and walked, as my brother did, with the help of a cane. At some point she moved from the big upstairs balconied room to the little study right at the back. I remained in the middle room, in between, and we let the big front room to a beautiful, rather pale music student, who didn't stay long. Jo's health was up and down. Sometimes her back was so painful she couldn't get out of bed. She missed work. Her diet was appalling. Sometimes she was up all night and I would hear her cry out.

She shied away from help.

PEOPLE MATTER TO ROSI BRAIDOTTI. EACH TIME I MET WITH HER in the Netherlands, her welcome was wonderfully generous. She always gave the impression that while you were with her, there was nothing more important going on. All this shouldn't be so rare, but it seems to me that it is. I wondered, later, whether this was what it meant to be in the company of someone who is skilled in being fully present.

We met three times over the course of my ten-day stay in Utrecht, and Braidotti talked a lot. In listening, I sometimes found myself in awe of just how comfortable she seemed in her own skin, but when we reached the point in her life story where she talked about meeting her life partner, Anneke Smelik, it explained something. 'We meet and this is it,' she told me. 'I remember seeing light, she remembers a voice, and we just stand still.' Thirty years have passed since. I know then that Braidotti's sense of ease with herself and with others is deeply connected to her partner. Here is a woman profoundly, consistently loved.

As she relayed to me the years she spent in Australia, Braidotti's story was knitted through with the serendipitous relationships she formed with friends, mentors, activists and teachers in circumstances she could rarely have anticipated. Chance meetings happened on railway station platforms, in factories, on footpaths, and many of them ignited lively, joyful friendships that would fuel Braidotti's journey all the way back to Europe, and last into the decades beyond.

It was in 1970 that Braidotti commenced a crash course in English on the boat from Italy and when she enrolled in fifth form at Fitzroy High School – at that time one of Australia's roughest and most disadvantaged schools – her English language skills were still very rudimentary. She was given extra tuition after school hours and when it became clear that she was an academically gifted student, her teachers kept an eye out for her, alerting her to scholarships and other opportunities and taking a personal interest in her success. She did so well in the school leaving exams that she had her picture on the front page of the *Age*, and was accepted into the Australian National University (ANU) under the auspices of a national undergraduate scholarship.

At the same time, Braidotti's Australian adventure was shot through with subtle but life-affirming acts of resistance. As a teenager she helped the Labor party campaign to change conditions in inner-city schools with a movement to embrace multiculturalism; then, despite her outstanding school-leaver's results, she refused to even contemplate 'doing law' at the University of Melbourne in the manner suggested suitable for good Italian migrant daughters in her neighbourhood. In Canberra, suddenly living in a residential college alongside the children of Australia's ruling elite, she sent the money she earned waitressing home to her younger sister in Fitzroy, but gave herself permission to do what *she* wanted to do – classical philosophy. As graduation approached, she did not even consider following her first serious romantic partner to a sensible diplomatic posting in Sweden. She had already applied for a French scholarship. 'I didn't even wait for the results,' she said, of completing her final exam at ANU. 'I didn't go to the graduation ceremony. There's no pictures of me graduating. I was already in Paris.'

In Paris, those decisions all seemed validated.

'It's high feminism,' she told me of the city in 1978, 'so I can't even remember how I got into a collective. It's only ten years after May 1968 and the fallout is still around. François Mitterrand would be elected three years later; it's a very open society. I meet incredible people. I just land on my feet. I am literate in the French language. I love the language. I love the culture, and it's the right moment to be there. I mean, it's so exciting. You'd have the choice between going to a Gilles Deleuze lecture or a Jean-François Lyotard lecture which was on at the same time. Not only would you talk to Simone de Beauvoir on a weekly basis, but you would meet everybody.

'It was a real intellectual elite moment. I suppose there's something about the life of the mind, the function of intellectual eroticisation or intelligence, or however you want to put it. It was not intellectually elite in a snobbish sense, but we all felt loaded with the task of being responsible for the world and making the world a better place.'

In Paris at that time, perhaps more than ever, philosophy was considered an important part of the social fabric. I didn't have any trouble imagining Braidotti in and amongst such a community. The energy this immersive period gave her thinking is still evident so many decades later.

BRAIDOTTI'S MOST RECENT WORK MAKES A CONVINCING CASE for re-appraising the work of Dutch-Jewish philosopher, Baruch or Benedict de Spinoza, and depends increasingly on Spinoza's monism as a central premise. Spinoza's *Ethics* was first published in 1677, and has been widely understood as a refutation of René Descartes' thinking on the mind/body problem, in which Descartes argued for the mind and body as two separate, and in some senses duelling, entities. But it is Spinoza's monistic worldview that is most relevant to Braidotti's thinking and especially her approach to friendship.

Ethics was Spinoza's major life's work, and was published only after his death. Even then, his friends, who edited and released the manuscript, felt it wise to remove their own names from the project given the supreme power of the church in Europe at that time. In *Ethics*, Spinoza expounds on the attributes of God, arguing through a mathematically inspired method that God is both one substance and everything. This is why the term 'monism' is appropriate. The Latinate prefix *mon* means singular; the productive suffix *ism* in this case denotes a state, condition or principle. Monism, in the simplest sense, refers to the idea that reality is one. It was, and still is, in many ways, a radical idea, for it directly opposes Cartesian dualism: the widely held belief, rooted in Greek classicism and upheld by many Christians, that mind and body are divided; that the material body and the immaterial (or divine) mind are two completely different kinds of substances.

Monism perhaps seems a simple idea, at first glance, but when you begin to look at its implications, particularly in light of how much of the classical Western philosophical tradition it contradicts, you start to appreciate both how controversial it can be, and the manner in which it is also potentially, infinitely complex. As Braidotti attests, Spinoza's philosophy was the subject of intense criticism in leading philosophical circles, in part because of its 'absence of any reference to negativity and to violent, dialectical oppositions'. One of the key reasons for Spinoza's rediscovery among Western philosophers in the 1970s was precisely because of the genuine possibilities it offered for setting aside such violent oppositions or binaries.

Gilles Deleuze was a professor at the Sorbonne when Braidotti studied there, and he was amongst those thinkers to argue for looking at Spinoza's philosophy anew. Deleuze's work implores us to consider matter as vital and self-organising. This is a very active reinvention of monism that rejects the transcendentalist or quasi-spiritualist slant that others have sometimes emphasised in reading Spinoza's work. The validity of Deleuze's approach has been reinforced by recent advances in the biological and environmental sciences, where evidence of the complex, self-organising structures of living matter has become more and more convincing over the course of the past century.

So, what has all this to do with friendship?

'We are structurally connected to multiple others of all kinds, human and non-human,' explains Braidotti on precisely this question. Surprisingly, it has taken her some time to fully embrace monistic theology as a key aspect of her work on nomadic subjectivity, in part because of the way Spinoza's monism clashes with some of the key concepts underpinning the psychoanalytic worldview she was so deeply immersed in as a young woman. When she was in her twenties and living in Paris, Braidotti, along with many of her peers, underwent psychoanalysis herself, in part as a means to better understand psychoanalysis as a philosophical phenomenon.

'Did you ever do it?' she asked me.

'No.'

'You know, if you go through the process it's a very different sensibility. I did my MA on Lacan, and in my day, you were encouraged very strongly to do psychoanalysis if you were going to write about it. Not to just theorise it, but to know what you're talking about.' Braidotti started working with an analyst at twenty-seven, and stayed with the same professional for seven years. 'I stayed to go through every bit of this from every possible angle of it. For me, it was pulling everything apart and then reconstructing it.' Braidotti described the relationship with her analyst during those years as her key relationship. Analysis 'catalyses everything and then things around you have to fall into place'.

When she took up the offer of the Chair of Women's Studies at Utrecht University in 1988, her analyst was careful to ask her whether such a move might become her fourth migration.

And Braidotti decided that it wouldn't be, not in those terms. It wouldn't be a repetition.

'So, I did things that I considered symbolically very important. I had come to Paris with the same trunk that we had used to emigrate to Australia, and so one of the things that I did was I said, "I have to leave this behind." So I shared all of this with my analyst and we made sort of a plan for what this could be: a brand-new start, not a repetition. If there are Italians here, I don't care. There are no Australians. I'm again on my own. It's again a suitcase, but there is a chance.

'Now, in the advisory board for the selection committee, Anneke Smelik – now my partner – was advising the committee.' As already mentioned, both women recognised the powerful connection between them at that first meeting and it would prove to be utterly transformative. 'So I got back from the interview to analysis in Paris and now all of this is happening. I'm doing something I've never done in my life. I'm putting every egg in the same basket. This is make it or break it, this is what I think life should be, I mean, could be. I don't know, I've never done this. I said to my analyst, "I can stay here and tell you about it, or I can go." I said this in French. It is better in French. *Je peux rester ici et vous dire à ce sujet, ou je peux suivre la vague.* So on a surfing metaphor, I catch it, just catch the wave, and then from then on it's a legend.' She laughed. 'I do think that Utrecht is not a fourth migration. I think Utrecht is something else, but I did work on this through analysis and it was important. An analyst is not a friend, it's a mentor, it's a Virgil to Dante, it's the coach. With her help, I pulled myself apart and reconstructed something manageable.'

How, then, did this very positive, deeply personal experience of psychoanalysis influence her later thinking on Deleuzian-inflected monism?

'The philosophy of otherness and difference as the other was very much imprinted in my mind and also in my body, because of the experience of analysis.' In psychoanalytic terms, the notion of the other is caught up with notions of desire and also of lack (or *manque*). The work of psychoanalyst Jacques Lacan, for example, which influenced many French intellectuals during the 1960s and 1970s, and had a lasting influence on post-structuralism, conceives of two kinds of others, the first with a small o (other) and the second with a capital 'O' (Other). For Lacan, the other is a projection of our selves (or Ego), while the Other designates a radical alterity, which can never be assimilated through identification. Lacan proposed that speech and language come from the Other, that is, they are outside of the control of the Ego, or, to put it differently, from outside of consciousness. According to Lacan's line of thinking, the mother is the first Other we encounter, and the castration complex is formed when we realise that this Other is not complete; she is a form of lack. It is perhaps not surprising that many feminists, including Luce Irigaray, have taken Lacan to task for maintaining a sexist tradition in psychoanalysis, but the point here is that the very idea of the other in psychoanalytic terms is markedly different from the way it is conceived of in Spinoza's monism. 'You notice in Deleuze's philosophies,' continued Braidotti, 'it advances, there is not an other, certainly not a capital O Other, it's others, it's multiplicities, a clustering of otherings and I think that's the monistic turn.'

Braidotti's most recent work rejects the approach to the other – or otherness – taken by the likes of Lacan and Derrida, where the emphasis is on vulnerability and lack. In this form of psychoanalytic thinking, she explained to me, our attachment to the other is read as something essential, however that can render us vulnerable, because the other is infinitely demanding but never giving in. 'I respect this is a very noble ethic,' she told me, 'but it is also a recipe for impotence. Moreover it locks the self to the other in a negative relationship. It is a recipe for self-obsession.'

One of the more interesting feminist psychoanalysts to have written on friendship is Jessica Benjamin. While Braidotti's more recent work has shifted away from psychoanalytic theory, it is useful to look back at her appraisal of Benjamin's work in *Nomadic Subjects*. Importantly, Benjamin sees self and other as inextricably linked, and argues that female desire should be conceptualised as the 'in-between space' (after Winnicott, whose work I have discussed in the chapter on play). 'Emphasising the genderedness of embodiment,' writes Braidotti, 'Benjamin collapses the inside/outside distinction of the body. She thus attempts to replace the mediation by the phallus with the capacity for interconnectedness and agency so that desire need not be conceptualised according to the murderous logic of dialectical oppositions.' For Benjamin, as for Braidotti, something in the ontological structure of the subject is related to the presence of the other. Or, to put it differently, and to imbue this idea with Spinoza's approach, subjectivity is formed through complex and layered interconnections that need not be read as dangerous or negative, but rather can be appreciated as vital and energetic aspects of being alive together.

EVENTUALLY, THE HOUSE I SHARED WITH JO IN DARLINGTON'S Lander Street dissolved amicably, as share houses sometimes do. My brother moved down to the south coast and fell in love. Jo moved to Melbourne, and once my Masters degree was submitted, it was my turn to travel. One of my sharpest memories of my friendship with Jo is the first visit I made to her in her new share house in Melbourne's inner-city suburb of Fitzroy. I remember lying beside her on her queen-sized futon late into the night, both of us unable to sleep. We were so happy to be together again that we couldn't stop talking, even beyond exhaustion. I was conscious that night of how much I loved her, and I thought it was a shame that we weren't physically attracted to each other. Or perhaps it was a blessing. We discussed this openly. It seemed that we had an understanding and an interest in each other that was different from the kind you have with lovers. Perhaps it was more stable, we pondered, perhaps less inclined to the giddy highs and lows of romantic love. In hindsight, I don't think that was true. Such stability as there was, was imagined, and eros is never entirely absent from any vital friendship.

By the following year Jo had paid work in a field she was passionate about – art therapy in the mental health sector. She worked for a number of mental health agencies and organisations around Melbourne. There were the usual frustrations with workmates or with short-term contracts that were not renewed, but for a while it looked as though she was doing exactly what she'd always aimed to do. After hours, she wrote songs on guitar, a practice she described as 'gently developing'. Soon she'd put together a demo. Life seemed full and good, and I was happy for her.

Meanwhile, my partner and I set out on a slow journey in a four-wheel drive up the east coast of the country to the northern-most tip, then west, around the gulf across to the Kimberley. I was absorbed by Australia's breadth and depth, camping on beaches and in deep tropical gorges, rattling along in the old Land Rover along dusty back roads and minor inlets.

Jo and I wrote often.

26 September 1993

Dear Julienne

Sunny Sunday in Melbourne and yesterday we cleaned the kitchen windows so all the sun can come in now. About two weeks ago S. and I confessed to each other that were harbouring secret fantasies about spring-cleaning the house. Once this knowledge was out in the open we had no choice but to go through with it, so yesterday, S., D. and I scrubbed the walls and ceilings, polished windows and kettles and stoves, cleaned out cupboards, washed tiles (bathroom and toilet) and so it all went on for six straight hours with the help of loud music, sugar soap and hot water until we found ourselves that evening sitting rather exhausted in a sparkly house downing some hard-earned beers.

Oh, Julienne, I miss you greatly. I think of you often when I am talking with people – or when I see or hear something I know you would like. This place makes me feel happy. Most of the time I like myself in Melbourne and the people here are absolutely lovely. Real and true and good. Even so, there is this Julienne-shaped space in my heart. At this point I pledge to maintain good letter contact with you until such time arises that we inhabit the same city or town again.

Undated postcard (probably 1996):

Dearest Julienne,

Are you orright? I heard that a big cyclone went thorugh Port Hedland … did you batten down the hatches? Take shelter in the basement? Cling tightly to Toto and sing songs about the other side of rainbows while having somewhat dubious and sexually ambiguous relations with tin men, lions and scarecrows?

In 1997, increasingly disillusioned with working in the mental health sector, Jo began to put more time into her music career. She was officially a singer-songwriter and began to perform in pubs around Melbourne. Then her grandmother died and she inherited a little money. Around this time the wheels fell off once more.

I wonder sometimes what became of all the letters I sent to Jo. The only one I have is a half-finished page I never sent, for lack of fixed address:

6 November 1997

Hi Jo

I don't know if you'll get this. I'm not sure whether you're still in hospital or not. Hope the food isn't too bad. I'm not sure what to say to you. I spent some time on the phone to J. and to D., talking about having you committed. These were difficult conversations. I hope you know that it's not something people who love you can do easily. I'm sure you resent us for our unanimous agreement. Who wouldn't? It's okay to resent me, just don't do it forever.

I don't know who I'm writing to when you're in hospital, because of the drugs. I think you must be a different person, though I know you're not.

Here in Perth, the sun is shining. I've been pretty down and busy with work, so much I find it hard to daydream. They say there's a snake in the Swan River, a large serpent shape, just

outside the Old Swan Brewery. I try to imagine I can see it –
but whitefellas can't, generally.

Sometimes I hate letter writing because I can't get the tone
right …

IN A WONDERFUL SHORT ARTICLE ON THE EROS-FUELLED
friendship between Virginia Woolf and Vita Sackville-West, Rosi
Braidotti focuses on the figure of Vita as a life-giving force whose
presence, for Virginia, has a particular energy about it – 'a shim-
mering intensity, a radiance, a sense of the acceleration of life'. The
article argues for Woolf's invention of a genre like no other, one
which Braidotti labels 'intensive' and she links this intensity to the
relationship between the two women, that is, to the entanglement
of creativity and desire. Braidotti quotes from Woolf's diaries:

> Vita was here, and when she went, I began to feel the quality
> of the evening – how it was spring coming; a silver light;
> mixing with the early lamps; the cabs all rushing through the
> streets; I had a tremendous sense of life beginning; mixed with
> the emotion, which is the essence of my feeling, but escapes
> description […] I felt the spring beginning and Vita's life so
> full and flush; and all the doors opening.

During one of our meetings, I confessed to Braidotti how much I
enjoyed this article, and asked whether we might talk a little about
Woolf and Sackville-West.

'My love for Woolf!' she said, nodding approvingly.

'I wondered if you could talk a little bit about Vita as a vector
for *zoe* in Woolf's life and work.'

Before I go to Braidotti's response to this question, let's

backtrack a little and look in more detail at the terms 'vector' and 'zoe' in Braidotti's discourse. The term 'vector' is used across a range of disciplines. In maths and physics, it is generally defined as a quantity that has magnitude and direction; in biology it operates as an agent, for example, a parasite that transfers a virus from one animal to another is said to be a vector for that virus. In the philosophy of Gilles Deleuze, the term has a related but slightly different meaning. In his two books on cinema, Deleuze draws on the mathematical understanding of the term 'vector' to talk about how cinema is able to convey fluctuations or transformations of various kinds. Where there is a gap in the narrative, for example, the vector makes the connection; in this way vectors are a sign that change or transformation has occurred.

For Braidotti, Woolf's creativity is transformed by 'difference as positivity', that is, by Vita as a vector. Her writing gathers force from the potential or joyful affirmation of their open-ended interaction. Woolf's nomadic becoming – in, through and with Vita – is crucial to her creativity, her imagination, and her affectivity. Becoming, as Braidotti reminds us in this piece, has to do with 'emptying out of the self, opening it out to possible encounters with the "outside"'. ('All the doors opening.') What gets activated in Woolf's writing, argues Braidotti, is 'a fluid sensibility that is porous to the outside and which our culture has coded as "feminine". This sensibility is central to the creative process.' As Woolf puts it, 'I am rooted, but I flow.'

Braidotti argues for Woolf's 'intensive genre' as a model for 'the plane of immanence' conceptualised by Deleuze. This is a way of being conceived of as a plane or two-dimensional space in which different elements can encounter one another, producing an energy without which there could be no *becoming*. Woolf, writes Braidotti, 'expresses with stark intensity the pain involved' in attempting to gather the contradictions and differences of 'life as *zoe*, [that is] as positive vitality'. This reading is consistent with Braidotti's larger philosophical and ethical project of encouraging us 'to experiment with different modes of inhabiting subjectivity, and different ways of inhabiting our corporeality' while at the same time acknowledging the potential pain involved in genuinely intense, sometimes wildly powerful change and transformation.

In the Greek language, there are three different words which can be translated to mean 'life' – and one of these is *zoe*. For Braidotti, this notion of *zoe* or of life as a vital force is of crucial ethical importance. 'Life is half animal: *zoe* and half discursive: *bios*,' she writes. Across centuries of Western European thinking, *bios* has been thought of as the divine aspect of life, while *zoe* was seen as the baser, poorer cousin, the 'gritty' animal aspect. Braidotti argues that mind/body dualism has operated as a 'reductive shortcut' around some of the complexities surrounding the relation between *zoe* and *bios*. She argues then, for an acknowledgment (and in fact, a celebration) of *zoe* as a life force that carries on independent of agency and perhaps even regardless of rational control. '*Zoe* is impersonal and inhuman in the monstrous, animal sense of radical alterity, whereas classical philosophy is logo centric,' she writes. Braidotti's thinking privileges *zoe*, and seeks to sing its praises 'by emphasizing its active, empowering force against all negative odds'. This thinking is at the heart of her approach to the school of philosophy now known as Posthumanist. And yet, Braidotti emphasises, too, that the sheer force of *zoe*'s vitality can be negative. We can get hurt: 'It is a constant challenge for us to rise to the occasion, to catch the wave of life's intensities and ride it on, exposing the boundaries or limits as we transgress them.'

Crucially, as subjects in Braidotti's *zoe*-inflected terms, we are 'physiologically embedded in the corporeal materiality of the self' but our subjectivity is nevertheless enabled and dependent on an 'in-between: a folding-in of external influences and a simultaneous unfolding-outwards of affects'. Read with this in mind, Braidotti's article on Virginia Woolf and Vita Sackville-West is an argument for the literary text as a laboratory in which life as *zoe* is approached as a splendid complexity. Vita is a vector for *zoe* and in this way enables the canonical creative work *Orlando*.

In answer to my question about Vita and Virginia, Braidotti embarked enthusiastically on a broader conversation about Woolf's life and work.

'I have been reading Woolf since I can't even remember,' she told me. 'Her diary is an extraordinary piece. It's interesting in terms of how she organised her thought processes, because this is someone who resisted psychoanalysis. She says that if she had undergone therapy she wouldn't have written, which I believe is true. So the function of the diary is also psychoanalytic, I mean she really works things out in it and I think when Vita read some of it, when it was published, she was really upset because she thought "What a nasty woman!" But it wasn't nasty. Virginia was working things out.

'I think the best writing on Vita is in the diaries and the letters. Virginia just loved her, there's no question about it. It was eros at work, but we all know that for Virginia eros was a complicated issue. Quite clearly, Vita was quite a seductress, a bit like Proust with his boy. She was 600 years old. She's Orlando. I mean Vita was really *vita*, she was life. And I think that it was a very ambiguous, ambivalent relationship in Woolf because she needed to be in life and on the side of it. Like all writers you need to sort of watch yourself living in order to be able to report it in writing, so she was attracted and disgusted simultaneously, which would have been also the key to the rather sort of sporadic sex life. But their intimacy was well beyond the genital, although it was absolutely part of that.

'In the case of Virginia and Vita it is a real chemical transformation, whereby Woolf writes *Orlando*. It is the longest and best love letter in English literature, and Vita, I think, comes to terms with her limitations and then you know the rest of her life was not great. Vita went on to have all kinds of other relationships, but nothing ever matched that particular one. They really got each other, literally.

'So my interest in them is in that mode, and in trying to look at eros as transitive, as a sort of factor of positivity. It's something that transforms as it goes and it creates the conditions of its own sustainability but demands quite a lot of work, epistemic [that is, involving knowledge or cognition] as well as emotional. And what I thought also was very clear here is that you see sexual difference at work, with individuals that are wrongly called all the same sex. Vita and Virginia are not of the same sex. So, what are you looking at when you're looking for sexual difference? If we're talking about levels of intensities that are expressed through bodily capacities, if we're looking at what bodies can do, we have to talk like different galaxies, so the gender system really, gender is not … it does not do any justice to the complexities. It really is a post-it, a kind of a mimeograph, a kind of a cookie cutter to express socially encoded relations, but that's not what happens in intimate life. That social encoding gets thrown away. So you see this work of crafting difference as they go, and of course *Orlando* had to be, it's essentially a trans-sex act, this woman changes sexes through the ages and becomes a man and woman, not just any kind of man or woman. It's just an endless becoming. Woolf nails it!'

I like Braidotti's reading of *Orlando* very much. I like it because, while I had always thought of this particular work of

Woolf's as setting out to capture something of the impossibility of representing subjective (especially women's) experience, Braidotti's reading grounds Woolf's writing practice as, above all, relational. She works to emphasise the positivity and a vitality of the shared – in fact deeply entangled – lived experience that enabled *Orlando* to come into being at all.

JO WROTE HER FINAL LETTER TO ME TOWARDS THE END OF 1997. 'No, you're wrong,' she wrote, 'you're not homesick for Port Hedland, you're homesick for me. I'm your home.'

I wonder that I didn't find this statement overly dramatic at the time. I remember smiling about it, and thinking, 'yes, I know', because in some ways, I felt the same. Perhaps it's not such a strange idea, this idea of being at home in one another. Perhaps it is what Virginia Woolf is describing when she writes of doors opening. Therapists Susie Orbach and Louise Eichenbaum, in their book-length study of women's friendships, *Between Women*, published in the 1980s, wrote that a woman's adult relationships are 'woven with the threads of merged attachment'. This psychoanalytic approach makes the threading sound almost like an illness. Particularly since becoming a mother, I have often wondered why this whole notion of independent selfhood ever made any sense to anybody in the first place, never mind it being continually held up as the norm or the ideal. In fact it seems increasingly clear to me that, as Rosi Braidotti has argued, material reality is all about connectedness. Friendship, validated in this way, is indeed 'a play of complexity that expresses the principle of not-One', as Braidotti has put it in her article on Virginia and Vita. Such becoming or openness to the outside is not only the source of life's energy and strength; it is actually what makes life both meaningful and sustainable.

IN OCTOBER 1998, I WAS STRUGGLING TO SURVIVE MY FIRST year as an academic in Perth. I worked a twelve-hour day, leaving for work early in the morning and returning home in the dark, then marking papers for several hours in the evening. Weekends were a blur of teaching preparation, juggled alongside my own further study. I had little energy for my live-in partner, never mind for maintaining friendships. It was a bleak time.

One day, mid-week, I returned to my office at the university with lunch in hand. I had just finished teaching two tutorials back to back, and I had another to do the same afternoon. When I reached my desk, I noticed that the phone was bleating with the short, urgent tones that indicated a message on the voicemail service. The message was from R, my old boss at the University of Wollongong. 'I've got a friend of yours with me in the office,' he said. 'Her name is Jo. She heard you might be in Wollongong. I said I didn't think so, but I thought, why not give you a call and see?' There was an odd tone to R.'s voice, a suggestion that he was not completely comfortable with Jo standing there in front of him while he spoke to my message service.

I tried to picture Jo there in R.'s office on the other side of the country. I knew she was having a relapse. I knew she'd recently escaped from professional care in Melbourne. Was her hair okay? I wondered. She had a habit of pulling it out strand by strand when she was unwell. It was a form of stimming. Was she doing it as R. relayed his message?

'If you get this message in the next little while give us a call back', R. finished. According to the message service, the call had come in less than ten minutes earlier. I put the phone down.

There had been many calls back and forth across the country about Jo in the past few months, and I was tired and deeply saddened by the same old pattern. Jo's escapes no longer amused me.

She was seriously unwell and I didn't know what to do or how to make sense of it any more. I would not call back, I decided, not straight away. I picked up my lunch and walked out of the office. It was a beautiful spring day. I sat out on the grass under the pine trees and ate. In another hour, I would teach the next class, and then after that, I would call R. back. Jo would be gone by then. I knew that. Perhaps I thought I could use whatever intelligence R. could provide to try and get someone I knew in Wollongong to help her locally. Perhaps I thought I was buying myself a little reprieve, some time to gather the energy to have the conversation about her health, yet again. I still regret my lack of immediate action. In the end, my afternoon call to R. was not helpful. Jo had been careful to give nothing about her circumstances away to him.

It was only ten days after R.'s call that Jo's dead body was found in Wattle Place, in Sydney's Ultimo. Delusional and paranoid, she had been on the run by then for several weeks. Homeless and itinerant, she had taken pains not to be recognised by anyone who knew her. She had taken on a new name – Rachel Winter – and shaved off her eyebrows. Before leaving Melbourne, she had deliberately 'terminated' (her word) many of her friendships, as well her relationship with her mother. On 6 November, a Friday, she had been asleep in the shade on one of several mattresses laid out in an Ultimo back lane between rubbish bins. Some time between six and eleven in the morning, she suffered a massive blow to the head. When found by a shopkeeper, several hours later, she was already dead. She was thirty years old.

Jo's was to become one of a series of murders of homeless people sleeping rough in inner-city Sydney that year, all under similar circumstances. The following year a man was charged for one of the murders, although Jo's particular case has never been solved. The three murders – and there was a fourth in 2003 – have since been dubbed by the Sydney media as 'The Starlight Hotel Murders'. The Starlight Hotel was the name one of the victims had been known to use as a euphemism for sleeping on the streets.

Back in 1998, when I flew from Perth to Sydney for Jo's funeral, one of the first things I did was visit the site of her death. In the cool of early morning, the sun barely reached along the quiet back lane and there was no one else in sight. A little way ahead of me, where the lane formed a dog-leg, a few couches and mattresses and some plastic debris marked a makeshift camp. I edged further forward and then stood still before an alcove attached to the rear entrance of one of the shops. My heart was beating fast. I was not prepared for what happened next.

When I closed my eyes and searched for Jo, I found myself dropped very suddenly right inside her head. There was confusion amid darkness. Sudden movement. A struggle to wake up, to properly see or prepare for the dark force of the stranger. There was not even time for language to form, hardly time for breath. Only the muffled sound of movement, as with the quick, violent dance of boots on hard ground. I tried to sit up. And then: ooffgh. Nothing.

I have never felt quite so frightened. When I turned to leave the laneway, I found I could barely walk.

IN ROSI BRAIDOTTI'S MOST INFLUENTIAL BOOK, *THE POSTHUMAN* (2013), she works to crystallise much of her earlier thinking around contemporary subjectivity and the book reads to me as her most powerful and accessible work yet. In it, she underlines how important it is for us to confront the sobering idea 'of a Life that may not have "me" or any "human" at the centre'. Such thinking is crucial, she argues, to an ethics of sustainability. She also continues and extends her investigation into the conditions that may facilitate the 'thinkability of positive difference' as outlined in her article on Woolf's *Orlando*.

During our conversation in Utrecht, I asked Braidotti whether friendship is one condition that might facilitate this notion of 'positive difference'.

'Yes, if by friendship you mean a practice, a project that is never accomplished. To go back a bit, I think there is a lot of eros in friendship, as well. By eros I mean the epistemophilic curiosity: where are you at?' The term 'epistemophilic' is related to epistemophilia, that is, having a love and longing for knowledge, perhaps to the extent that we strive excessively for it. And so in choosing the phrase 'epistemophilic curiosity', Braidotti is referencing a form of curiosity motivated by this intense thirst for learning and for the recognition of some form of knowledge. Thus, the question 'where are you at?' goes well beyond a question about one's whereabouts. It becomes a question we can never fully satisfy, for all our striving. And yet we must ask it of our friends. We are driven to ask it.

At sixty, and having moved countries so many times, Braidotti remains geographically distanced from many of her very good friends. 'Friends are the people that you continuously try to keep in touch with,' she says, 'whose different moments in evolution, sometimes implosion, you try to be close to. It's hard work. My own life,' she told me, 'is in between. We will go to Australia in November and I will check on my, by now, few remaining friends, because a lot of the Australians have gone to the States. There is that kind of needing to touch base, and it's never to be taken for granted. I'm somebody who gets on planes to go to birthday parties, to go to weddings, to go soon to funerals.

'Having a good time together is more important than other things. Growing older, things change. A project I would like to do is to look at a new pattern of female friendships, at a sort of post-competitive [and post-menopausal] stage, a process influenced by years of clashes with institutions and [the competitiveness of the job market we're in]. I have experienced the 2016 presidential campaign of Hillary Clinton, for example, as a personal project. I recognise everything, I mean on a different scale, but everything that happens to her has happened to all of us as professional women. The commentary focusses on your lack of qualification, and you laugh too much, and you do that, and now … what is the latest? Oh, yes, you lack. The lack has entered the American campaign: she lacks judgment, ladies and gentlemen, says the twerp who has been in the Senate for twenty-five years saying nothing but no, the lack is in the picture. It drives me crazy. So, that recognition of what it took to confront this, and what it continues to take. I would love to do a project on the possibility of female friendship post-menopause.'

'Can we talk about an ethics of friendship?'

'That would be, in a sense, a more classical ethics. If you think of Seneca, and also of the classical Greek definition of friendship: Socrates and his students, really. The problem with the classical notion is obvious. It is very exclusionary; it is not all-inclusive. It is very, very masculine and it's very much in the realm of legal citizens: Immanuel Kant walking around town or sitting in a café reading the papers. I think the fact that it is contaminated by this, however, does not disqualify. I think it is a notion we will need to bring back in, and see how it would work in cases where there is attrition due to significant disparities in power, so negative differences. That attrition would challenge the harmonious nature of the concept. I think we have not done enough work on it. I think it is a notion that has been for one thing drowned in the binary of friend/enemy.

'I was always distressed when the left turned to that particular model, either friend or enemy. Why do that? It's so reductive, it just kills the kind of opening threshold for the function of proper friendship. There has been hospitality and that type of friendship in Derrida but always with a notion of an internal attrition due to the antagonism. It's always caught in the dialectics, in other words, and I would like to imagine a notion of friendship as openness and receptivity, connected to a Spinozist monistic ontology [the study of the nature of being, becoming, existence or reality] where openness and receptivity to others is what propels you in life, it's what moves you, it's what affects you and makes you capable of affect.

'Let's think about an affective turn in this receptive, relational mode, including the multiplicity of non-human others: machines, bacteria, air, all the non-humans to whom we are intimately connected, and to activate it in a direction of an ethics of affirmation. But it would again be a praxis: it would not be a recognition of we're all equal, elite, and *we* are the friends. I would like to redefine it as this – affective – and not deprived of potential disagreements, but not dialectically inscribed. But I think that the left is incapable of discourse on friendship, to be completely in my anti-left mode – I am a woman of the left – friend or enemies, it's just a dialectical mode. We're cramped by the dialectics. We don't seem to be able to move beyond.'

In classical philosophical terms, dialectics is a word used to describe a conventional method of argument that involves a contradictory process involving two opposing sides. Braidotti has made reference here to the way in which this very mode of thinking – a combative back and forth that strives towards linear progression as a path to evolution – can occlude new forms of understanding. To properly understand friendship, in particular, she has called here for an inclusive, receptive, relational mode of thinking, one that in foregrounding affect, takes properly into account our embodied experience. It is a speculative and therefore controversial approach to philosophy: exploratory and open. It rejects pure combativeness and duality as method. Others have criticised it for lacking in 'seriousness'.

'Immediately, such alternatives get suspected of spirituality and mysticism, which is a standard critique of monism, including of Deleuze,' Braidotti continued. 'It was Hegel's critique of Spinoza and that's, of course, a total misreading. There's nothing mystical. This is very real: embedded. It may be spiritual but it's not spiritual in the same way that Georges Bataille is spiritual. It is spiritual in recognising the vitality of matter in a relation, but not in any way transcendentalist, let alone in a Christian sort of way. So, it's a complicated one. I think we have neglected it, and there are not very many splendid examples of female friendships or post-colonial friendships. It's oppositional; our culture is oppositional more than friendly.'

Sadly, I'm afraid Braidotti is right about the tendency for so much discourse – both scholarly and public – to privilege the dialectical or 'us and them' mode, and I wonder how more of us might work to call mainstream political culture to account on this, and to do so more effectively, more often.

WHILE I WAS WRITING THIS CHAPTER, I COMMENCED A VOLUNTARY role on a not-for-profit board based in Sydney. The new role required me to travel from my home in Melbourne to Sydney four times a year, and the offices in which the board meets are situated just a few hundred metres from the site in Wattle Lane in which Jo was killed. From the windows of the hotel in which I now regularly stay, I can just see the laneway entrance.

When Jo was alive our friendship was indeed a complex to-and-fro, layered by travel and movement and illness and care, but even beyond her death, I am still open to her influence. These days I sometimes imagine a stop-and-start exchange between us about this place and that, or this person or that. In my new home town, I hear her commentary on the subtlety of Melbourne's light, or her appreciation of the sound a bike tyre makes along the city's old bluestone laneways. Since she died, I have gone on, of course, to create and dwell in different sorts of friendships, and yet I find that many friendships made later in life, in the midst of work and family commitments and against the pressures of limited time and energy, lack the fullness and positive vitality made possible by the life force – *zoe* – Jo and I had enabled in each other during our twenties.

For some time after Jo's death, I pondered her use of the pseudonym Rachel Winter. My first thought was that it might have come from the writing of Janet Frame, and the family so beautifully represented in her novel *Owls Do Cry*. Had we both studied that text at high school? I recalled the Shakespeare verse quoted in the novel:

Where the bee sucks, there suck I:
In a cowslip's bell I lie.
There I couch when owls do cry.

It is the voice of Ariel from *The Tempest*.

One day, I reread *Owls Do Cry* and discovered I had remembered the fictional family's name incorrectly. Their surname was Withers.

Later, I read about Rachel of the Bible story. Rachel is betrothed to Jacob. He works hard for seven years to win her hand, but on the night of the wedding fails to notice that beneath the veil is Leah, Rachel's sister. He has married the wrong woman. Rachel has been cruelly substituted for someone else.

Sometimes, from my Ultimo hotel room, I consider how different this part of town was when Jo and I shared our Lander Street house in the 1990s, only ten minutes away from here by foot. Wattle Lane, back then, was a narrow rear-access lane, grey and empty of pedestrians, scattered with overflowing rubbish bins and old mattresses. The 44-gallon drum that used to double as a fireplace and gathering point for the small group of homeless men on the Wattle Street corner is long gone. Wattle Lane is now home to several bright new multi-storey apartment buildings aimed at the lucrative student-accommodation market. Balconies filled with plants and clothes-airers look over the laneway, and a fairly constant stream of students attending the nearby University of Sydney and UTS Broadway campuses walk the lane, day and night. This part of the city has re-invented itself, as inner-city spaces so often do.

One morning en route to the board meeting, I pass a young homeless woman sitting cross-legged on an Ultimo footpath and I stop. The woman is not Jo, but between us an energy drifts and when I look into her eyes I am overwhelmed by her loneliness. I put all the cash I have into her upturned woollen hat. The smile the woman gives me is both too much and not enough, and I remember Braidotti's phrase about friendship as a praxis, as a project that has no end. I walk away from the seated woman with tears flowing.

Without openness, without relation, what have we, I wonder? Spinoza, on the way to his theory of monism, contemplated three numbers: zero, infinity and one. In an important sense, there is no difference between each of those figures.

I now look back at the movement – the nomadism – that formed such an integral part of my relationship with Jo and I consider that strange dance from one city to another and one country to another that we each engaged in as an integral aspect of what developed between us. Sackville-West and Woolf, too, came and went, came and went from one another's physical presence. It could not be otherwise. There is a link here, I think, back to Braidotti's last days in Italy as a fifteen year old. Perhaps there was something about that putting on the train – even as it was and perhaps remains steeped in grief and shock – that oriented Braidotti towards her life's work of 'rethinking the lived processes of existence'. While, like Braidotti, I have come to understand that identity formation is a collective project, it seems in some ways an understanding enabled in and through movement and upheaval, in and through the ever-present prospect of separation, whether forced or choreographed. Does this kind of movement somehow make more visible to us the idea that 'life may not have "me" or any "human" at the centre'?

Even through all this looking back at myself and Jo, there remains something about Rosi Braidotti's approach to the philosophy of friendship that continues to call me to attention. The conditions in which we now find ourselves are complex and challenging, Braidotti argues, and so she urges us to think 'critically and creatively about who and what we are actually in the process of becoming'. Importantly, Braidotti urges us all to be *worthy* of the present, and perhaps in and through that attention, to equip ourselves and one another for that which is yet to come. Her robustly central concern, her ongoing argument, is that the self-other dialectic needs to be radically displaced and reconfigured so that we can begin to see ourselves in relation rather than in opposition to one another. For Braidotti, relationality is exactly where our potential for transformation lies. It is a form of thinking that may be crucial to survival in the midst of the environmental catastrophe that is climate change. It is a thinking at home in multiplicity, open-doored-ness, the sheer force of vitality (*zoe*), and the very site of our curiosity about limits: friendship. Where are you at? We so clearly need to keep asking one another – human and non-human – this powerful question.

Notes

Epigraph

think we must: Woolf, Virginia. 'Three Guineas'. 1938. In *Women's Political and Social Thought*, eds Hilda L. Smith, Berenice A Carroll, Indiana UP, 2000, p. 342.

Chapter One: Love

kind of grace: O'Connor, Flannery. *Mystery and Manners: Occasional Prose*. Farrar, Straus and Giroux, 1969.

the realm of sleep: Barthes, Roland. *A Lover's Discourse: Fragments*. Translated by Richard Howard, Farrar, Straus and Giroux, 1978, p. 126.

an essay she published: Kipnis, Laura. 'Adultery'. *Critical Inquiry*, vol. 24, no. 2, 1998, pp. 289–327.

Against Love: Kipnis, Laura. *Against Love*. Random House, 2003.

her first book: Kipnis, Laura. *Bound and Gagged: Pornography and the Politics of Fantasy in America*. Duke UP, 1999.

a later publication: Kipnis, Laura. *How to Become a Scandal: Adventures in Bad Behavior*. Henry Holt, 2010.

her most recent: Kipnis, Laura. *Unwanted Advances*. HarperCollins, 2017.

only a handful of words: Kipnis, Laura. Personal interview. 7 Jan. 2014.

who would dream: *Against Love*, p. 3.

two influential books: Marcuse, Herbert. *Eros and Civilization*. 1955. The Marcuse Internet Archive; *One Dimensional Man*. 1964. The Marcuse Internet Archive <www.marxists.org/reference/archive/marcuse/index.htm>.

we all know that Good Marriages: *Against Love*, p. 18.

Wilhelm Reich: Reich, Wilhelm. *Mass Psychology of Fascism*. Translated by Vincent R Carfagno, Farrar, Straus and Giroux, 1970.

several reviewers: See, for example, Cox, Ted. 'Why work at marriage when adultery is so much easier?' *Daily Herald*. 28 Oct. 2003.

I think so: Kipnis, Laura. Personal interview. 7 Jan. 2014.

shuttle between two:. 'Adultery', p. 304.

man watches TV: *Against Love*, p. 103.

secular society needed: *Against Love*, p. 103.

Yes. It's huge: Kipnis, Laura. Personal interview. 7 Jan. 2014.

I kind of think: Kipnis, Laura. Personal interview. 7 Jan. 2014.

the best of Kipnis's: Schwartz, Madeleine. 'The People vs. Laura Kipnis'. 'Review of *Men: Notes from an Ongoing Investigation* by Laura Kipnis'. *Dissent*, Winter 2015, www.dissentmagazine.com.

let's hear it: Kipnis, Laura. *The Female Thing: Dirt, Sex, Envy, Vulnerability*. Random House, 2006, p. 14.

what offers greater regulation: *Against Love*, p. 93.

Discipline and Punish: Foucault, Michel. 1975. *Discipline and Punish: The Birth of the Prison*. Trans. Alan Sheridan, Random House, 1995.

you can't leave the house: *Against Love*, pp. 84–92.

I did interview: Kipnis, Laura. Personal interview. 7 Jan. 2014.

the all-subsuming, all-organising: Tanner, Tony. *Adultery in the Novel: Contract and Transgression*. John Hopkins UP, 1979, p. 15.

Marriage, a History: Coontz, Stephanie. *Marriage, a History: How Love Conquered Marriage*. Penguin, 2005.

we were two of a kind: de Beauvoir, quoted in Appignanesi, Lisa. 'Did Simone de Beauvoir's Open Marriage Make Her Happy?' *The Guardian*, 10 Jun. 2005, <www.theguardian.com/world/2005/jun/10/gender.politicsphilosophyandsociety>

The Second Sex: de Beauvoir, Simone. *The Second Sex*. 1949. Translated H.M. Parshley, New English Library, 1970.

now widely agreed: See, for example, the discussion of de Beauvoir's contribution to philosophy in Sarah Bakewell's *At the Existentialist Café: Freedom, Being and Apricot Cocktails*. Vintage, 2016.

we … feel like failures: Kipnis, Laura. 'Love in the Twenty-First Century: Against Love.' The *New York Times Magazine*, 14 Oct. 2001, <www.nytimes.com/2001/10/14/magazine/love-in-the-21st-century-against-love.html>

the anti-love story: *Against Love*, pp. 97–99.

this place with no laws: Cixous, Hélène. *Three Steps on the Ladder of Writing*. Columbia UP, p. 59.

it's not that we … don't register: 'Adultery,' p. 304.

what you read really does influence: Joyce Goodfellow, quoted in Forster, Penny and Imogen Sutton. *Daughters of de Beauvoir*. Women's Press, 1989. p. 6.

it was post-industrialism: Kipnis, Laura. 'The State of the Unions: Should This Marriage be Saved?' *New York Times*, 25 Jan. 2004, <www.nytimes.com/2004/01/25/opinion/the-state-of-the-unions-should-this-marriage-be-saved.html>

the great disruption: Fukuyama, Francis. *The Great Disruption: Human Nature and the Reconstitution of Social Order*. Touchstone, 2000.

we live in sexually interesting times: *Against Love*, p. 11.

I get the sense: Kipnis, Laura. Personal interview. 7 Jan. 2014.

there are degrees: Kipnis, Laura. Personal interview. 7 Jan. 2014.

experiencing utopia: *Against Love*, p. 40.

like Soma in *Brave:* *Against Love*, p. 40.

how people negotiate: Kofman, Lee. *The Dangerous Bride*. U Melbourne P, 2014, p. 36.

I should probably declare: Kofman, Lee. Personal interview. 29 Apr. 2017.

Chapter Two: Play

to be playful is to: Paraphrased from 'play, v.' *OED Online*. Oxford UP, July 2018, <www.oed.com/view/Entry/145475> Accessed 31 October 2018

early play theorist Johan Huizinga: Huizinga, Johan. 1949. *Homo Ludens*. Routledge and Kegan Paul, 2001.

Miguel Sicart: Sicart, Miguel. *Play Matters*. MIT P, 2014.

first and perhaps most important: Government of Western Australia, Department of Health. 'Child Development 0–3 Months.' Child and Adolescent Health Service, 2008.

children must acquire: Hustvedt, Siri. *The Shaking Woman or A History of My Nerves*. Sceptre, 2010, p. 92.

her bestselling fourth novel: Hustvedt, Siri. *What I Loved*. Sceptre, 2003.

so many forms of human endeavour: Hustvedt, Siri. Personal interview. 8 Jan. 2014.

for Winnicott, every human: Hustvedt, Siri. Personal interview. 8 Jan. 2014.

Playing and Reality: Winnicott, D[onald] W. *Playing and Reality*. Tavistock, 1971.

The Piggle: Winnicott, D[onald] W. *The Piggle: An Account of the Psychoanalytic Treatment of a Little Girl*. Hogarth Press, 1971.

no human being is free: Winnicott, D[onald] W. 'Transitional objects and transitional phenomena.' *International Journal of Psychoanalysis*, vol. 34, 1953, p. 96.

The Magic Years: Fraiberg, Selma H. *The Magic Years: Understanding and Handling the Problems of Early Childhood*. Charles Scribner, 1959.

her first novel: Hustvedt, Siri. *The Blindfold*. Henry Holt, 1993.

Winnicott talks about adults: Hustvedt, Siri. Personal interview. 8 Jan 2014.

The Sorrows: Hustvedt, Siri. *The Sorrows of an American*. Henry Holt, 2008.

Lavinia in Slovenia: *The Sorrows of an American*, pp. 94–95.

art is essentially intersubjective: Hustvedt, Siri. Personal interview. 8 Jan. 2014.

there is overwhelming evidence: Hustvedt, Siri. Personal interview. 8 Jan. 2014.

when I was a child: Hustvedt, Siri. Personal interview. 8 Jan. 2014.

a new formation: Vygotsky, L(ev) S. 'Play and its Role in the Mental Development of the Child.' 1933. Translated by Catherine Mulholland, 2002. *Lev Vygotsky Archive*, <www.marxists.org/archive/vygotsky/>, par. 16.

the child is free: Vygotsky, ibid., par. 33.

most commercially successful novel: Hustvedt, Siri. *What I Loved*. Sceptre, 2003.

I found the motion: *What I Loved*, p. 146.

what is it: *What I Loved*, p. 352.

in his book: Sicart, ibid.

in an interesting review: Michael deAnda, 'Review of *Play Matters*.' *American Journal of Play*, Winter 2015, p. 254.

Nina Huntemann and Mia Consalvo: deAnda, Michael, p. 254.

The Blazing World: Hustvedt, Siri. *The Blazing World*. Hodder and Stoughton, 2014.

a cock and a pair: *The Blazing World*, p. 1.

the opposite of play: Brown, Stuart. *Play*. Penguin, 2009, p. 126.

I thought of a novel: Scott, John. *The Architect*. Penguin, 2001.

it used to be: Hustvedt, Siri. Personal interview. 16 Jan. 2014.

we feel that something: Robert Fagen, quoted in Brian Sutton-Smith. *The Ambiguity of Play*. Harvard UP, 2001, p. 2.

this is really fascinating: Hustvedt, Siri. Personal interview. 16 Jan. 2014.

Hustvedt quoted Einstein: Hustvedt, Siri. Personal interview. 16 Jan. 2014.

the shaking woman felt: Hustvedt, Siri. *The Shaking Woman or A History of My Nerves*. Sceptre, 2010, p. 7.

I seem to translate: *The Shaking Woman*, p. 117.

in one essay: Hustvedt, Siri. Personal interview, 16 Jan. 2014.

in her essay 'Freud's Playground': Hustvedt, Siri. 'Freud's Playground.' *Salmagundi*, no. 174–5, Spring–Summer 2012, pp. 59–78.

this is a nice place: Hustvedt, Siri. Personal interview. 16 Jan. 2014.

they were both human actors: *The Shaking Woman*, p. 134.

it is important to understand: Hustvedt, Siri. Personal interview. 16 Jan. 2014

deep bodily metaphors: See George Lakoff and Mark Johnson. *Metaphors We Live By*. 1980. U Chicago P, 2003.

I wrote a short essay: Hustvedt, Siri. 'Underground Sexism: What Was That You Just Said?' in Appignanesi, Lisa, Rachel Holmes and Susie Orbach, eds., *Fifty Shades of Feminism*, Hachette Digital, 2013.

we live in a culture: Hustvedt, Siri. Personal interview. 16 Jan. 2014.

researchers I spoke to: For a fuller discussion of this research project, see van Loon, Julienne. 'In defense of play: a manifesto arrived at through dialogues' in James Oliver, ed., *Associations: Creative Practice and Research*. Melbourne UP, 2018, pp. 149–157.

I think of play: Hustvedt, Siri. Personal interview. 8 Jan. 2014.

there was a girl: Hustvedt, Siri. Personal interview. 8 Jan. 2014.

Chapter Three: Work

to call labour power a commodity: 'Sex, Work and Capitalism', par. 19.

essentially a legal fiction: Holmstrom, Nancy. 'Sex, Work and Capitalism'. *Logos*, vol. 13, nos. 2–3, 2014, par. 19. <logosjournal.com/2014/holmstrom/>.

Capitalism, For and Against: Ann E. Cudd and Nancy Holmstrom, *Capitalism, For and Against: A Feminist Debate.* Cambridge UP, 2011.

wherever my labour power goes: 'Sex, Work and Capitalism', par. 19.

very different values: *Capitalism, For and Against*, p. 259.

it is time to reject: *Capitalism, For and Against*, p. 252.

obtained by asking: Ayto, John. *Dictionary of Word Origins*. A. & C. Black, 2002, p. 408.

depending on: *Dictionary of Word Origins*, p. 408.

do individuals own: *Capitalism, For and Against*, p. 156.

by capitalism: *Capitalism, For and Against*, p. 6.

income inequality: Piketty, Thomas. *Capital in the Twenty-first Century*. Translated by Arthur Goldhammer, Harvard UP, 2014.

sharp distinction between: *Capitalism, For and Against*, p. 7.

sixty per cent: *Capital in the Twenty-first Century*, p. 297.

incubator of ideas: *Capitalism, For and Against*, p. 4.

private ownership: *Capitalism, For and Against*, p. 6.

but the structure: *Capitalism, For and Against*, p. 199.

more importantly: Holmstrom, Nancy. Personal interview. 5 Jan. 2015.

what is the prostitute: 'Sex, Work and Capitalism', par. 29.

emotional labour: Hochschild, Arlie. *The Managed Heart.* University of California Press, Berkeley CA. 2012.

freedom is always relative: 'Sex, Work and Capitalism', par. 8.

sexual services cannot: 'Sex, Work and Capitalism', par. 8.

the original site of emotions: 'Sex, Work and Capitalism', par. 32.

the fiction at the heart: 'Sex, Work and Capitalism', par. 35.

an appendage of the machine: *Capitalism, For and Against,* p. 206.

it gets into everything: *Capitalism, For and Against,* p. 206.

my father was: Holmstrom, Nancy. Personal interview. 5 Jan. 2015.

I think it was in graduate school: Holmstrom, Nancy. Personal interview. 9 Jan. 2015.

the later work: Marx, Karl. *Capital: Volume 1.* 1867, Translated by Samuel Moore and Edward Aveling, <www.marxists.org/archive/marx/works/1867-c1>.

two souls: Draper, Hal. 'The Two Souls of Socialism'. *New Politics*, vol. 5, no. 1, Winter 1966, pp. 57–84.

the influence of Christian doctrines: See Svendsen, Lars Fredrik. *Work.* Acumen, 2008.

Max Weber: Weber, Max. 'The Protestant Ethic and the Spirit of Capitalism'. 1904–05. *Essays in Economic Sociology.* Ed. Richard Swedberg, Princeton UP, 1999, p. 2.

perennial nobleness: Carlyle, Thomas. *Past and Present.* 1843. New York UP, 1977, p. 122.

sacred halo: Lafargue, Paul. *The Right to Be Lazy.* 1883. Translated by Charles Kerr, *Lafargue Internet Archive*, 2000, <www.marxists.org/archive/lafargue/1883/lazy/index.htm>.

a survey conducted in 2013: Jump, Paul. 'Work and other labours of love'. *Times Higher Education Supplement*, 6 June 2013, <www.timeshighereducation.com>.

the creative class: Florida, Richard. *The Rise of the Creative Class.* Basic Books, 2002.

why do we work: Weeks, Kathi. *The Problem with Work.* Duke UP, 2011, p. 1.

we often experience: *The Problem with Work*, p. 3.

material inequalities … are also: *Capitalism, For and Against,* p. 194.

Cruel Optimism: Berlant, Lauren. *Cruel Optimism.* Duke UP, 2011.

affective attachment: *Cruel Optimism*, p. 27.

ride the wave: *Cruel Optimism*, p. 28.

cruel optimism afflicts the colleague: Warner, Marina. 'Learning my Lesson'. *London Review of Books*, 19 Mar. 2015, <www.lrb.co.uk/v37/n06/marina-warner/learning-my-lesson>.

neither take hire nor give hire: *Capitalism, For and Against,* p. 157.

either by oppression or murder or theft: *Capitalism, For and Against,* p. 157.

substantive and robust: Drabinski, Kate. Review of *Capitalism, For and Against* by Ann E. Cudd and Nancy Holmstrom. *Marx and Philosophy*, 29 June 2011. <www.marxandphilosophy.org.uk/reviewofbooks/reviews/2011/341>.

until England is free: *Capitalism, For and Against,* p. 157.

buried, literally and metaphorically: Duran, Jane. *Eight Women Philosophers.* U Illinois P, 2006, p. 14.

I did analytic philosophy: Holmstrom, Nancy. Personal interview. 9 Jan. 2015.

the challenge to come: *Capitalism, For and Against,* p. 318.

Chapter Four: Fear

there is no emotion: Montaigne, Michel de. *The Complete Essays*. Translated by
M.A. Screech, Penguin, 1993. p. 81.

bother your head: Bakewell, Sarah. *How to Live: A Life of Montaigne in One Question
and Twenty Attempts at an Answer.* Kindle ed., Vintage, 2011, loc. 550.

a number of scholarly studies: See Stanko, Elizabeth A. 'Women, Crime and Fear.'
The Annals of the American Academy of Political and Social Science, vol. 539, 1995,
pp. 43–58.

more recent research: See 'Women, Crime and Fear.'

the latest statistics: Our Watch. 'Understanding Violence: Facts and Figures.'
<ourwatch.org.au> Accessed 8 Jan. 2016.

almost twice as likely: Australian Institute of Family Studies. 'Child Abuse and Neglect
Statistics: CFCS Resource Sheet'. Australian Government, Oct. 2016, <aifs.gov.
au/cfca/publications/child-abuse-and-neglect-statistics>.

fail to participate: Wesely, Jennifer K. and Emily Gaarder. 'The Gendered Nature of the
Urban Outdoors.' *Gender and Society*, vol. 18, no. 5, 2004, pp. 645–663.

in a state of change: McAfee, Noëlle. *Julia Kristeva*. Kindle ed., Routledge, 2004,
loc. 177.

'Stabat Mater': Kristeva, Julia and Arthur Goldhammer. 'Stabat Mater'. *Poetics Today*,
vol. 6, no. 1–2, 1985, pp. 133–152.

I plant my feet: Kristeva and Goldhammer, ibid, p. 141.

Powers of Horror: Kristeva, Julia. *Powers of Horror*. Translated by Leon S Rudiez,
Columbia UP, 1982.

"I" want none of that: *Powers of Horror*, p. 3.

she published her autobiography: Batty, Rosie and Bryce Corbett. *A Mother's Story*.
Kindle ed., Harper Collins, 2015.

I tried to stop him: Batty and Corbett, loc. 2405.

the dad hit the boy: Batty and Corbett, loc. 3575.

in perpetual danger: *Powers of Horror*, p. 9.

oft-cited examples: *Alien*. Dir. Ridley Scott. Twentieth Century Fox, 1979.

biological freaks: Creed, Barbara. *The Monstrous-Feminine: Film, Feminism,
Psychoanalysis*. Routledge, 2007, p. 6.

literally a monster: Aristotle quoted in Ussher, Jane. *Managing the Monstrous Feminine:
Regulating the Female Body*. Routledge, 2006, p. 1.

as much airtime: Hogan, J. Michael and Sarah Ann Mehltretter. 'Helen Caldicott,
"Stop the Nuclear Madness" (17 April 1986)'. *Voices of Democracy: The US Oratory
Project*, vol. 3, 2008.

in her autobiography: Caldicott, Helen. *A Passionate Life*. Random House, 1996.

I remember the hair: Caldicott, Helen. Personal interview. 10 Nov. 2015.

she read the novel: Shute, Nevil. 1957. *On the Beach*. Vintage, 2009.

the image of the people of Melbourne: *A Passionate Life*, p. 1.

I guess I was frightened: Caldicott, Helen. Personal interview. 10 Nov. 2015.

disturbing body of knowledge: See, for example, the following titles written and/
or edited by Helen Caldicott: *Missile Envy: The Arms Race and Nuclear War*,
Bantam, 1985; *If You Love This Planet*, WW Norton, 1992; *Nuclear Power Is
Not the Answer*, New Press, 2006; *Loving This Planet: Leading Thinkers Talk*

about How to Make a Better World, New Press, 2012; *Crisis Without End: The Medical and Ecological Consequences of the Fukushima Nuclear Catastrophe*, New Press, 2014.

not without controversy: See, for example, Paul Boyer. *Fallout: A Historian Reflects on America's Half-century with Nuclear Weapons*. Ohio State UP, 1998.

a totally appropriate response: Caldicott, Helen. Personal interview. 10 Nov. 2015.

fear is utterly central: Hobbes, quoted in Blits, Jan H. 'Hobbesian Fear'. *Political Theory*, vol. 7, no. 3, 1989, pp. 417–431.

an attack on her reputation: See, for example, Monbiot, George. 'Nuclear opponents have a moral duty to get their facts right.' *The Guardian*, 14 Apr. 2011, <www.theguardian.com/environment/georgemonbiot/2011/apr/13/anti-nuclear-lobby-interrogate-beliefs>.

other environmental-science journalists: Green, Jim. 'What is the Chernobyl deathtoll?' *Green Left Weekly*, no. 877, 16 Apr. 2011, <www.greenleft.org.au/content/what-chernobyl-death-toll>.

used to work against you: Caldicott, Helen. Personal interview. 10 Nov. 2015.

a difficult few days: Batty, quoted in Price, Jenna. 'Mark Latham needs to stop his unfair, rage-fuelled attacks on Rosie Batty'. The *Sydney Morning Herald*. 2 Nov. 2016, <www.smh.com.au/lifestyle/mark-latham-needs-to-stop-his-unfair-ragefuelled-attacks-on-rosie-batty-20161102-gsfxef.html>.

when I was very young: Caldicott, Helen. Personal interview. 12 Nov. 2015.

using pornography to encourage: Jeffreys, Sheila. 'Double Jeopardy: Women, the US military and the war in Iraq'. *Women's Studies International Forum*, vol. 30, 2007, pp. 16–25.

more pronounced maternal behaviour: See, for example, Marlin, Bianca J. et al. 'Oxytocin enables maternal behaviour by balancing cortical inhibition'. *Nature*, vol. 520, no. 7548, 23 Apr. 2015, pp. 499–504, doi: <10.1038/nature14402>.

hormonal responses: Trainor, Brian C. et al. 'Sex differences in hormonal responses to social conflict in the monogamous mouse'. *Hormones and Behaviour*, vol. 58, no. 3, 2010, pp. 506–512, doi: <10.1016/j.yhbeh.2010.04.008>

men and violence: Niehoff, Debra. 'Not Hard Wired: The Complex Neurobiology of Sex Difference in Violence'. *Violence and Gender*, vol. 1, no.1, 2014, pp. 19–24.

why the hell: Caldicott, Helen. Personal interview. 12 Nov. 2015.

there looms, within abjection: Kristeva, Julia. *Powers of Horror: An Essay on Abjection*. Translated by Leon S. Roudiez, Columbia UP, 1982, p. 1.

not me: *Powers of Horror*, p. 2.

power as a force: See Ann J. Cahill. 'The Phenomenology of Fear'. *The Feminist Philosophy Reader*. Eds Alison Bailey and Chris Cuomo. McGraw Hill, 2008, p. 813.

likely to carry themselves: 'The Phenomonology of Fear', p. 810.

woman follows man: Batty and Corbett, loc. 1263.

a public forum: 'On Julia Kristeva's Couch'. *25th Chicago Humanities Festival*. 13 Oct. 2013. <www.stitcher.com/podcast/chicago-humanities-festival-podcast/e/on-julia-kristevas-couch>.

according to Kant: Card, Claudia. 'Kant's Theory of Radical Evil'. *The Atrocity Paradigm*. Oxford Scholarship Online, 2002.

we cannot conceive: Hannah Arendt, quoted in Bernstein, Richard J. 'Reflections on radical evil: Arendt and Kant'. *Soundings*, vol. 85, no. 1–2, 2002, p. 17.

a beautiful passage: Kristeva, Julia. *New Maladies of the Soul*. Translated by Ross Guberman, Columbia UP, 1995.

the only reason: Batty and Corbett, loc. 222.

we nearly got there: Caldicott, Helen. Personal interview. 10 Nov. 2015.

other people say: Caldicott, Helen. Personal interview. 10 Nov. 2015.

temporality of fear: Martin Heidegger, quoted in Lars Fredrik Svendsen. *A Philosophy of Fear*. Translated by John Irons. Reaktion Books, 2008, p. 43.

international crime victims survey: Yodanis, Carrie L. 'Gender Inequality, Violence against Women, and Fear'. *Journal of Interpersonal Violence*, vol. 19, no. 6, 2004, p. 655.

Chapter Five: Wonder

why do ladies: Warner, Marina. 'Contradictory Curiosity'. *Curiosity: Art and the Pleasure of Knowing*. Hayman Publishing, 2013, p. 31.

Alice *falls* down: 'Contradictory Curiosity', p. 25.

the first of her essays: Warner, Marina. 'Out of an Old Toy Chest'. *Journal of Aesthetic Education*, vol. 43, no. 2, 2009, p. 3–18.

where is the soul?: Baudelaire, quoted in Warner, 'Out of an Old Toy Chest', p. 3.

curious by mistake: 'Contradictory Curiosity', p. 32.

descended from a long line: Warner, Marina. *Signs and Wonders: Essays on Literature and Culture*. Vintage, 2003, p. 298.

beautiful and voluptuous: *Signs and Wonders*, p. 301.

her first biography: Warner, Marina. *The Dragon Empress*. 1972, Vintage, 1993.

a cultural biography: Warner, Marina. *Alone of All Her Sex: The Myth and the Cult of the Virgin Mary*. Vintage, 1976.

on Joan of Arc: Marina Warner. *Joan of Arc: The Image of Female Heroism*. Vintage, 1981.

a key early influence: Ardener, Shirley. *Perceiving Women*. Halsted, 1975.

I became very interested: Warner, Marina. Personal interview, 3 Jul. 2014.

Reith Lecture series: Warner, Marina. *Managing Monsters: Six Myths of Our Time*. Vintage, 1994.

a major book: Warner, Marina. *Stranger Magic: Charmed States and the Arabian Nights*. Chatto & Windus, 2011.

the technique of the book: Moog, Nina. 'The Rumpus Interview with Marina Warner'. *The Rumpus,* 17 Oct. 2012, <therumpus.net/2012/10/the-rumpus-interview-with-marina-warner/>.

she's telling stories: Warner, Marina. Personal interview, 3 Jul. 2014.

the first of the passions: Warner, Marina. Personal interview, 3 Jul. 2014.

curiouser and curiouser: Carroll, Lewis. 1865. *Alice's Adventures in Wonderland*. Penguin, 1998, p. 6.

the great questioner: Warner, Marina. Personal interview, 3 Jul. 2014.

Thomas Aquinas posited: quoted in Vasalou, Sophia. *Wonder: A Grammar*. SUNY, 2015, p. 52.

a form of vulnerability: Vasalou, p. 72.

her essay: 'St Paul: Let women be silent'. *Signs and Wonders*, pp. 55–63.

intrepid, unstoppable: *Signs and Wonders*, p. 59.

let the women: quoted in *Signs and Wonders*, p. 59.

the paradox: Warner, Marina. Personal interview. 3 Jul. 2014.

some Antipodean literature: Frame, Janet. *Owls Do Cry*. 1961, The Women's Press, 1985; Anderson, Jessica. *Tirra Lirra By the River*. Penguin, 1980; Winton, Tim. *An Open Swimmer*. Allen & Unwin, 1982.

wonder is enchantment: Warner, Marina. Personal interview. 3 Jul. 2014.

the prettiest undergraduate: Wroe, Nicholas. 'Absolutely Fabulist.' *The Guardian*, 21 Jan. 2000, <www.theguardian.com/books/2000/jan/22/history>.

two essays: Warner, Marina. 'Diary: Why I Quit'. *London Review of Books*, vol. 36, no. 17, 11 Sept. 2014, pp. 42–43; Warner, Marina. 'Learning My Lesson'. *London Review of Books*, vol. 37, no. 6, 19 Mar. 2015, pp. 8–14.

we go to poetry: Seamus Heaney quoted in 'Learning My Lesson'. p. 5.

good knowledge: 'Learning My Lesson,' p. 5.

honestly difficult: Bernard Williams quoted in 'Learning My Lesson'. p. 5.

all men [sic] begin: Aristotle quoted in Vasalou, p. 57.

I always had: Walwicz, Ania. 'Little Red Riding Hood.' *Overland*. No. 74, 1979, p. 26.

essay on botanical artist Maria Sibylla Merian: Warner, Marina. 'Hatching'. *Fantastic Metamorphoses, Other Worlds: Ways of Telling the Self*. Kindle ed., Oxford UP, 2002, loc.1243–1881.

Metamorphosis insectorum Surinamensium: Merian, Maria Sybilla. *Metamorphosis insectorum Surinamensium*. 1705. National Library of the Netherlands, 2016.

there were elements: Warner, Marina. Personal interview. 10 Jul. 2014.

thaumazein: Vasalou, p. 86.

admiratio: Vasalou, p. 86.

awakening the mind: Wordsworth quoted in Vasalou, p. 82.

miraculousness of the common: Emerson quoted in Vasalou, p. 114.

leaving a paper trail: Vasalou, p. 82.

the most neglected: Fisher, Philip. *Wonder, the Rainbow and the Aesthetics of Rare Experiences*. Harvard UP, 2003, p. 2.

emerges as an emotion: Vasalou, p. 19.

too slippery: Vasalou, p. 20.

the association of magical power: *Signs and Wonders*, p. 392.

argued elsewhere: van Loon, Julienne. 'Where do writers get their ideas from?' *Sydney Review of Books*. 8 Mar. 2017, <sydneyreviewofbooks.com/where-do-writers-get-their-ideas-from/>.

getting lost: Kim Scott quoted in Wood, Charlotte. *The Writer's Room*. Allen and Unwin, 2016, p. 344.

an emotion or movement: Smith, Adam. 'The History of Anatomy.' *Essays on Philosophical Subjects*. Eds WPD Wightman and JC Boyce. Clarendon, 1980, p. 39.

on a stand: Warner, Marina. Personal interview. 10 Jul. 2014.

when Rousseau and Locke: Warner, Marina. Personal interview. 10 Jul. 2014.

Dawkins' dislike: Warner's reference is to Dawkins, Richard. *Unweaving the Rainbow: Science, Delusion and the Appetite for Wonder*. Mariner, 2000.

open sea: Mary-Jane Rubenstein, quoted in Vasalou, p. 56.

Chapter Six: Friendship

you've got to be: Braidotti, Rosi. Personal interview. 7 Apr. 2016.

when I look back: Braidotti, Rosi. Personal interview. 7 Apr. 2016.

transform the lives: Fradinger, Moira. Introduction to the Tanner Lecture 'Memoirs of a Posthumanist' by Rosi Braidotti, 1 March 2017, Yale University. <www.youtube.com/watch?v=OjxelMWLGCo>

rethinking the living processes: Braidotti, Rosi. *Nomadic Subjects: Embodiment and Sexual Difference in Contemporary Feminist Theory*. Second edition, Columbia UP, 2011, p. 274.

Patterns of Dissonance: Braidotti, Rosi. *Patterns of Dissonance*. Polity, 1991.

Nomadic Subjects: Braidotti, Rosi. *Nomadic Subjects: Embodiment and Sexual Difference in Contemporary Feminist Theory*. Columbia UP, 1994.

the motivation to explore: Braidotti, Rosi. 'Writing as a Nomadic Subject'. Transcript of a presentation given at Oxford University, May 2013, p. 1.

an ideal of bodily perfection: Braidotti, Rosi. *The Posthuman*. Polity, 2013, p. 13.

Metamorphoses: Braidotti, Rosi. *Metamorphoses: Towards a Materialist Theory of Becoming*. Polity, 2002.

Transpositions: Braidotti, Rosi. *Transpositions: On Nomadic Ethics*. Polity, 2006.

her more recent books: Braidotti, Rosi. *The Posthuman*. Polity, 2013; Braidotti, Rosi and Maria Hlavajova (eds). *Posthuman Glossary*. Bloomsbury, 2018.

a play of complexity: Braidotti, Rosi. 'Intensive Genre and the Demise of Gender'. *Angelaki*, vol. 13, no. 2, 2008, p. 46.

written elsewhere: van Loon, Julienne. 'In Broad Daylight', *Just Between Us: Australian Women Tell the Truth about Friendship*. Edited by Maya Linden et al, Pan Macmillan, 2013. pp. 35–56.

joyfully discontinuous subject: 'Intensive Genre and the Demise of Gender', p. 46.

she always escaped: Ray Franklin quoted in Crawford, Barclay. 'Anger, grief, but daughter's murder no surprise'. The *Australian*, 20 Nov. 1998, p. 6.

learning to love: Nietzsche, Friedrich. *The Gay Science*. 1910. Translated by Thomas Common. Dover, 2006.

we meet and this is it: Braidotti, Rosi. Personal interview. 3 Apr. 2016.

Ethics: Spinoza, Benedict de. *Ethics*. 1677. Translated by Edwin Curley, Penguin, 2005.

even then, his friends: Scruton, Roger. *A Short Introduction to Spinoza*. Oxford UP, 2002.

absence of any reference: Braidotti, Rosi. *The Posthuman*. Columbia UP, 2013, p. 56.

we are structurally connected: Braidotti, Rosi. Personal interview. 13 Apr. 2016.

things that I considered symbolically very important: Braidotti, Rosi. Personal interview. 3 Apr. 2016.

the philosophy of otherness: Braidotti, Rosi. Personal interview. 13 Apr. 2016.

Jacques Lacan: 'Jacques Lacan'. *Stanford Encyclopedia of Philosophy*. 2 Apr. 2013, Rev. 10 Jul. 2018, <plato.stanford.edu/entries/lacan/#OthOedComSex>.

Luce Irigaray: See, for example, Irigaray, Luce. *An Ethics of Sexual Difference*. 1984. Translated by Carolyn Burke and Gillian C. Gill, Cornell UP, 1993.

the genderedness of embodiment: *Nomadic Subjects*, second edition, p. 131.

Vita was here: Woolf quoted in Braidotti, Rosi, *Nomadic Theory: The Portable Rosi Braidotti*. Columbia UP, 2011, p. 157.

My love for Woolf!: Braidotti, Rosi. Personal interview. 13 Apr. 2016.

in his two books on cinema: Discussed in, for example, Colman, Felicity. *Deleuze and Cinema*. Berg, 2011.

emptying out of the self: *Nomadic Theory*, p. 152.

a fluid sensibility: *Nomadic Theory*, p. 152.

plane of immanence: *Nomadic Theory*, p. 155.

different modes of inhabiting subjectivity: Braidotti, Rosi. 'The Ethics of Becoming Imperceptible'. *Deleuze and Philosophy*. Ed. Constantin Boundas. Edinburgh University Press, 2006, p. 133.

zoe is impersonal: *The Posthuman*, p. 131.

it is a constant challenge: *The Posthuman*, p. 131.

physiologically embedded: 'The Ethics of Becoming Imperceptible'. p. 136.

I have been reading Woolf: Braidotti, Rosi. Personal interview. 13 Apr. 2016.

threads of merged attachment: Orbach, Susie and Louise Eichenbaum. *Between Women: Love, Envy and Competition in Women's Friendships*. Penguin, 1989, pp. 53–54.

a play of complexity: *Nomadic Theory*, p. 151.

the Starlight Hotel: Kennedy, Les. 'The Starlight Hotel Murders'. The *Sydney Morning Herald*, 10 October 2003, <www.smh.com.au/articles/2003/10/09/1065676093775.html>

of a Life that may not: *The Posthuman*, p. 121.

yes, if by friendship: Braidotti, Rosi. Personal interview. 13 Apr. 2016.

that would be: Braidotti, Rosi. Personal interview. 14 Apr. 2016.

lacking in 'seriousness': See, for example, van Ingen, Michiel. 'Beyond the nature/culture divide? The contradictions of Rosi Braidotti's The Posthuman'. Journal of Critical Realism, vol. 15, iss. 5, 2016, pp. 530–542.

rethinking the lived processes: *Nomadic Subjects*, p. 274.

critically and creatively: *The Posthuman*, p. 12.

Note: Sections of the chapter titled 'Friendship' were published as memoir in 'In Broad Daylight' in *Just Between Us: Australian Women Tell the Truth about Friendship* (Pan Macmillan) in 2013. Some excerpts from the chapter titled 'Play' were published in the essay 'Where do writers get their ideas from?' in *The Sydney Review of Books*, 8 May 2017.

Bibliography

Alien. Dir. Ridley Scott. Twentieth Century Fox, 1979.

Anderson, Jessica. *Tirra Lirra by the River*, Penguin, 1980.

Appignanesi, Lisa. *Simone de Beauvoir*, Haus, 2005.

Appignanesi, Lisa, Rachel Holmes and Susie Orbach, eds. *Fifty Shades of Feminism*. Hachette Digital, 2013.

Ardener, Shirley. *Perceiving Women*. Halsted, 1975.

Aristotle. *The Nicomachean Ethics*. Transl. David Ross. Oxford UP, 2009.

Australian Institute of Family Studies. 'Child Abuse and Neglect Statistics: CFCS Resource Sheet'. Australian Government. Oct. 2016. <aifs.gov.au/cfca/publications/child-abuse-and-neglect-statistics>.

Ayto, John. *Dictionary of Word Origins*. A. & C. Black, 2002.

Bakewell, Sarah. *How to Live: A Life of Montaigne in One Question and Twenty Attempts at an Answer*. Vintage, 2011.

—. *At the Existentialist Café: Freedom, Being and Apricot Cocktails*. Vintage, 2016.

Barthes, Roland. *A Lover's Discourse: Fragments*. Trans. Richard Howard. Farrar, Straus and Giroux, 1978.

Batty, Rosie and Bryce Corbett. *A Mother's Story*. Harper Collins, 2015.

Berlant, Lauren. *Cruel Optimism*. Duke UP, 2011.

Bernstein, Richard J. 'Reflections on radical evil: Arendt and Kant'. *Soundings*, vol. 85, no. 1–2, 2002, p. 17.

Blits, Jan H. 'Hobbesian Fear.' *Political Theory*, vol. 7, no. 3, 1989, pp. 417–431.

Boyer, Paul. *Fallout: A Historian Reflects on America's Half-century with Nuclear Weapons*. Ohio State UP, 1998.

Braidotti, Rosi. 'Intensive Genre and the Demise of Gender'. *Angelaki*, vol. 13, no. 2, August 2008, pp. 45–57.

—. *Metamorphoses: Towards a Materialist Theory of Becoming*. Polity, 2002.

—. *Nomadic Subjects: Embodiment and Sexual Difference in Contemporary Feminist Theory*. Columbia UP, 1994.

—. *Nomadic Theory: The Portable Rosi Braidotti*. Columbia UP, 2011.

—. *Patterns of Dissonance*. Polity, 1991.

—. 'Posthuman Humanities'. *European Educational Research Journal*, vol. 12, no. 1, 2013, pp. 1–14.

—. 'The Ethics of Becoming Imperceptible.' *Deleuze and Philosophy*. Edited by Constantin Boundas. Edinburgh University Press, 2006, pp. 133–159.

—. *The Posthuman*. Polity, 2013.

Braidotti, Rosi and Maria Hlavajova, eds. *Posthuman Glossary*. Bloomsbury, 2018.

Brown, Stuart. *Play*. Penguin, 2009.

Cahill, Ann J. 'The Phenomenology of Fear'. *The Feminist Philosophy Reader*. Edited by Alison Bailey and Chris Cuomo. McGraw Hill, 2008, pp. 810–825.

Caldicott, Helen. *A Passionate Life*. Random House, 1996.

—. *Crisis Without End: The Medical and Ecological Consequences of the Fukushima Nuclear Catastrophe*. New Press, 2014.

—. *If You Love This Planet*. WW Norton, 1992.

—. *Loving This Planet: Leading Thinkers Talk About How to Make a Better World*. New Press, 2012.

—. *Missile Envy: The Arms Race and Nuclear War*. Bantam, 1985.

—. *Nuclear Madness: What You Can Do*. WW Norton, 1978.

—. *Nuclear Power Is Not the Answer*. New Press, 2006.

Card, Claudia. 'Kant's Theory of Radical Evil'. *The Atrocity Paradigm*. Oxford Scholarship Online, 2002.

Carroll, Lewis. 1865. *Alice's Adventures in Wonderland*. Claremont, 1999.

Colman, Felicity. *Deleuze and Cinema*. Berg, 2011.

Coontz, Stephanie. *Marriage, a History: How Love Conquered Marriage*. Penguin, 2005.

Cox, Ted. 'Why work at marriage when adultery is so much easier?', *Daily Herald*, 28 Oct. 2003, p. 1.

Creed, Barbara. *The Monstrous-Feminine: Film, Feminism, Psychoanalysis*. Routledge, 2007.

Cudd, Ann E. and Nancy Holmstrom. *Capitalism, For and Against: A Feminist Debate*. Cambridge UP, 2011.

Dawkins, Richard. *Unweaving the Rainbow: Science, Delusion and the Appetite for Wonder*. Mariner, 2000.

DeAnda, Michael. Review of '*Play Matters*'. *American Journal of Play*, Winter 2015, p. 254.

Drabinski, Kate. Review of *Capitalism, For and Against* by Ann E. Cudd and Nancy Holmstrom. *Marx and Philosophy*, 29 June 2011. <www.marxandphilosophy. uk./reviewofbooks/reviews/2011/341>

Draper, Hal. 'The Two Souls of Socialism'. *New Politics*, vol. 5, no. 1, Winter 1966, pp. 57–84.

Durran, Jane. *Eight Women Philosophers*. University of Illinois Press, 2006.

Fagen, Robert. *Animal Play Behaviour*. Oxford UP, 1981.

Florida, Richard. *The Rise of the Creative Class*. Basic Books, 2002.

Foucault, Michel. 1975. *Discipline and Punish: The Birth of the Prison*. Trans. Alan Sheridan. Random House, 1995.

Fradinger, Moira. Introduction to The Tanner Lecture 'Memoirs of a Posthumanist' by Rosi Braidotti, 1 March 2017, Yale University. Available: <www.youtube.com/ watch?v=OjxelMWLGCo>.

Fraiberg, Selma H. *The Magic Years: Understanding and Handling the Problems of Early Childhood*. Charles Scribner, 1959.

Frame, Janet. *Owls Do Cry*. 1961, The Women's Press, 1985.

Fukuyama, Roland. *The Great Disruption: Human Nature and the Reconstitution of Social Order*. Touchstone, 2000.

Gay, Peter, ed. *The Freud Reader*. WW Norton, 1989.

Green, Jim. 'George Monbiot vs Helen Caldicott: Who is right about the Chernobyl death toll?', *Green Left Weekly*, 17 April 2011.

Greer, Germaine. 1970. *The Female Eunuch*. Harper Perennial, 2006.

Hogan, J Michael and Sarah Ann Mehltretter. 'Helen Caldicott, "Stop the Nuclear Madness" (17 April 1986)'. *Voices of Democracy: The US Oratory Project*, vol. 3, 2008.

Holmstrom, Nancy, ed. 'Sex, Work and Capitalism'. *Logos*, vol. 13, no. 2–3, 2014. <logosjournal.com/2014/holmstrom>

—. *The Socialist Feminist Project: A Contemporary Reader in Theory and Politics*. Monthly Review Press, 2002.

Huizinga, Johan. 1958. *Homo Ludens*. Routledge and Kegan, 2001.

Hustvedt, Siri. *Living, Thinking, Looking*. Sceptre, 2012.

—. *The Blazing World*. Hodder and Stoughton, 2014.

—. *The Blindfold*. Henry Holt, 1993.

—. *The Shaking Woman or A History of My Nerves*. Sceptre, 2010.

—. *The Sorrows of an American*. Henry Holt, 2008.

—. *The Summer Without Men*. Sceptre, 2011.

—. 'Underground Sexism: What Was That You Just Said?' in Appignanesi, Lisa; Rachel Holmes and Susie Orbach, eds, *Fifty Shades of Feminism*, Hachette Digital, 2013.

—. *What I Loved*. Henry Holt, 2003.

Jump, Paul. 'Work and other labours of love'. *Times Higher Education Supplement*. 6 June 2013. <www.timeshighereducation.com>.

Kennedy, Les. 'The Starlight Hotel Murders.' The *Sydney Morning Herald*, 10 October 2003. <www.smh.com.au/articles/2003/10/09/1065676093775.html>

Kipnis, Laura. 'Adultery.' *Critical Inquiry*, vol. 24, no. 2, 1998, pp. 289–327.

—. *Against Love*. Random House, 2003.

—. 'A Treatise on the Tyranny of Two'. The *New York Times*, 14 Oct. 2001. <www.nytimes.com>.

—. *Bound and Gagged: Pornography and the Politics of Fantasy in America*. Duke University Press, 1999.

—. *How to Become a Scandal: Adventures in Bad Behaviour*. Henry Holt, 2010.

—. *The Female Thing: Dirt, Sex, Envy, Vulnerability*. Random House, 2006.

—. *Unwanted Advances*. Verso, 2018.

Kristeva, Julia. *New Maladies of the Soul*. Translated by Ross Guberman. Columbia University Press, 1995.

—. *Powers of Horror: An Essay on Abjection*. Translated by Leon S. Roudiez. Columbia University Press, 1982.

Kristeva, Julia and Arthur Goldhammer. 'Stabat Mater'. *Poetics Today*, vol. 6, nos. 1–2, 1985, pp. 133–152.

Lafargue, Paul. *The Right to Be Lazy*. 1883. Translated by Charles Kerr. Lafargue Internet Archive, 2000. <www.marxists.org/archive/lafargue/1883/lazy/index.htm>.

Lakoff, George and Mark Johnson. *Metaphors We Live By*. 1980. University of Chicago Press, 2003.

Marcuse, Herbert. 'Eros and Civilisation'. 1955. *The Marcuse Internet Archive*. <www.marxists.org/reference/archive/marcuse/>.

—. 'One Dimensional Man.' 1964. *The Marcuse Internet Archive*. <www.marxists.org/reference/archive/marcuse/>.

Marx, Karl. 1867. *Capital: Volume 1*. Translated by Samuel Moore and Edward Aveling. <www.marxists.org/archive/marx/works/1867-c1>.

McAfee, Noëlle. *Julia Kristeva*. Routledge, 2004.

Meacham, Steve. 'More Affinities: Whiteley and Rees'. *Sydney Morning Herald*, 8 Dec. 2005.

Midgley, Mary. *Wisdom, Information and Wonder: What is knowledge for?* Routledge, 1989.

Moog, Nina. 'The Rumpus Interview with Marina Warner.' <therumpus.net>.

Nabokov, Vladimir. *Bend Sinister*. Henry Holt, 1942.

Niehoff, Debra. 'Not Hard Wired: The Complex Neurobiology of Sex Difference in Violence'. *Violence and Gender*, vol. 1, no.1, 2014, pp. 19–24.

Nietzsche, Friedrich. *The Gay Science*. 1910. Translated by Thomas Common. Dover, 2006.

O'Connor, Flannery. *Mystery and Manners: Occasional Prose*. Farrar, Straus and Giroux, 1969.

Orbach, Susie and Louise Eichenbaum. *Between Women: Love, Envy and Competition in Women's Friendships*. Penguin, 1989.

Orwell, George. 'You and the Atomic Bomb'. The *Tribune*, 19 Oct. 1945. <orwell.ru>.

Our Watch. 'Understanding Violence: Facts and Figures'. <ourwatch.org.au>.

Piketty, Thomas. *Capital in the Twenty-first Century*. Translated by Arthur Goldhammer. Harvard UP, 2014.

Retallack, Joan. *The Poethical Wager*. U California P, 2004.

Russell, Bertrand. *The Autobiography of Bertrand Russell*. George Allen and Unwin, 1967–1969.

Schwartz, Madeleine. 'The People vs. Laura Kipnis.' Review of *Men: Notes from an Ongoing Investigation* by Laura Kipnis. *Dissent*. Winter 2015. <www.dissentmagazine.org>

Shute, Nevil. 1957. *On the Beach*. Vintage, 2009.

Sicart, Miguel. *Play Matters*. MIT Press, 2014.

Smith, Adam. *Essays on Philosophical Subjects*. Eds W.P.D. Wightman and J.C. Boyce. Clarendon, 1980.

Spinoza, Benedict de. *Ethics*. 1677. Translated by Edwin Curley. Penguin, 2005.

Stanko, Elizabeth A. 'Women, Crime and Fear'. *The Annals of the American Academy of Political and Social Science*, vol. 539, 1995, pp. 43–58.

Sutton-Smith, Brian. *The Ambiguity of Play*. Harvard UP, 2001.

Svendsen, Lars Fredrik. *A Philosophy of Fear*. Translated by John Irons. Reaktion Books, 2008.

—. *Work*. Acumen, 2008.

Tanner, Tony. *Adultery in the Novel: Contract and Transgression*. Johns Hopkins UP, 1979.

Trainor, Brian C., Elizabeth Y. Takahashi, Andrea L. Silva, Katie K. Crean and Caroline Hosteller. 'Sex Differences in Hormonal Responses to Social Conflict in the Monogamous Mouse'. *Hormones and Behaviour*, vol. 58, no. 3, 2010, pp. 506–512.

Ussher, Jane. *Managing the Monstrous Feminine: Regulating the Female Body*. Routledge, 2006.

van Loon, Julienne. 'In Broad Daylight.' *Just Between Us: Australian Women Tell the Truth about Friendship*. Eds Maya Linden et al, Pan Macmillan, 2013. pp. 35–56.

—. 'Where do writers get their ideas from?', *Sydney Review of Books*, 8 Mar. 2017. <sydneyreviewofbooks.com/where-do-writers-get-their-ideas-from/>.

Vasalou, Sophia. *Wonder: A Grammar*. SUNY, 2015.

Vygotsky, L(ev) S. 'Play and its Role in the Mental Development of the Child'. 1933. *The Vygotsky Internet Archive*.

Warner, Marina. *Alone of All Her Sex: The Myth and Cult of the Virgin Mary*. Vintage, 1976.

—. 'Contradictory Curiosity'. *Curiosity: Art and the Pleasure of Knowing*. Hayman Publishing, 2013. pp. 25–39.

—. *Dragon Empress*. 1972. Vintage, 1993.

—. *Fantastic Metamorphoses, Other Worlds: Ways of Telling the Self*. Vintage, 2004.

—. *Joan of Arc: The Image of Female Heroism*. Vintage, 1981.

—. 'Learning my Lesson'. *London Review of Books*, 19 March 2015, <www.lrb.co.uk/v37/n06/marina-warner/learning-my-lesson>.

—. *Managing Monsters: Six Myths of Our Time*. Vintage, 1994.

—. *Signs and Wonders: Essays on Literature and Culture*. Vintage, 2004.

—. *Stranger Magic: Charmed States and the Arabian Nights*. Chatto & Windus, 2011.

Weber, Max. 1904–05. 'The Protestant Ethic and the Spirit of Capitalism'. *Essays in Economic Sociology*. Ed. Richard Swedberg. Princeton University Press, 1999, p. 2.

Weeks, Kathi. *The Problem with Work*. Duke UP, 2011.

Weseley, Jennifer K and Emily Gaarder. 'The Gendered Nature of the Urban Outdoors' *Gender and Society*. 18.5 (2004): 645–663.

Winnicott, D[onald] W. *Playing and Reality*. Tavistock, 1971.

—. *The Piggle: An Account of the Psychoanalytic Treatment of a Little Girl*. Hogarth Press, 1971.

Winton, Tim. *An Open Swimmer*. Allen & Unwin, 1982.

Wood, Charlotte. *The Writer's Room*. Allen and Unwin, 2016.

Yodanis, Carrie L. 'Gender Inequality, Violence against Women, and Fear'. *Journal of Interpersonal Violence*, 19.6 (2004): 655–675.

Acknowledgments

This work was made possible with the financial support of RMIT University through a Vice Chancellor's Senior Research Fellowship (2015–2019). It has also been supported by Creative Victoria, the Australia Council for the Arts, and Varuna: The National Writers House, and the Paul and Hauling Engle Fund of the International Writing Program at the University of Iowa. I am very grateful for the material difference the support of these organisations has made to my ability to research and develop this project, and to my capacity to see it through to completion.

I would also like to thank the generous, intelligent and inspiring women who agreed to be subjects of the work and to speak to me about their lives, their work and their ideas: Rosi Braidotti, Helen Caldicott, Nancy Holmstrom, Siri Hustvedt, Laura Kipnis, and Marina Warner. The work you do is important to so many of us. Thank you also to Julia Kristeva, Rosie Batty, Lee Kofman and Maureen Gibbons for their input, both direct and indirect.

Writing reflectively in the first person about real-life experience inevitably involves writing about others, and I want to acknowledge those who are represented via my own personal reflections here: my partner and son, my parents and siblings, my ex-partners, and several of my good friends, colleagues and acquaintances. Please forgive me for any errors or misinterpretations. I hope you can sympathise with my quest to better understand how things work and I acknowledge the discomfort and difficulties involved in being dragged, often unwittingly, into such a quest. Mine is only ever going to be a partial and subjective version of events and I'm sure there are other stories to be told and other emphases to be made in and around the experiences I've reflected on here.

For support, advice, feedback, discussion and encouragement as the manuscript developed, thank you to John Byron, Liz Byrski, David Carlin, Nadine Davidoff, Lisa French, Lee Kofman, Natalie Kon-Yu, Antoni Jach, Amanda Lohrey, Sonia Orchard, Francesca Rendle-Short, Georgia Richter, Lyn Tranter and many of my excellent colleagues in the non/fictionLab research group at RMIT University. Thank you to Phillipa McGuinness, Paul O'Beirne, Jocelyn Hungerford, and the whole team at NewSouth for your enthusiasm and your investment in this book. Thanks, too, to Amanda Lohrey (again!), Christopher Merville, and, especially, Anne Summers, for your generous contributions as we prepared the book in its final form for readers.

Finally, thank you to my partner, John Byron, who arrived in my world quite unexpectedly during the early stages of writing *The Thinking Woman*, and whose loving presence since makes everything seem possible.

Index